The Chronology of Ancient Kingdoms Amended

by

Isaac Newton

The Echo Library 2007

Published by

The Echo Library

Echo Library
131 High St.
Teddington
Middlesex TW11 8HH

www.echo-library.com

Please report serious faults in the text to complaints@echo-library.com

ISBN 1-40683-453-X

TO THE QUEEN

MADAM,

As I could never hope to write any thing my self, worthy to be laid before YOUR MAJESTY; *I think it a very great happiness, that it should be my lot to usher into the world, under Your Sacred Name, the last work of as great a Genius as any Age ever produced: an Offering of such value in its self, as to be in no danger of suffering from the meanness of the hand that presents it.*

The impartial and universal encouragement which YOUR MAJESTY *has always given to Arts and Sciences, entitles You to the best returns the learned world is able to make: And the many extraordinary Honours* YOUR MAJESTY *vouchsafed the Author of the following sheets, give You a just right to his Productions. These, above the rest, lay the most particular claim to Your Royal Protection; For the* Chronology *had never appeared in its present Form without* YOUR MAJESTY's *Influence; and the* Short Chronicle, *which precedes it, is entirely owing to the Commands with which You were pleased to honour him, out of your singular Care for the education of the Royal Issue, and earnest desire to form their minds betimes, and lead them early into the knowledge of Truth.*

The Author has himself acquainted the Publick, that the following Treatise was the fruit of his vacant hours, and the relief he sometimes had recourse to, when tired with his other studies. What an Idea does it raise of His abilities, to find that a Work of such labour and learning, as would have been a sufficient employment and glory for the whole life of another, was to him diversion only, and amusement! The Subject is in its nature incapable of that demonstration upon which his other writings are founded, but his usual accuracy and judiciousness are here no less observable; And at the same time that he supports his suggestions, with all the authorities and proofs that the whole compass of Science can furnish, he offers them with the greatest caution; And by a Modesty, that was natural to Him and always accompanies such superior talents, sets a becoming example to others, not to be too presumptuous in matters so remote and dark. Tho' the Subject be only Chronology, *yet, as the mind of the Author abounded with the most extensive variety of Knowledge, he frequently intersperses Observations of a different kind; and occasionally instills principles of Virtue and Humanity, which seem to have been always uppermost in his heart, and, as they were the Constant Rule of his actions, appear Remarkably in all his writings.*

Here YOUR MAJESTY *will see* Astronomy, *and a just Observation on the course of Nature, assisting other parts of Learning to illustrate Antiquity; and a Penetration and Sagacity peculiar to the great Author, dispelling that Mist, with which Fable and Error had darkened it; and will with pleasure contemplate the first dawnings of Your favourite Arts and Sciences, the noblest and most beneficial of which He alone carried farther in a few years, than all the most Learned who went before him, had been able to do in many Ages. Here too,* MADAM, *You will observe, that an Abhorrence of Idolatry and Persecution (the very essence and foundation of that Religion, which makes so bright a part of* YOUR MAJESTY's *character) was one of the* earliest Laws *of the Divine Legislator, the* Morality of the first Ages, and the primitive Religion of both Jews and Christians; *and, as the Author adds,* ought to be the standing Religion of all Nations; it being for the honour of God, and good of Mankind. *Nor will* YOUR MAJESTY *be displeased to find his sentiments so agreeable to Your own, whilst he condemns* all oppression; *and every kind of* cruelty, even to brute beasts; *and, with so much warmth, inculcates* Mercy, Charity, *and the indispensable duty of* doing good, *and promoting the general* welfare of mankind: *Those great ends, for which Government was first instituted, and to which alone it is administred in this happy Nation, under a KING, who distinguished himself early in opposition to the Tyranny which threatned* Europe, *and chuses to reign in the hearts of his subjects; Who, by his innate Benevolence, and Paternal Affection to his People, establishes and confirms all their Liberties; and, by his Valour and Magnanimity, guards and defends them.*

That Sincerity and Openness of mind, which is the darling quality of this Nation, is become more conspicuous, by being placed upon the Throne; And we see, with Pride, OUR SOVEREIGN *the most eminent for a Virtue, by which our country is so desirous to be distinguished. A Prince, whose views and heart are above all the mean arts of Disguise, is far out of the reach of any temptation to Introduce Blindness and Ignorance. And, as* HIS MAJESTY *is, by his incessant personal cares, dispensing Happiness at home, and Peace abroad; You,* MADAM, *lead us on by Your great Example to the most noble use of that Quiet and Ease, which we enjoy under His Administration, whilst all Your hours of leisure are employed in cultivating in Your Self That Learning, which You so warmly patronize in Others.*

YOUR MAJESTY does not think the instructive Pursuit, an entertainment below Your exalted Station; and are Your Self a proof, that the abstruser parts of it are not beyond the reach of Your Sex. Nor does this Study end in barren speculation; It discovers itself in a steady attachment to true Religion; in Liberality, Beneficence, and all those amiable Virtues, which increase and heighten the Felicities of a Throne, at the same time that they bless All around it. Thus, MADAM, to enjoy, together with the highest state of publick Splendor and Dignity all the retired Pleasures and domestick Blessings of private life; is the perfection of human Wisdom, as well as Happiness.

The good Effects of this Love of knowledge, will not stop with the present Age; It will diffuse its Influence with advantage to late Posterity: And what may we not anticipate in our minds for the Generations to come under a Royal Progeny, so descended, so educated, and formed by such Patterns!

The glorious Prospect gives us abundant reason to hope, that Liberty and Learning will be perpetuated together; and that the bright Examples of Virtue and Wisdom, set in this Reign by the Royal Patrons of Both, will be transmitted with the Scepter to their Posterity, till this and the other Works of Sir ISAAC NEWTON shall be forgot, and Time it self be no more: Which is the most sincere and ardent wish of

MADAM,

May it please YOUR MAJESTY,

YOUR MAJESTY's most obedient and most dutiful subject and servant, *John Conduitt.*

THE CONTENTS

Advertisement

THO' The Chronology of Ancient Kingdoms amended, *was writ by the Author many years since; yet he lately revis'd it, and was actually preparing it for the Press at the time of his death. But* The Short Chronicle *was never intended to be made public, and therefore was not so lately corrected by him. To this the Reader must impute it, if he shall find any places where* the Short Chronicle *does not accurately agree with the Dates assigned in the larger Piece. The Sixth Chapter was not copied out with the other Five, which makes it doubtful whether he intended to print it: but being found among his Papers, and evidently appearing to be a Continuation of the same Work, and (as such) abridg'd in* the Short Chronicle; *it was thought proper to be added.*

    Had the Great Author *himself liv'd to publish this Work, there would have been no occasion for this Advertisement; But as it is, the Reader is desired to allow for such imperfections as are inseparable from Posthumous Pieces; and, in so great a number of proper names, to excuse some errors of the Press that have escaped.*

INTRODUCTION

THE *Greek* Antiquities are full of Poetical Fictions, because the *Greeks* wrote nothing in Prose, before the Conquest of *Asia* by *Cyrus* the *Persian*. Then *Pherecydes Scyrius* and *Cadmus Milesius* introduced the writing in Prose. *Pherecydes Atheniensis*, about the end of the Reign of *Darius Hystaspis*, wrote of Antiquities, and digested his work by Genealogies, and was reckoned one of the best Genealogers. *Epimenides* the Historian proceeded also by Genealogies; and *Hellanicus*, who was twelve years older than *Herodotus*, digested his History by the Ages or Successions of the Priestesses of *Juno Argiva*. Others digested theirs by the Kings of the *Lacedæmonians*, or Archons of *Athens*. *Hippias* the *Elean*, about thirty years before the fall of the *Persian* Empire, published a breviary or list of the Olympic Victors; and about ten years before the fall thereof, *Ephorus* the disciple of *Isocrates* formed a Chronological History of *Greece*, beginning with the return of the *Heraclides* into *Peloponnesus*, and ending with the siege of *Perinthus*, in the twentieth year of *Philip* the father of *Alexander* the great: But he digested things by Generations, and the reckoning by Olympiads was not yet in use, nor doth it appear that the Reigns of Kings were yet set down by numbers of years. The *Arundelian* marbles were composed sixty years after the death of *Alexander* the great (*An.* 4. *Olymp.* 128.) and yet mention not the Olympiads: But in the next Olympiad, *Timæus Siculus* published an history in several books down to his own times, according to the Olympiads, comparing the Ephori, the Kings of *Sparta*, the Archons of *Athens*, and the Priestesses of *Argos*, with the Olympic Victors, so as to make the Olympiads, and the Genealogies and Successions of Kings, Archons, and Priestesses, and poetical histories suit with one another, according to the best of his judgment. And where he left off, *Polybius* began and carried on the history.

So then a little after the death of *Alexander* the great, they began to set down the Generations, Reigns and Successions, in numbers of years, and by putting Reigns and Successions equipollent to Generations, and three Generations to an hundred or an hundred and twenty years (as appears by their Chronology) they have made the Antiquities of *Greece* three or four hundred years older than the truth. And this was the original of the Technical Chronology of the *Greeks*. *Eratosthenes* wrote about an hundred years after the death of *Alexander* the great: He was followed by *Apollodorus*, and these two have been followed ever since by Chronologers.

But how uncertain their Chronology is, and how doubtful it was reputed by the *Greeks* of those times, may be understood by these passages of *Plutarch*. *Some reckon*, saith he,[1] Lycurgus *contemporary to* Iphitus, *and to have been his companion in ordering the Olympic festivals: amongst whom was* Aristotle *the Philosopher, arguing from the Olympic Disc, which had the name of* Lycurgus *upon it. Others supputing the times by the succession of the Kings of the* Lacedæmonians, *as* Eratosthenes *and* Apollodorus, *affirm that he was not a few years older than the first Olympiad*. First *Aristotle* and some others made him as old as the first Olympiad; then *Eratosthenes*, *Apollodorus*, and some others made him above an hundred years older: and in another place

Plutarch[2] tells us: *The congress of* Solon *with* Croesus, *some think they can confute by Chronology. But an history so illustrious, and verified by so many witnesses, and (which is more) so agreeable to the manners of* Solon, *and so worthy of the greatness of his mind and of his wisdom, I cannot persuade my self to reject because of some Chronological Canons, as they call them: which hundreds of authors correcting, have not yet been able to constitute any thing certain, in which they could agree among themselves, about repugnancies.* It seems the Chronologers had made the Legislature of *Solon* too ancient to consist with that Congress.

For reconciling such repugnancies, Chronologers have sometimes doubled the persons of men. So when the Poets had changed *Io* the daughter of *Inachus* into the *Egyptian Isis*, Chronologers made her husband *Osiris* or *Bacchus* and his mistress *Ariadne* as old as *Io*, and so feigned that there were two *Ariadnes*, one the mistress of *Bacchus*, and the other the mistress of *Theseus*, and two *Minos's* their fathers, and a younger *Io* the daughter of *Jasus*, writing *Jasus* corruptly for *Inachus*. And so they have made two *Pandions*, and two *Erechtheus's*, giving the name of *Erechthonius* to the first; *Homer* calls the first, *Erechtheus*: and by such corruptions they have exceedingly perplexed Ancient History.

And as for the Chronology of the *Latines*, that is still more uncertain. *Plutarch* represents great uncertainties in the Originals of *Rome*: and so doth *Servius*. The old records of the *Latines* were burnt by the *Gauls*, sixty and four years before the death of *Alexander* the great; and *Quintus Fabius Pictor*, the oldest historian of the *Latines*, lived an hundred years later than that King.

In Sacred History, the *Assyrian* Empire began with *Pul* and *Tiglathpilaser*, and lasted about 170 years. And accordingly *Herodotus* hath made *Semiramis* only five generations, or about 166 years older than *Nitocris*, the mother of the last King of *Babylon*. But *Ctesias* hath made *Semiramis* 1500 years older than *Nitocris*, and feigned a long series of Kings of *Assyria*, whose names are not *Assyrian*, nor have any affinity with the *Assyrian* names in Scripture.

The Priests of *Egypt* told *Herodotus*, that *Menes* built *Memphis* and the sumptuous temple of *Vulcan*, in that City: and that *Rhampsinitus*, *Moeris*, *Asychis* and *Psammiticus* added magnificent porticos to that temple. And it is not likely that *Memphis* could be famous, before *Homer's* days who doth not mention it, or that a temple could be above two or three hundred years in building. The Reign of *Psammiticus* began about 655 years before Christ, and I place the founding of this temple by *Menes* about 257 years earlier: but the Priests of *Egypt* had so magnified their Antiquities before the days of *Herodotus*, as to tell him that from *Menes* to *Moeris* (who reigned 200 years before *Psammiticus*) there were 330 Kings, whose Reigns took up as many Ages, that is eleven thousand years, and had filled up the interval with feigned Kings, who had done nothing. And before the days of *Diodorus Siculus* they had raised their Antiquities so much higher, as to place six, eight, or ten new Reigns of Kings between those Kings, whom they had represented to *Herodotus* to succeed one another immediately.

In the Kingdom of *Sicyon*, Chronologers have split *Apis Epaphus* or *Epopeus* into two Kings, whom they call *Apis* and *Epopeus*, and between them have inserted eleven or twelve feigned names of Kings who did nothing, and thereby they have made its Founder *Ægialeus*, three hundred years older than his brother *Phoroneus*. Some have made the Kings of *Germany* as old as the Flood: and yet before the use of letters, the names and actions of men could scarce be remembred above eighty or an hundred years after their deaths: and therefore I admit no Chronology of things done in *Europe*, above eighty years before *Cadmus* brought letters into *Europe*; none, of things done in *Germany*, before the rise of the *Roman* Empire.

Now since *Eratosthenes* and *Apollodorus* computed the times by the Reigns of the Kings of *Sparta*, and (as appears by their Chronology still followed) have made the seventeen Reigns of these Kings in both Races, between the Return of the *Heraclides* into *Peloponnesus* and the Battel of *Thermopylæ*, take up *622* years, which is after the rate of 36½ years to a Reign, and yet a Race of seventeen Kings of that length is no where to be met with in all true History, and Kings at a moderate reckoning Reign but 18 or 20 years a-piece one with another: I have stated the time of the return of the *Heraclides* by the last way of reckoning, placing it about 340 years before the Battel of *Thermopylæ*. And making the Taking of *Troy* eighty years older than that Return, according to *Thucydides*, and the *Argonautic* Expedition a Generation older than the *Trojan* War, and the Wars of *Sesostris* in *Thrace* and death of *Ino* the daughter of *Cadmus* a Generation older than that Expedition: I have drawn up the following Chronological Table, so as to make Chronology suit with the Course of Nature, with Astronomy, with Sacred History, with *Herodotus* the Father of History, and with it self; without the many repugnancies complained of by *Plutarch*. I do not pretend to be exact to a year: there may be Errors of five or ten years, and sometimes twenty, and not much above.

A SHORT
CHRONICLE

FROM THE

First Memory of things in Europe *to
the Conquest of* Persia *by* Alexander
the great.

The Times are set down in years before Christ.

THE *Canaanites* who fled from *Joshua,* retired in great numbers into *Egypt,* and there conquered *Timaus, Thamus,* or *Thammuz* King of the lower *Egypt,* and reigned there under their Kings *Salatis, Boeon, Apachnas, Apophis, Janias, Assis,* &c. untill the days of *Eli* and *Samuel.* They fed on flesh, and sacrificed men after the manner of the *Phoenicians,* and were called Shepherds by the *Egyptians,* who lived only on the fruits of the earth, and abominated flesh-eaters. The upper parts of *Egypt* were in those days under many Kings, Reigning at *Coptos, Thebes, This, Elephantis,* and other Places, which by conquering one another grew by degrees into one Kingdom, over which *Misphragmuthosis* Reigned in the days of *Eli.*

In the year before Christ 1125 *Mephres* Reigned over the upper *Egypt* from *Syene* to *Heliopolis,* and his Successor *Misphragmuthosis* made a lasting war upon the Shepherds soon after, and caused many of them to fly into *Palestine, Idumæa, Syria,* and *Libya;* and under *Lelex, Æzeus, Inachus, Pelasgus, Æolus* the first, *Cecrops,* and other Captains, into *Greece.* Before those days *Greece* and all *Europe* was peopled by wandring *Cimmerians,* and *Scythians* from the backside of the *Euxine Sea,* who lived a rambling wild sort of life, like the *Tartars* in the northern parts of *Asia.* Of their Race was *Ogyges,* in whose days these *Egyptian* strangers came into *Greece.* The rest of the Shepherds were shut up by *Misphragmuthosis,* in a part of the lower *Egypt* called *Abaris* or *Pelusium.*

In the year 1100 the *Philistims,* strengthned by the access of the Shepherds, conquer *Israel,* and take the Ark. *Samuel* judges *Israel.*

1085. *Hæmon* the son of *Pelasgus* Reigns in *Thessaly.*

1080. *Lycaon* the son of *Pelasgus* builds *Lycosura; Phoroneus* the son of *Inachus, Phoronicum,* afterwards called *Argos; Ægialeus* the brother of *Phoroneus* and son of *Inachus, Ægialeum,* afterwards called *Sicyon:* and these were the oldest towns in *Peloponnesus.* 'Till then they built only single houses scattered up and down in the fields. About the same time *Cecrops* built *Cecropia* in *Attica,* afterwards called *Athens;* and *Eleusine,* the son of *Ogyges,* built *Eleusis.* And these towns gave a beginning to the Kingdoms of the *Arcadians, Argives, Sicyons, Athenians, Eleusinians,* &c. *Deucalion* flourishes.

1070. *Amosis,* or *Tethmosis,* the successor of *Misphragmuthosis,* abolishes the *Phoenician* custom in *Heliopolis* of sacrificing men, and drives the Shepherds out of *Abaris.* By their access the *Philistims* become so numerous, as to bring into the field against *Saul* 30000 chariots, 6000 horsemen, and people as the sand on the sea shore for multitude. *Abas*, the father of *Acrisius* and *Proetus*, comes from *Egypt*.

1069. *Saul* is made King of *Israel*, and by the hand of *Jonathan* gets a great victory over the *Philistims*. *Eurotas* the son of *Lelex*, and *Lacedæmon* who married *Sparta* the daughter of *Eurotas*, Reign in *Laconia*, and build *Sparta*.

1060. *Samuel* dies.

1059. *David* made King.

1048. The *Edomites* are conquered and dispersed by *David*, and some of them fly into *Egypt* with their young King *Hadad*. Others fly to the *Persian Gulph* with their Commander *Oannes*; and others from the *Red Sea* to the coast of the *Mediterranean*, and fortify *Azoth* against *David*, and take *Zidon*; and the *Zidonians* who fled from them build *Tyre* and *Aradus*, and make *Abibalus* King of *Tyre*. These *Edomites* carry to all places their Arts and Sciences; amongst which were their Navigation, Astronomy, and Letters; for in *Idumæa* they had Constellations and Letters before the days of *Job*, who mentions them: and there *Moses* learnt to write the Law in a book. These *Edomites* who fled to the *Mediterranean*, translating the word *Erythræa* into that of *Phoenicia*, give the name of *Phoenicians* to themselves, and that of *Phoenicia* to all the sea-coasts of *Palestine* from *Azoth* to *Zidon*. And hence came the tradition of the *Persians*, and of the *Phoenicians* themselves, mentioned by *Herodotus*, that the *Phoenicians* came originally from the *Red Sea*, and presently undertook long voyages on the *Mediterranean*.

1047. *Acrisius* marries *Eurydice*, the daughter of *Lacedæmon* and *Sparta*. The *Phoenician* mariners who fled from the *Red Sea*, being used to long voyages for the sake of traffic, begin the like voyages on the *Mediterranean* from *Zidon*; and sailing as far as *Greece*, carry away *Io* the daughter of *Inachus*, who with other *Grecian* women came to their ships to buy their merchandize. The *Greek Seas* begin to be infested with Pyrates.

1046. The *Syrians* of *Zobah* and *Damascus* are conquered by *David*. *Nyctimus*, the son of *Lycaon*, reigns in *Arcadia*. *Deucalion* still alive.

1045. Many of the *Phoenicians* and *Syrians* fleeing from *Zidon* and from *David*, come under the conduct of *Cadmus*, *Cilix*, *Phoenix*, *Membliarius*, *Nycteus*, *Thasus*, *Atymnus*, and other Captains, into *Asia minor*, *Crete*, *Greece*, and *Libya*; and introduce Letters, Music, Poetry, the *Octaeteris*, Metals and their Fabrication, and other Arts, Sciences and Customs of the *Phoenicians*. At this time *Cranaus* the successor of *Cecrops* Reigned in *Attica*, and in his Reign and the beginning of the Reign of *Nyctimus*, the *Greeks* place the flood of *Deucalion*. This flood was succeeded by four Ages or Generations of men, in the first of which *Chiron* the son of *Saturn* and *Philyra* was born, and the last of which according to *Hesiod* ended with the *Trojan* War; and so places the Destruction of *Troy* four Generations or about 140 years later than that flood, and the coming of *Cadmus*, reckoning with the ancients three Generations to an hundred years. With these *Phoenicians* came a sort of men skilled in the Religious Mysteries, Arts, and Sciences of *Phoenicia*, and settled in several places under the names of *Curetes*, *Corybantes*, *Telchines*, and *Idæi Dactyli*.

1043. Hellen, the son of *Deucalion*, and father of *Æolus*, *Xuthus*, and *Dorus*, flourishes.

1035. *Erectheus* Reigns in *Attica*. *Æthlius*, the grandson of *Deucalion* and father of *Endymion*, builds *Elis*. The *Idæi Dactyli* find out Iron in mount *Ida* in *Crete*, and work it into armour and iron tools, and thereby give a beginning to the trades of smiths and armourers in *Europe*; and by singing and dancing in their armour, and keeping time by striking upon one another's armour with their swords, they bring in Music and Poetry; and at the same time they nurse up the *Cretan Jupiter* in a cave of the same mountain, dancing about him in their armour.

1034. *Ammon* Reigns in *Egypt*. He conquered *Libya*, and reduced that people from a wandering savage life to a civil one, and taught them to lay up the fruits of the earth; and from him *Libya* and the desert above it were anciently called *Ammonia*. He was the first that built long and tall ships with sails, and had a fleet of such ships on the *Red Sea*, and another on the *Mediterranean* at *Irasa* in *Libya*. 'Till then they used small and round vessels of burden, invented on the *Red Sea*, and kept within sight of the shore. For enabling them to cross the seas without seeing the shore, the *Egyptians* began in his days to observe the Stars: and from this beginning Astronomy and Sailing had their rise. Hitherto the Lunisolar year had been in use: but this year being of an uncertain length, and so, unfit for Astronomy, in his days and in the days of his sons and grandsons, by observing the Heliacal Risings and Setting of the Stars, they found the length of the Solar year, and made it consist of five days more than the twelve calendar months of the old Lunisolar year. *Creusa* the daughter of *Erechtheus* marries *Xuthus* the son of *Hellen*. *Erechtheus* having first celebrated the *Panathenæa* joins horses to a chariot. *Ægina*, the daughter of *Asopus*, and mother of *Æacus*, born.

1030. *Ceres* a woman of *Sicily*, in seeking her daughter who was stolen, comes into *Attica*, and there teaches the *Greeks* to sow corn; for which Benefaction she was Deified after death. She first taught the Art to *Triptolemus* the young son of *Celeus* King of *Eleusis*.

1028. *Oenotrus* the youngest son of *Lycaon*, the *Janus* of the *Latines*, led the first Colony of *Greeks* into *Italy*, and there taught them to build houses. *Perseus* born.

1020. *Arcas*, the son of *Callisto* and grandson of *Lycaon*, and *Eumelus* the first King of *Achaia*, receive bread-corn from *Triptolemus*.

1019. *Solomon* Reigns, and marries the daughter of *Ammon*, and by means of this affinity is supplied with horses from *Egypt*; and his merchants also bring horses from thence for all the Kings of the *Hittites* and *Syrians*: for horses came originally from *Libya*; and thence *Neptune* was called *Equestris*. *Tantalus* King of *Phrygia* steals *Ganimede* the son of *Tros* King of *Troas*.

1017. *Solomon* by the assistance of the *Tyrians* and *Aradians*, who had mariners among them acquainted with the *Red Sea*, sets out a fleet upon that sea. Those assistants build new cities in the *Persian Gulph*, called *Tyre* and *Aradus*.

1015. The Temple of *Solomon* is founded. *Minos* Reigns in *Crete* expelling his father *Asterius*, who flees into *Italy*, and becomes the *Saturn* of the *Latines*. *Ammon* takes *Gezer* from the *Canaanites*, and gives it to his daughter, *Solomon's* wife.

1014. *Ammon* places *Cepheus* at *Joppa*.

1010. *Sesac* in the Reign of his father *Ammon* invades *Arabia Foelix*, and sets up pillars at the mouth of the *Red Sea*. *Apis*, *Epaphus* or *Epopeus*, the son of *Phroroneus*, and *Nycteus* King of *Boeotia*, slain. *Lycus* inherits the Kingdom of his brother *Nycteus*. *Ætolus* the son of *Endymion* flies into the Country of the *Curetes* in *Achaia*, and calls it *Ætolia*; and of *Pronoe* the daughter of *Phorbas* begets *Pleuron* and *Calydon*, who built cities in *Ætolia* called by their own names. *Antiopa* the daughter of *Nycteus* is sent home to *Lycus* by *Lamedon* the successor of *Apis*, and in the way brings forth *Amphion* and *Zethus*.

1008. *Sesac*, in the Reign of his father *Ammon*, invades *Afric* and *Spain*, and sets up pillars in all his conquests, and particularly at the mouth of the *Mediterranean*, and returns home by the coast of *Gaul* and *Italy*.

1007. *Ceres* being dead *Eumolpus* institutes her Mysteries in *Eleusine*. The Mysteries of *Rhea* are instituted in *Phrygia*, in the city *Cybele*. About this time Temples begin to be built in *Greece*. *Hyagnis* the *Phrygian* invents the pipe. After the example of the common-council of the five Lords of the *Philistims*, the *Greeks* set up the *Amphictyonic* Council, first at *Thermopylæ*, by the influence of *Amphictyon* the son of *Deucalion*; and a few years after at *Delphi* by the influence of *Acrisius*. Among the cites, whose deputies met at *Thermopylæ*, I do not find *Athens*, and therefore doubt whether *Amphictyon* was King of that city. If he was the son of *Deucalion* and brother of *Hellen*, he and *Cranaus* might Reign together in several parts of *Attica*. But I meet with a later *Amphictyon* who entertained the great *Bacchus*. This Council worshipped *Ceres*, and therefore was instituted after her death.

1006. *Minos* prepares a fleet, clears the *Greek* seas of Pyrates, and sends Colonies to the Islands of the *Greeks*, some of which were not inhabited before. *Cecrops* II. Reigns in *Attica*. *Caucon* teaches the Mysteries of *Ceres* in *Messene*.

1005. *Andromeda* carried away from *Joppa* by *Perseus*. *Pandion* the brother of *Cecrops* II. Reigns in *Attica*. *Car*, the son of *Phoroneus*, builds a Temple to *Ceres*.

1002. *Sesac* Reigns in *Egypt* and adorns *Thebes*, dedicating it to his father *Ammon* by the name of *No-Ammon* or *Ammon-No*, that is the people or city of *Ammon*: whence the *Greeks* called it *Diospolis*, the city of *Jupiter*. *Sesac* also erected Temples and Oracles to his father in *Thebes*, *Ammonia*, and *Ethiopia*, and thereby caused his father to be worshipped as a God in those countries, and I think also in *Arabia Foelix*: and this was the original of the worship of *Jupiter Ammon*, and the first mention of Oracles that I meet with in Prophane History. War between *Pandion* and *Labdacus* the grandson of *Cadmus*.

994. *Ægeus* Reigns in Attica.

993. *Pelops* the son of *Tantalus* comes into *Peloponnesus*, marries *Hippodamia* the granddaughter of *Acrisius*, takes *Ætolia* from *Ætolus* the son of *Endymion*, and by his riches grows potent.

990. *Amphion* and *Zethus* slay *Lycus*, put *Laius* the son of *Labdacus* to flight, and Reign in *Thebes*, and wall the city about.

989. *Dædalus* and his nephew *Talus* invent the saw, the turning-lath, the wimble, the chip-ax, and other instruments of Carpenters and Joyners, and

thereby give a beginning to those Arts in *Europe*. *Dædalus* also invented the making of Statues with their feet asunder, as if they walked.

988. *Minos* makes war upon the *Athenians*, for killing his son *Androgeus*. *Æacus* flourishes.

987. *Dædalus* kills his nephew *Talus*, and flies to *Minos*. A Priestess of *Jupiter Ammon*, being brought by *Phoenician* merchants into *Greece*, sets up the Oracle of *Jupiter* at *Dodona*. This gives a beginning to Oracles in *Greece*: and by their dictates, the Worship of the Dead is every where introduced.

983. *Sisyphus*, the son of *Æolus* and grandson of *Hellen*, Reigns in *Corinth*, and some say that he built that city.

980. *Laius* recovers the Kingdom of *Thebes*. *Athamas*, the brother of *Sisyphus* and father of *Phrixus* and *Helle*, marries *Ino* the daughter of *Cadmus*.

979. *Rehoboam* Reigns. *Thoas* is sent from *Crete* to *Lemnos*, Reigns there in the city *Hephoestia*, and works in copper and iron.

978. *Alcmena* born of *Electryo* the son of *Perseus* and *Andromeda*, and of *Lysidice* the daughter of *Pelops*.

974. *Sesac* spoils the Temple, and invades *Syria* and *Persia*, setting up pillars in many places. *Jeroboam*, becoming subject to *Sesac*, sets up the worship of the *Egyptian* Gods in *Israel*.

971. *Sesac* invades *India*, and returns with triumph the next year but one: whence *Trieterica Bacchi*. He sets up pillars on two mountains at the mouth of the river *Ganges*.

968. *Theseus* Reigns, having overcome the *Minotaur*, and soon after unites the twelve cities of *Attica* under one government. *Sesac*, having carried on his victories to *Mount Caucasus*, leaves his nephew *Prometheus* there, and *Æetes* in *Colchis*.

967. *Sesac*, passing over the *Hellespont* conquers *Thrace*, kills *Lycurgus* King thereof, and gives his Kingdom and one of his singing-women to *Oeagrus* the father of *Orpheus*. *Sesac* had in his army *Ethiopians* commanded by *Pan*, and *Libyan* women commanded by *Myrina* or *Minerva*. It was the custom of the *Ethiopians* to dance when they were entring into a battel, and from their skipping they were painted with goats feet in the form of Satyrs.

966. *Thoas*, being made King of *Cyprus* by *Sesac*, goes thither with his wife *Calycopis*, and leaves his daughter *Hypsipyle* in *Lemnos*.

965. *Sesac* is baffled by the *Greeks* and *Scythians*, loses many of his women with their Queen *Minerva*, composes the war, is received by *Amphiction* at a feast, buries *Ariadne*, goes back through *Asia* and *Syria* into *Egypt*, with innumerable captives, among whom was *Tithonus*, the son of *Laomedon* King of *Troy*; and leaves his *Libyan Amazons*, under *Marthesia* and *Lampeto*, the successors of *Minerva*, at the river *Thermodon*. He left also in *Colchos* Geographical Tables of all his conquests: And thence Geography had its rise. His singing-women were celebrated in *Thrace* by the name of the Muses. And the daughters of *Pierus* a *Thracian*, imitating them, were celebrated by the same name.

964. *Minos*, making war upon *Cocalus* King of *Sicily*, is slain by him. He was eminent for his Dominion, his Laws and his Justice: upon his sepulchre visited

by *Pythagoras*, was this inscription, [Greek: TOU DIOS] the Sepulchre of *Jupiter.* *Danaus* with his daughters flying from his brother *Egyptus* (that is from *Sesac*) comes into *Greece*. *Sesac* using the advice of his Secretary *Thoth*, distributes *Egypt* into xxxvi *Nomes*, and in every *Nome* erects a Temple, and appoints the several Gods, Festivals and Religions of the several *Nomes*. The Temples were the sepulchres of his great men, where they were to be buried and worshipped after death, each in his own Temple, with ceremonies and festivals appointed by him; while He and his Queen, by the names of *Osiris* and *Isis*, were to be worshipped in all *Egypt*. These were the Temples seen and described by *Lucian* eleven hundred years after, to be of one and the same age: and this was the original of the several *Nomes* of *Egypt*, and of the several Gods and several Religions of those *Nomes*. *Sesac* divided also the land of *Egypt* by measure amongst his soldiers, and thence *Geometry* had its rise. *Hercules* and *Eurystheus* born.

963. *Amphictyon* brings the twelve Gods of *Egypt* into *Greece*, and these are the *Dii magni majorum gentium*, to whom the Earth and Planets and Elements are dedicated.

962. *Phryxus* and *Helle* fly from their stepmother *Ino* the daughter of *Cadmus*. *Helle* is drowned in the *Hellespont*, so named from her, but *Phryxus* arrived at *Colchos*.

960. The war between the *Lapithæ* and the people of *Thessaly* called *Centaurs*.

958. *Oedipus* kills his father *Laius*. *Sthenelus* the son of *Perseus* Reigns in *Mycene*.

956. *Sesac* is slain by his brother *Japetus*, who after death was deified in *Afric* by the name of *Neptune*, and called *Typhon* by the *Egyptians*. *Orus* Reigns and routs the *Libyans*, who under the conduct of *Japetus*, and his Son *Antæus* or *Atlas*, invaded *Egypt*. *Sesac* from his making the river *Nile* useful, by cutting channels from it to all the cities of *Egypt*, was called by its names, *Sihor* or *Siris*, *Nilus* and *Egyptus*. The *Greeks* hearing the *Egyptians* lament, O *Siris* and *Bou Siris*, called him *Osiris* and *Busiris*. The *Arabians* from his great acts called him *Bacchus*, that is, the Great. The *Phrygians* called him *Ma-fors* or *Mavors*, the valiant, and by contraction *Mars*. Because he set up pillars in all his conquests, and his army in his father's Reign fought against the *Africans* with clubs, he is painted with pillars and a club: and this is that *Hercules* who, according to *Cicero*, was born upon the *Nile*, and according to *Eudoxus*, was slain by *Typhon*; and according to *Diodorus*, was an *Egyptian*, and went over a great part of the world, and set up the pillars in *Afric*. He seems to be also the *Belus* who, according to *Diodorus*, led a Colony of *Egyptians* to *Babylon*, and there instituted Priests called *Chaldeans*, who were free from taxes, and observed the stars, as in *Egypt*. Hitherto *Judah* and *Israel* laboured under great vexations, but henceforward *Asa* King of *Judah* had peace ten years.

947. The *Ethiopians* invade *Egypt*, and drown *Orus* in the *Nile*. Thereupon *Bubaste* the sister of *Orus* kills herself, by falling from the top of an house, and their mother *Isis* or *Astræa* goes mad: and thus ended the Reign of the Gods of *Egypt*.

946. *Zerah* the *Ethiopian* is overthrown by *Asa*. The people of the lower *Egypt* make *Osarsiphus* their King, and call in two hundred thousand *Jews* and *Phoenicians*

against the *Ethiopians*. *Menes* or *Amenophis* the young son of *Zerah* and *Cissia* Reigns.

944. The *Ethiopians*, under *Amenophis*, retire from the lower *Egypt* and fortify *Memphis* against *Osarsiphus*. And by these wars and the *Argonautic* expedition, the great Empire of *Egypt* breaks in pieces. *Eurystheus* the son of *Sthenelus* Reigns in *Mycenæ*.

943. *Evander* and his mother *Carmenta* carry Letters into *Italy*.

942. *Orpheus* Deifies the son of *Semele* by the name of *Bacchus*, and appoints his Ceremonies.

940. The great men of *Greece*, hearing of the civil wars and distractions of *Egypt*, resolve to send an embassy to the nations, upon the *Euxine* and *Mediterranean* Seas, subject to that Empire, and for that end order the building of the ship *Argo*.

939. The ship *Argo* is built after the pattern of the long ship in which *Danaus* came into *Greece*: and this was the first long ship built by the *Greeks*. *Chiron*, who was born in the Golden Age, forms the Constellations for the use of the *Argonauts*; and places the Solstitial and Equinoctial Points in the fifteenth degrees or middles of the Constellations of *Cancer*, *Chelæ*, *Capricorn*, and *Aries*. *Meton* in the year of *Nabonassar* 316, observed the Summer Solstice in the eighth degree of *Cancer*, and therefore the Solstice had then gone back seven degrees. It goes back one degree in about seventytwo years, and seven degrees in about 504 years. Count these years back from the year of *Nabonassar* 316, and they will place the *Argonautic* expedition about 936 years before *Christ*. *Gingris* the son of *Thoas* slain, and Deified by the name of *Adonis*.

938. *Theseus*, being fifty years old, steals *Helena* then seven years old. *Pirithous* the son of *Ixion*, endeavouring to steal *Persephone* the daughter of *Orcus* King of the *Molossians*, is slain by the Dog of *Orcus*; and his companion *Theseus* is taken and imprisoned. *Helena* is set at liberty by her brothers.

937. The *Argonautic* expedition. *Prometheus* leaves *Mount Caucasus*, being set at liberty by *Hercules*. *Laomedon* King of *Troy* is slain by *Hercules*. *Priam* succeeds him. *Talus* a brazen man, of the Brazen Age, the son of *Minos*, is slain by the *Argonauts*. *Æsculapius* and *Hercules* were *Argonauts*, and *Hippocrates* was the eighteenth from *Æsculapius* by the father's side, and the nineteenth from *Hercules* by the mother's side; and because these generations, being noted in history, were most probably by the chief of the family, and for the most part by the eldest sons; we may reckon 28 or at the most 30 years to a generation: and thus the seventeen intervals by the father's side and eighteen by the mother's, will at a middle reckoning amount unto about 507 years; which being counted backwards from the beginning of the *Peloponnesian* war, at which time *Hippocrates* began to flourish, will reach up to the time where we have placed the *Argonautic* expedition.

936. *Theseus* is set at liberty by *Hercules*.

934. The hunting of the *Calydonian* boar slain by *Meleager*.

930. *Amenophis*, with an army out of *Ethiopia* and *Thebais*, invades the lower *Egypt*, conquers *Osarsiphus*, and drives out the *Jews* and *Canaanites*: and this is

reckoned the second expulsion of the Shepherds. *Calycopis* dies, and is Deified by *Thoas* with Temples at *Paphos* and *Amathus* in *Cyprus*, and at *Byblus* in *Syria*, and with Priests and sacred Rites, and becomes the *Venus* of the ancients, and the *Dea Cypria* and *Dea Syria*. And from these and other places where Temples were erected to her, she was also called *Paphia*, *Amathusia*, *Byblia*, *Cytherea*, *Salaminia*, *Cnidia*, *Erycina*, *Idalia*, &c. And her three waiting-women became the three Graces.

928. The war of the seven Captains against *Thebes*.

927. *Hercules* and *Æsculapius* are Deified. *Eurystheus* drives the *Heraclides* out of *Peloponnesus*. He is slain by *Hyllus* the son of *Hercules*. *Atreus* the son of *Pelops* succeeds him in the Kingdom of *Mycenæ*. *Menestheus*, the great grandson of *Erechtheus*, Reigns at *Athens*.

925. *Theseus* is slain, being cast down from a rock.

924. *Hyllus* invading *Peloponnesus* is slain by *Echemus*.

919. *Atreus* dies. *Agamemnon* Reigns. In the absence of *Menelaus*, who went to look after what his father *Atreus* had left to him, *Paris* steals *Helena*.

918. The second war against *Thebes*.

912. *Thoas*, King of *Cyprus* and part of *Phoenicia* dies; and for making armour for the Kings of *Egypt*; is Deified with a sumptuous Temple at *Memphis* by the name of *Baal Canaan*, *Vulcan*. This Temple was said to be built by *Menes*, the first King of *Egypt* who reigned next after the Gods, that is, by *Menoph* or *Amenophis* who reigned next after the death of *Osiris*, *Isis*, *Orus*, *Bubaste* and *Thoth*. The city, *Memphis* was also said to be built by *Menes*; he began to build it when he fortified it against *Osarsiphus*. And from him it was called *Menoph*, *Moph*, *Noph*, &c; and is to this day called *Menuf* by the *Arabians*. And therefore *Menes* who built the city and temple Was *Menoph* or *Amenophis*. The Priests of *Egypt* at length made this temple above a thousand years older then *Amenophis*, and some of them five or ten thousand years older: but it could not be above two or three hundred years older than the Reign of *Psammiticus* who finished it, and died 614 years before *Christ*. When *Menoph* or *Menes* built the city, he built a bridge there over the *Nile*. a work too great to be older than the Monarchy of *Egypt*.

909. *Amenophis*, called *Memnon* by the *Greeks*, built the *Memnonia* at *Susa*, whilst *Egypt* was under the government of *Proteus* his Viceroy.

904. *Troy* taken. *Amenophis* was still at *Susa*; the *Greeks* feigning that he came from thence to the *Trojan* war.

903. *Demophoon*, the son of *Theseus* by *Phoedra* the daughter of *Minos*, Reigns at *Athens*.

901. *Amenophis* builds small Pyramids in *Cochome*.

896. *Ulysses* leaves *Calypso* in the Island *Ogygie* (perhaps *Cadis* or *Cales*.) She was the daughter of *Atlas*, according to *Homer*. The ancients at length feigned that this Island, (which from *Atlas* they called *Atlantis*) had been as big as all *Europe*, *Africa* and *Asia*, but was sunk into the Sea.

895. *Teucer* builds *Salamis* in *Cyprus*. *Hadad* or *Benhadad* King of *Syria* dies, and is Deified at *Damascus* with a Temple and Ceremonies.

887. *Amenophis* dies, and is succeeded by his son *Ramesses* or *Rhampsinitus*, who builds the western Portico of the Temple of *Vulcan*. The *Egyptians* dedicated to *Osiris*, *Isis*, *Orus* senior, *Typhon*, and *Nephthe* the sister and wife of *Typhon*, the five days added by the *Egyptians* to the twelve Calendar months of the old Luni-solar year, and said that they were added when these five Princes were born. They were therefore added in the Reign of *Ammon* the father of these five Princes: but this year was scarce brought into common use before the Reign of *Amenophis*: for in his Temple or Sepulchre at *Abydus*, they placed a Circle of 365 cubits in compass, covered on the upper side with a plate of gold, and divided into 365 equal parts, to represent all the days of the year; every part having the day of the year, and the Heliacal Risings and Settings of the Stars on that day, noted upon it. And this Circle remained there 'till *Cambyses* spoiled the temples of *Egypt*: and from this monument I collect that it was *Amenophis* who established this year, fixing the beginning thereof to one of the four Cardinal Points of the heavens. For had not the beginning thereof been now fixed, the Heliacal Risings and Settings of the Stars could not have been noted upon the days thereof. The Priests of *Egypt* therefore in the Reign of *Amenophis* continued to observe the Heliacal Risings and Settings of the Stars upon every day. And when by the Sun's Meridional Altitudes they had found the Solstices and Equinoxes according to the Sun's mean motion, his Equation being not yet known, they fixed the beginning of this year to the Vernal Equinox, and in memory thereof erected this monument. Now this year being carried into *Chaldæa*, the *Chaldæans* began their year of *Nabonassar* on the same *Thoth* with the *Egyptians*, and made it of the same length. And the *Thoth* of the first year of *Nabonassar* fell upon the 26th day of *February*: which was 33 days and five hours before the Vernal Equinox, according to the Sun's mean motion. And the *Thoth* of this year moves backwards 33 days and five hours in 137 years, and therefore fell upon the Vernal Equinox 137 years before the *Æra* of *Nabonassar* began; that is, 884 years before *Christ*. And if it began upon the day next after the Vernal Equinox, it might begin three or four years earlier; and there we may place the death of this King. The *Greeks* feigned that he was the Son of *Tithonus*, and therefore he was born after the return of *Sesac* into *Egypt*, with *Tithonus* and other captives, and so might be about 70 or 75 years old at his death.

883. *Dido* builds *Carthage*, and the *Phoenicians* begin presently after to sail as far as to the *Straights Mouth*, and beyond. *Æneas* was still alive, according to *Virgil*.

870. *Hesiod* flourishes. He hath told us himself that he lived in the age next after the wars of *Thebes* and *Troy*, and that this age should end when the men then living grew hoary and dropt into the grave; and therefore it was but of an ordinary length: and *Herodotus* has told us that *Hesiod* and *Homer* were but 400 years older than himself. Whence it follows that the destruction of *Troy* was not older than we have represented it.

860. *Moeris* Reigns in *Egypt*. He adorned *Memphis*, and translated the seat of his Empire thither from *Thebes*. There he built the famous Labyrinth, and the northern portico of the Temple of *Vulcan*, and dug the great Lake called the Lake of *Moeris*, and upon the bottom of it built two great Pyramids of brick: and

these things being not mentioned by *Homer* or *Hesiod*, were unknown to them, and done after their days. *Moeris* wrote also a book of Geometry.

852. *Hazael* the successor of *Hadad* at *Damascus* dies and is Deified, as was *Hadad* before: and these Gods, together with *Arathes* the wife of *Hadad*, were worship in their Sepulchres or Temples, 'till the days of *Josephus* the *Jew*; and the *Syrians* boasted their antiquity, not knowing, saith *Josephus*, that they were novel.

844. The *Æolic* Migration. *Boeotia*, formerly called *Cadmeis*, is seized by the *Boeotians*.

838. *Cheops* Reigns in *Egypt*. He built the greatest Pyramid for his sepulchre, and forbad the worship of the former Kings; intending to have been worshipped himself.

825. The *Heraclides*, after three Generations, or an hundred years, reckoned from their former expedition, return into *Peloponnesus*. Henceforward, to the end of the first *Messenian* war, reigned ten Kings of *Sparta* by one Race, and nine by another; ten of *Messene*, and nine of *Arcadia*: which, by reckoning (according to the ordinary course of nature) about twenty years to a Reign, one Reign with another, will take up about 190 years. And the seven Reigns more in one of the two Races of the Kings of *Sparta*, and eight in the other, to the battle at *Thermopylæ*; may take up 150 years more: and so place the return of the *Heraclides*, about 820 years before *Christ*.

824. *Cephren* Reigns in *Egypt*, and builds another great Pyramid.

808. *Mycerinus* Reigns there, and begins the third great Pyramid. He shut up the body of his daughter in a hollow ox, and caused her to be worshipped daily with odours.

804. The war, between the *Athenians* and *Spartans*, in which *Codrus*, King of the *Athenians*, is slain.

801. *Nitocris*, the sister of *Mycerinus*, succeeds him, and finishes the third great Pyramid.

794. The *Ionic* Migration, under the conduct of the sons of *Codrus*.

790. *Pul* founds the *Assyrian* Empire.

788. *Asychis* Reigns in *Egypt*, and builds the eastern Portico of the Temple of *Vulcan* very splendidly; and a large Pyramid of brick, made of mud dug out of the Lake of *Moeris*. *Egypt* breaks into several Kingdoms. *Gnephactus* and *Bocchoris* Reign successively in the upper *Egypt*; *Stephanathis*, *Necepsos* and *Nechus*, at *Sais*; *Anysis* or *Amosis*, at *Anysis* or *Hanes*; and *Tacellotis*, at *Bubaste*.

776. *Iphitus* restores the Olympiads. And from this *Æra* the Olympiads are now reckoned. *Gnephactus* Reigns at *Memphis*.

772. *Necepsos* and *Petosiris* invent Astrology in *Egypt*.

760. *Semiramis* begins to flourish; *Sanchoniatho* writes.

751. *Sabacon* the *Ethiopian*, invades *Egypt*, now divided into various Kingdoms, burns *Bocchoris*, slays *Nechus*, and makes *Anysis* fly.

747. *Pul*, King of *Assyria*, dies, and is succeeded at *Nineveh* by *Tiglathpilasser*, and at *Babylon* by *Nabonassar*. The *Egyptians*, who fled from *Sabacon*, carry their Astrology and Astronomy to *Babylon*, and found the *Æra* of *Nabonassar* in *Egyptian* years.

740. *Tiglathpilasser*, King of *Assyria*, takes *Damascus*, and captivates the *Syrians*.

729. *Tiglathpilasser* is succeeded by *Salmanasser*.

721. *Salmanasser*, King of *Assyria*, carries the Ten Tribes into captivity.

719. *Sennacherib* Reigns over *Assyria*. *Archias* the son of *Evagetus*, of the stock of *Hercules*, leads a Colony from *Corinth* into *Sicily*, and builds *Syracuse*.

717. *Tirhakah* Reigns in *Ethiopia*.

714. *Sennacherib* is put to flight by the *Ethiopians* and *Egyptians*, with great slaughter.

711. The *Medes* revolt from the *Assyrians*. *Sennacherib* slain. *Asserhadon* succeeds him. This is that *Asserhadon-Pul*, or *Sardanapalus*, the son of *Anacyndaraxis*, or *Sennacherib*, who built *Tarsus* and *Anchiale* in one day.

710. *Lycurgus*, brings the poems of *Homer* out of *Asia* into *Greece*.

708. *Lycurgus*, becomes tutor to *Charillus* or *Charilaus*, the young King of *Sparta*. *Aristotle* makes *Lycurgus* as old as *Iphitus*, because his name was upon the Olympic Disc. But the Disc was one of the five games called the *Quinquertium*, and the *Quinquertium* was first instituted upon the eighteenth Olympiad. *Socrates* and *Thucydides* made the institutions of *Lycurgus* about 300 years older than the end of the *Peloponnesian* war, that is, 705 years before *Christ*.

701. *Sabacon*, after a Reign of 50 years, relinquishes *Egypt* to his son *Sevechus* or *Sethon*, who becomes Priest of *Vulcan*, and neglects military affairs.

698. *Manasseh* Reigns.

697. The *Corinthians* begin first of any men to build ships with three orders of oars, called *Triremes*. Hitherto the *Greeks* had used long vessels of fifty oars.

687. *Tirhakah* Reigns in *Egypt*.

681. *Asserhadon* invades *Babylon*.

673. The *Jews* conquered by *Asserhadon*, and *Manasseh* carried captive to *Babylon*.

671. *Asserbadon* invades *Egypt*. The government of *Egypt* committed to twelve princes.

668. The western nations of *Syria*, *Phoenicia* and *Egypt*, revolt from the *Assyrians*. *Asserhadon* dies, and is succeeded by *Saosduchinus*. *Manasseh* returns from Captivity.

658. *Phraortes* Reigns in *Media*. The *Prytanes* Reign in *Corinth*, expelling their Kings.

657. The *Corinthians* overcome the *Corcyreans* at sea: and this was the oldest sea fight.

655. *Psammiticus* becomes King of all *Egypt*, by conquering the other eleven Kings with whom he had already reigned fifteen years: he reigned about 39 years more. Henceforward the *Ionians* had access into *Egypt*; and thence came the *Ionian* Philosophy, Astronomy and Geometry.

652. The first *Messenian* war begins: it lasted twenty years.

647. *Charops*, the first decennial Archon of the *Athenians*. Some of these Archons might dye before the end of the ten years, and the remainder of the ten years be supplied by a new Archon. And hence the seven decennial Archons might not take up above forty or fifty years. *Saosduchinus* King of *Assyria* dies, and is succeeded by *Chyniladon*.

640. *Josiah* Reigns in *Judæa*.

636. *Phraortes*] King of the *Medes*, is slain in a war against the *Assyrians*. *Astyages* succeeds him.

635. The *Scythians* invade the *Medes* and *Assyrians*.

633. *Battus* builds *Cyrene*, where *Irasa*, the city of *Antæus*, had stood.

627. *Rome* is built.

625. *Nabopolassar* revolts from the King of *Assyria*, and Reigns over *Babylon*. *Phalantus* leads the *Parthenians* into *Italy*, and builds *Tarentum*.

617. *Psammiticus* dies. *Nechaoh* reigns in *Egypt*.

611. *Cyaxeres* Reigns over the *Medes*.

610. The Princes of the *Scythians* slain in a feast by *Cyaxeres*.

609. *Josiah* slain. *Cyaxeres* and *Nebuchadnezzar* overthrow *Nineveh*, and, by sharing the *Assyrian* Empire, grow great.

607. *Creon* the first annual Archon of the *Athenians*. The second *Messenian* war begins. *Cyaxeres* makes the *Scythians* retire beyond *Colchos* and *Iberia*, and seizes the *Assyrian* Provinces of *Armenia*, *Pontus* and *Cappadocia*.

606. *Nebuchadnezzar* invades *Syria* and *Judæa*.

604. *Nabopolassar* dies, and is succeeded by his Son *Nebuchadnezzar*, who had already Reigned two years with his father.

600. *Darius* the *Mede*, the son of *Cyaxeres*, is born.

599. *Cyrus* is born of *Mandane*, the Sister of *Cyaxeres*, and daughter of *Astyages*.

596. *Susiana* and *Elam* conquered by *Nebuchadnezzar*. *Caranus* and *Perdiccas* fly from *Phidon*, and found the Kingdom of *Macedon*. *Phidon* introduces Weights and Measures, and the Coining of Silver Money.

590. *Cyaxeres* makes war upon *Alyattes* King of *Lydia*.

588. The Temple of *Solomon* is burnt by *Nebuchadnezzar*. The *Messenians* being conquered, fly into *Sicily*, and build *Messana*.

585. In the sixth year of the *Lydian* war, a total Eclipse of the Sun, predicted by *Thales*, *May* the 28th, puts an end to a Battel between the *Medes* and *Lydians*. Whereupon they make Peace, and ratify it by a marriage between *Darius Medus* the son of *Cyaxeres*, and *Ariene* the daughter of *Alyattes*.

584. *Phidon* presides in the 49th Olympiad.

580. *Phidon* is overthrown. Two men chosen by lot, out of the city *Elis*, to preside in the Olympic Games.

572. *Draco* is Archon of the *Athenians*, and makes laws for them.

568. The *Amphictions* make war upon the *Cirrheans*, by the advice of *Solon*, and take *Cirrha*. *Clisthenes*, *Alcmæon* and *Eurolicus* commanded the forces of the *Amphictions*, and were contemporary to *Phidon*. For *Leocides* the son of *Phidon*, and *Megacles* the son of *Alcmæon*, at one and the same time, courted *Agarista* the daughter of *Clisthenes*.

569. *Nebuchadnezzar* invades *Egypt*. *Darius* the *Mede* Reigns.

562. *Solon*, being Archon of the *Athenians*, makes laws for them.

557. *Periander* dies, and *Corinth* becomes free from Tyrants.

555. *Nabonadius* Reigns at *Babylon*. His Mother *Nitocris* adorns and fortifies that City.

550. *Pisistratus* becomes Tyrant at *Athens*. The Conference between *Croesus* and *Solon*.

549. *Solon* dies, *Hegestratus* being Archon of *Athens*.

544. *Sardes* is taken by *Cyrus*. *Darius* the *Mede* recoins the *Lydian* money into *Darics*.

538. *Babylon* is taken by *Cyrus*.

536. *Cyrus* overcomes *Darius* the *Mede*, and translates the Empire to the *Persians*. The *Jews* return from Captivity, and found the second Temple.

529. *Cyrus* dies. *Cambyses* Reigns,

521. *Darius* the son of *Hystaspes* Reigns. The *Magi* are slain. The various Religions of the several Nations of *Persia*, which consisted in the worship of their ancient Kings, are abolished; and by the influence of *Hystaspes* and *Zoroaster*, the worship of One God, at Altars, without Temples is set up in all *Persia*.

520. The second Temple is built at *Jerusalem* by the command of *Darius*.

515. The second Temple is finished and dedicated.

513. *Harmodius* and *Aristogiton*, slay *Hipparchus* the son of *Pisistratus*, Tyrant of the *Athenians*.

508. The Kings of the *Romans* expelled, and Consuls erected.

491. The Battle of *Marathon*.

485. *Xerxes* Reigns.

480. The Passage of *Xerxes* over the *Hellespont* into *Greece*, and Battles of *Thermopylæ* and *Salamis*.

464. *Artaxerxes Longimanus* Reigns.

457. *Ezra* returns into *Judæa. Johanan* the father of *Jaddua* was now grown up, having a chamber in the Temple.

444. *Nehemiah* returns into *Judæa. Herodotus* writes.

431. The *Peloponnesian* war begins.

428. *Nehemiah* drives away *Manasseh* the brother of *Jaddua*, because he had married *Nicaso* the daughter of *Sanballat*.

424. *Darius Nothus* Reigns.

422. *Sanballat* builds a Temple in *Mount Gerizim* and makes his son-in-law *Manasseh* the first High-Priest thereof.

412. Hitherto the Priests and Levites were numbered, and written in the Chronicles of the *Jews*, before the death of *Nehemiah*: at which time either *Johanan* or *Jaddua* was High-Priest, And here Ends the Sacred History of the *Jews*.

405. *Artaxerxes Mnemon* Reigns. The end of the *Peloponnesian* war.

359. *Artaxerxes Ochus* Reigns.

338. *Arogus* Reigns.

336. *Darius Codomannus* Reigns.

332. The *Persian* Empire conquered by *Alexander* the great.

331. *Darius Codomannus*, the last King of *Persia*, slain.

THE
CHRONOLOGY
OF ANCIENT KINGDOMS AMENDED.

CHAP. I

Of the Chronology of the First Ages of the Greeks.

ALL Nations, before they began to keep exact accounts of Time, have been prone to raise their Antiquities; and this humour has been promoted, by the Contentions between Nations about their Originals. *Herodotus* [3] tells us, that the Priests of *Egypt* reckoned from the Reign of *Menes* to that of *Sethon*, who put *Sennacherib* to flight, three hundred forty and one Generations of men, and as many Priests of *Vulcan*, and as many Kings of *Egypt*: and that three hundred Generations make ten thousand years; *for*, saith he, *three Generations of men make an hundred years*: and the remaining forty and one Generations make 1340 years: and so the whole time from the Reign of *Menes* to that of *Sethon* was 11340 years. And by this way of reckoning, and allotting longer Reigns to the Gods of *Egypt* than to the Kings which followed them, *Herodotus* tells us from the Priests of *Egypt*, that from *Pan* to *Amosis* were 15000 years, and from *Hercules* to *Amosis* 17000 years. So also the *Chaldæans* boasted of their Antiquity; for *Callisthenes*, the Disciple of *Aristotle*, sent Astronomical Observations from *Babylon* to *Greece*, said to be of 1903 years standing before the times of *Alexander* the great. And the *Chaldæans* boasted further, that they had observed the Stars 473000 years; and there were others who made the Kingdoms of *Assyria*, *Media* and *Damascus*, much older than the truth.

Some of the *Greeks* called the times before the Reign of *Ogyges*, Unknown, because they had No History of them; those between his flood and the beginning of the Olympiads, Fabulous, because their History was much mixed with Poetical Fables: and those after the beginning of the Olympiads, Historical, because their History was free from such Fables. The fabulous Ages wanted a good Chronology, and so also did the Historical, for the first 60 or 70 Olympiads.

The *Europeans*, had no Chronology before the times of the *Persian* Empire: and whatsoever Chronology they now have of ancienter times, hath been framed since, by reasoning and conjecture. In the beginning of that Monarchy, *Acusilaus* made *Phoroneus* as old as *Ogyges* and his flood, and that flood 1020 years older than the first Olympiad; which is above 680 years older than the truth: and to make out this reckoning his followers have encreased the Reigns of Kings in length and number. *Plutarch* [4] tells us that the Philosophers anciently delivered their Opinions in Verse, as *Orpheus, Hesiod, Parmenides, Xenophanes, Empedocles, Thales*; but afterwards left off the use of Verses; and that *Aristarchus, Timocharis, Aristillus, Hipparchus*, did not make Astronomy the more contemptible by describing it in Prose; after *Eudoxus, Hesiod*, and *Thales* had wrote of it in Verse. *Solon* wrote [5] in Verse, and all the Seven Wise Men were addicted to Poetry, as

Anaximenes [6] affirmed. 'Till those days the *Greeks* wrote only in Verse, and while they did so there could be no Chronology, nor any other History, than such as was mixed with poetical fancies. *Pliny,* [7] in reckoning up the Inventors of things, tells us, *that* Pherecydes Syrius *taught to compose discourses in Prose in the Reign of* Cyrus, *and* Cadmus Milesius *to write History.* And in [8] another place he saith *that* Cadmus Milesius *was the first that wrote in Prose. Josephus* tells us [9] that *Cadmus Milesius* and *Acusilaus* were but a little before the expedition of the *Persians* against the *Greeks:* and *Suidas* [10] calls *Acusilaus* a most ancient Historian, and saith that *he wrote Genealogies out of tables of brass, which his father, as was reported, found in a corner of his house.* Who hid them there may be doubted: For the *Greeks* [11] had no publick table or inscription older than the Laws of *Draco. Pherecydes Atheniensis,* in the Reign of *Darius Hystaspis,* or soon after, wrote of the Antiquities and ancient Genealogies of the *Athenians,* in ten books; and was one of the first *European* writers of this kind, and one of the best; whence he had the name of *Genealogus;* and by *Dionysius* [12] *Halicarnassensis* is said to be second to none of the Genealogers. *Epimenides,* not the Philosopher, but an Historian, wrote also of the ancient Genealogies: and *Hellanicus,* who was twelve years older than *Herodotus,* digested his History by the Ages or Successions of the Priestesses of *Juno Argiva.* Others digested theirs by those of the Archons of *Athens,* or Kings of the *Lacedæmonians. Hippias* the *Elean* published a Breviary of the Olympiads, supported by no certain arguments, as *Plutarch* [13] tells us: he lived in the 105th Olympiad, and was derided by *Plato* for his Ignorance. This Breviary seems to have contained nothing more than a short account of the Victors in every Olympiad. Then [14] *Ephorus,* the disciple of *Isocrates,* formed a Chronological History of *Greece,* beginning with the Return of the *Heraclides* into *Peloponnesus,* and ending with the Siege of *Perinthus,* in the twentieth year of *Philip* the father of *Alexander* the great, that is, eleven years before the fall of the *Persian* Empire: but [15] he digested things by Generations, and the reckoning by the Olympiads, or by any other *Æra,* was not yet in use among the *Greeks.* The *Arundelian* Marbles were composed sixty years after the death of *Alexander* the great (*An.* 4. *Olymp.* 128.) and yet mention not the Olympiads, nor any other standing *Æra,* but reckon backwards from the time then present. But Chronology was now reduced to a reckoning by Years; and in the next Olympiad *Timæus Siculus* improved it: for he wrote a History in Several books, down to his own times, according to the Olympiads; comparing the *Ephori,* the Kings of *Sparta,* the Archons of *Athens,* and the Priestesses of *Argos* with the Olympic Victors, so as to make the Olympiads, and the Genealogies and Successions of Kings and Priestesses, and the Poetical Histories suit with one another, according to the best of his judgment: and where he left off, *Polybius* began, and carried on the History. *Eratosthenes* wrote above an hundred years after the death of *Alexander* the great: He was followed by *Apollodorus;* and these two have been followed ever since by Chronologers.

But how uncertain their Chronology is, and how doubtful it was reputed by the *Greeks* of those times, may be understood by these passages of *Plutarch. Some reckon* Lycurgus, saith he, [16] *contemporary to* Iphitus, *and to have been his companion in ordering the Olympic festivals, amongst whom was* Aristotle *the Philosopher; arguing from the Olympic Disc, which had the name of* Lycurgus *upon it. Others supputing the times by the Kings of* Lacedæmon, *as* Eratosthenes *and* Apollodorus, *affirm that he was not a few years older than the first Olympiad.* He began to flourish in the 17th or 18th Olympiad, and at length *Aristotle* made him as old as the first Olympiad; and so did *Epaminondas,* as he is cited by *Ælian* and *Plutarch:* and then *Eratosthenes, Apollodorus,* and their followers, made him above an hundred years older.

And in another place *Plutarch*[17] tells us: The Congress of Solon *with* Croesus, *some think they can confute by Chronology. But a History so illustrious, and verified by so many witnesses, and which is more, so agreeable to the manners of* Solon, *and worthy of the greatness of his mind, and of his wisdom, I cannot persuade my self to reject because of some Chronological Canons, as they call them, which hundreds of authors correcting, have not yet been able to constitute any thing certain, in which they could agree amongst themselves, about repugnancies.*

As for the Chronology of the *Latines,* that is still more uncertain. *Plutarch*[18] represents great uncertainties in the Originals of *Rome,* and so doth *Servius*[19.] The old Records of the *Latines* were burnt[20] by the *Gauls,* an hundred and twenty years after the Regifuge, and sixty-four years before the death of *Alexander* the great: and *Quintus Fabius Pictor,*[21] the oldest Historian of the *Latines,* lived an hundred years later than that King, and took almost all things from *Diocles Peparethius,* a *Greek.* The Chronologers of *Gallia, Spain, Germany, Scythia, Swedeland, Britain* and *Ireland* are of a date still later; for *Scythia* beyond the *Danube* had no letters, 'till *Ulphilas* their Bishop formed them; which was about six hundred years after the death of *Alexander* the great: and *Germany* had none 'till it received them, from the western Empire of the *Latines,* above seven hundred years after the death of that King. The *Hunns,* had none in the days of *Procopius,* who flourished 850 years after the death of that King: and *Sweden* and *Norway* received them still later. And things said to be done above one or two hundred years before the use of letters, are of little credit.

Diodorus,[22] in the beginning of his History tells us, that he did not define by any certain space the times preceding the *Trojan* War, because he had no certain foundation to rely upon: but from the *Trojan* war, according to the reckoning of *Apollodorus,* whom he followed, there were eighty years to the Return of the *Heraclides* into *Peloponnesus;* and that from that Period to the first Olympiad, there were three hundred and twenty eight years, computing the times from the Kings of the *Lacedæmonians. Apollodorus* followed *Eratosthenes,* and both of them followed *Thucydides,* in reckoning eighty years from the *Trojan* war to the Return of the *Heraclides:* but in reckoning 328 years from that Return to the first Olympiad, *Diodorus* tells us, that the times were computed from the Kings of the *Lacedæmonians;* and *Plutarch*[23] tells us, that *Apollodorus, Eratosthenes* and others followed that computation: and since this reckoning is still received by Chronologers, and was gathered by computing the times from the Kings of the *Lacedæmonians,* that is from their number, let us re-examin that Computation.

The *Egyptians* reckoned the Reigns of Kings equipollent to Generations of men, and three Generations to an hundred years, as above; and so did the *Greeks* and *Latines*: and accordingly they have made their Kings Reign one with another thirty and three years a-piece, and above. For they make the seven Kings of *Rome* who preceded the Consuls to have Reigned 244 years, which is 35 years a-piece: and the first twelve Kings of *Sicyon*, *Ægialeus*, *Europs*, &c. to have Reigned 529 years, which is 44 years a-piece: and the first eight Kings of *Argos*, *Inachus*, *Phoroneus*, &c. to have Reigned 371 years, which is above 46 years a-piece: and between the Return of the *Heraclides* into *Peloponnesus*, and the end of the first *Messenian* war, the ten Kings of *Sparta* in one Race; *Eurysthenes*, *Agis*, *Echestratus*, *Labotas*, *Doryagus*, *Agesilaus*, *Archelaus*, *Teleclus*, *Alcamenes*, and *Polydorus*: the nine in the other Race; *Procles*, *Sous*, *Eurypon*, *Prytanis*, *Eunomus*, *Polydectes*, *Charilaus*, *Nicander*, *Theopompus*: the ten Kings of *Messene*; *Cresphontes*, *Epytus*, *Glaucus*, *Isthmius*, *Dotadas*, *Sibotas*, *Phintas*, *Antiochus*, *Euphaes*, *Aristodemus*: and the nine of *Arcadia*; *Cypselus*, *Olæas*, *Buchalion*, *Phialus*, *Simus*, *Pompus*, *Ægineta*, *Polymnestor*, *Æchmis*, according to Chronologers, took up 379 years: which is 38 years a-piece to the ten Kings, and 42 years a-piece to the nine. And the five Kings of the Race of *Eurysthenes*, between the end of the first *Messenian* war, and the beginning of the Reign of *Darius Hystaspis*; *Eurycrates*, *Anaxander*, *Eurycrates II*, *Leon*, *Anaxandrides*, Reigned 202 years, which is above 40 years a-piece.

Thus the *Greek* Chronologers, who follow *Timæus* and *Eratosthenes*, have made the Kings of their several Cities, who lived before the times of the *Persian* Empire, to Reign about 35 or 40 years a-piece, one with another; which is a length so much beyond the course of nature, as is not to be credited. For by the ordinary course of nature Kings Reign, one with another, about eighteen or twenty years a-piece: and if in some instances they Reign, one with another, five or six years longer, in others they Reign as much shorter: eighteen or twenty years is a medium. So the eighteen Kings of *Judah* who succeeded *Solomon*, Reigned 390 years, which is one with another 22 years a-piece. The fifteen Kings of *Israel* after *Solomon*, Reigned 259 years, which is 17¼ years a-piece. The eighteen Kings of *Babylon*, *Nabonassar* &c. Reigned 209 years, which is 11-2/3 years a-piece. The ten Kings of *Persia*; *Cyrus*, *Cambyses*, &c. Reigned 208 years, which is almost 21 years a piece. The sixteen Successors of *Alexander* the great, and of his brother and son in *Syria*; *Seleucus*, *Antiochus Soter*, &c. Reigned 244 years, after the breaking of that Monarchy into various Kingdoms, which is 15¼ years a-piece. The eleven Kings of *Egypt*; *Ptolomæus Lagi*, &c. Reigned 277 years, counted from the same Period, which is 25 years a-piece. The eight in *Macedonia*; *Cassander*, &c. Reigned 138 years, which is 17¼ years a-piece. The thirty Kings of *England*; *William* the Conqueror, *William Rufus*, &c. Reigned 648 years, which is 21½ years a-piece. The first twenty four Kings of *France*; *Pharamundus*, &c. Reigned 458 years, which is 19 years a-piece: the next twenty four Kings of *France*; *Ludovicus Balbus*, &c. 451 years, which is 18¾ years a-piece: the next fifteen, *Philip Valesius*, &c. 315 years, which is 21 years a-piece: and all the sixty three Kings of *France*, 1224 years, which is 19½ years a-piece. Generations from father to son, may be reckoned one with another at about 33 or 34 years a-piece, or about three Generations to an hundred years: but if the reckoning proceed by the eldest sons, they are shorter, so that three of them may be reckoned at about

75 or 80 years: and the Reigns of Kings are still shorter, because Kings are succeeded not only by their eldest sons, but sometimes by their brothers, and sometimes they are slain or deposed; and succeeded by others of an equal or greater age, especially in elective or turbulent Kingdoms. In the later Ages, since Chronology hath been exact, there is scarce an instance to be found of ten Kings Reigning any where in continual Succession above 260 years: but *Timæus* and his followers, and I think also some of his Predecessors, after the example of the *Egyptians*, have taken the Reigns of Kings for Generations, and reckoned three Generations to an hundred, and sometimes to an hundred and twenty years; and founded the Technical Chronology of the *Greeks* upon this way of reckoning. Let the reckoning be reduced to the course of nature, by putting the Reigns of Kings one with another, at about eighteen or twenty years a-piece: and the ten Kings of *Sparta* by one Race, the nine by another Race, the ten Kings of *Messene*, and the nine of *Arcadia*, above mentioned, between the Return of the *Heraclides* into *Peloponnesus*, and the end of the first *Messenian* war, will scarce take up above 180 or 190 years: whereas according to Chronologers they took up 379 years.

For confirming this reckoning, I may add another argument. *Euryleon* the son of *Ægeus*,[24] commanded the main body of the *Messenians* in the fifth year of the first *Messenian* war, and was in the fifth Generation from *Oiolicus* the son *Theras*, the brother-in-law of *Aristodemus*, and tutor to his sons *Eurysthenes* and *Procles*, as *Pausanias*[25] relates: and by consequence, from the return of the *Heraclides*, which was in the days of *Theras*, to the battle which was in the fifth year of this war, there were six Generations, which, as I conceive, being for the most part by the eldest sons, will scarce exceed thirty years to a Generation; and so may amount unto 170 or 180 years. That war lasted 19 or 20 years: add the last 15 years, and there will be about 190 years to the end of that war: whereas the followers of *Timæus* make it about 379 years, which is above sixty years to a Generation.

By these arguments, Chronologers have lengthned the time, between the return of the *Heraclides* into *Peloponnesus* and the first *Messenian* war, adding to it about 190 years: and they have also lengthned the time, between that war and the rise of the *Persian* Empire. For in the Race of the *Spartan* Kings, descended from *Eurysthenes*; after *Polydorus*, reigned[26] these Kings, *Eurycrates, Anaxander, Eurycratides, Leon, Anaxandrides, Clomenes, Leonidas,* &c. And in the other Race descended from *Procles*; after *Theopompus*, reigned[27] these, *Anaxandrides, Archidemus, Anaxileus, Leutychides, Hippocratides, Ariston, Demaratus, Leutychides* II. &c. according to *Herodotus*. These Kings reigned 'till the sixth year of *Xerxes*, in which *Leonidas* was slain by the *Persians* at *Thermopylæ*; and *Leutychides* II. soon after, flying from *Sparta* to *Tegea*, died there. The seven Reigns of the Kings of *Sparta*, which follow *Polydorus*, being added to the ten Reigns above mentioned, which began with that of *Eurysthenes*; make up seventeen Reigns of Kings, between the return of the *Heraclides* into *Peloponnesus* and the sixth year of *Xerxes*: and the eight Reigns following *Theopompus*, being added to the nine Reigns above mentioned, which began with that of *Procles*, make up also seventeen Reigns: and these seventeen Reigns, at twenty years a-piece one with another, amount unto three hundred and forty years. Count these 340 years upwards from the sixth year of *Xerxes*, and one or two years more for the war of the *Heraclides*, and Reign of *Aristodemus*, the father of *Eurysthenes* and *Procles*; and they will place the Return of the *Heraclides* into *Peloponnesus*, 159 years after the death of *Solomon*, and 46 years before the first Olympiad, in which *Corœbus* was victor. But the followers of *Timœus* have placed this Return two hundred and eighty years earlier. Now this being the computation upon which the *Greeks*, as you have heard from *Diodorus* and *Plutarch*, have founded the Chronology of their Kingdoms, which were ancienter than the *Persian* Empire; that Chronology is to be rectified, by shortening the times which preceded the death of *Cyrus*, in the proportion of almost two to one; for the times which follow the death of *Cyrus* are not much amiss.

The Artificial Chronologers, have made *Lycurgus*, the legislator, as old as *Iphitus*, the restorer of the Olympiads; and *Iphitus*, an hundred and twelve years, older than the first Olympiad: and, to help out the Hypothesis, they have feigned twenty eight Olympiads older than the first Olympiad, wherein *Corœbus* was victor. But these things were feigned, after the days of *Thucydides* and *Plato*: for *Socrates* died three years after the end of the *Peloponnesian* war, and *Plato*[28] introduceth him saying, that *the institutions of* Lycurgus *were but of three hundred years standing, or not much more*. And[29] *Thucydides*, in the reading followed by *Stephanus*, saith, that *the* Lacedæmonians, *had from ancient times used good laws, and been free from tyranny; and that from the time that they had used one and the same administration of their commonwealth, to the end of the* Peloponnesian *war, there were three hundred years and a few more*. Count three hundred years back from the end of the *Peloponnesian* war, and they will place the Legislature of *Lycurgus* upon the 19th Olympiad. And, according to *Socrates*, it might be upon the 22d or 23d. *Athenœus*[30] tells us out of ancient authors (*Hellanicus*, *Sosimus* and *Hieronymus*) that *Lycurgus* the Legislator, was contemporary to *Terpander* the Musician; and that *Terpander* was the first man who got the victory in the *Carnea*, in a solemnity of music instituted in those festivals in the 26th Olympiad. He overcame four times in those *Pythic* games, and therefore lived at least 'till the 29th Olympiad: and beginning to flourish in the days of *Lycurgus*, it is not likely that *Lycurgus* began to flourish, much before the 18th Olympiad. The name of *Lycurgus* being on the Olympic Disc, *Aristotle* concluded thence, that *Lycurgus* was the companion of *Iphitus*, in restoring the Olympic games: and this argument might be the ground of the opinion of Chronologers, that *Lycurgus* and *Iphitus* were contemporary. But *Iphitus* did not restore all the Olympic games. He[31] restored indeed the Racing in the first Olympiad, *Corœbus* being victor. In the 14th Olympiad, the double *stadium* was added, *Hypœnus* being victor. And in the 18th Olympiad the *Quinquertium* and Wrestling were added, *Lampus* and *Eurybatus*, two *Spartans*, being victors: And the Disc was one of the games of the *Quinquertium*.[32] *Pausanias* tells us that there were three Discs kept in the Olympic treasury at *Altis*: these therefore having the name of *Lycurgus* upon them, shew that they were given by him, at the institution of the *Quinquertium*, in the 18th Olympiad. Now *Polydectes* King of *Sparta*, being slain before the birth of his son *Charillus* or *Charilaus*, left the Kingdom to

Lycurgus his brother; and *Lycurgus*, upon the birth of *Charillus*, became tutor to the child; and after about eight months travelled into *Crete* and *Asia*, till the child grew up, and brought back with him the poems of *Homer*, and soon after published his laws, suppose upon the 22d or 23d Olympiad; for he was then growing old: and *Terpander* was a Lyric Poet, and began to flourish about this time; for[33] he imitated *Orpheus* and *Homer*, and sung *Homer's* verses and his own, and wrote the laws of *Lycurgus* in verse, and was victor in the *Pythic* games in the 26th Olympiad, as above. He was the first who distinguished the modes of Lyric music by several names. *Ardalus* and *Clonas* soon after did the like for wind music: and from henceforward, by the encouragement of the *Pythic* games, now instituted, several eminent Musicians and Poets flourished in *Greece*: as *Archilochus, Eumelus Corinthius, Polymnestus, Thaletas, Xenodemus, Xenocritus, Sacadas, Tyrtæus, Tlesilla, Rhianus, Alcman, Arion, Stesichorus, Mimnermnus, Alcæus, Sappho, Theognis, Anacreon, Ibycus, Simonides, Æschylus, Pindar*, by whom the Music and Poetry of the *Greeks* were brought to perfection.

Lycurgus, published his laws in the Reign of *Agesilaus*, the son and successor of *Doryagus*, in the Race of the Kings of *Sparta* descended from *Eurysthenes*. From the Return of the *Heraclides* into *Peloponnesus*, to the end of the Reign of *Agesilaus*, there were six Reigns: and from the same Return to the end of the Reign of *Polydectes*, in the Race of the *Spartan* Kings descended from *Procles*, there were also six Reigns: and these Reigns, at twenty years a-piece one with another, amount unto 120 years; besides the short Reign of *Aristodemus*, the father of *Eurysthenes* and *Procles*, which might amount to a year or two: for *Aristodemus* came to the crown, as[34] *Herodotus* and the *Lacedæmonians* themselves affirmed. The times of the deaths of *Agesilaus* and *Polydectes* are not certainly known: but it may be presumed that *Lycurgus* did not meddle with the Olympic games before he came to the Kingdom; and therefore *Polydectes* died in the beginning of the 18th Olympiad, or but a very little before. If it may be supposed that the 20th Olympiad was in, or very near to the middle time between the deaths of the two Kings *Polydectes* and *Agesilaus*, and from thence be counted upwards the aforesaid 120 years, and one year more for the Reign of *Aristodemus*, the reckoning will place the Return of the *Heraclides*, about 45 years before the beginning of the Olympiads.

Iphitus, who restored the Olympic games,[35] was descended from *Oxylus*, the son of *Hæmon*, the son of *Thoas*, the son of *Andræmon*: Hercules and *Andræmon* married two sisters: *Thoas* warred at *Troy*: *Oxylus* returned into *Peloponnesus* with the *Heraclides*. In this return he commanded the body of the *Ætolians*, and recovered *Elea*;[36] from whence his ancestor *Ætolus*, the son of *Endymion*, the son of *Aethlius*, had been driven by *Salmoneus* the grandson of *Hellen*. By the friendship of the *Heraclides*, *Oxylus* had the care of the Olympic Temple committed to him: and the *Heraclides*, for his service done them, granted further upon oath that the country of the *Eleans* should be free from invasions, and be defended by them from all armed force: And when the *Eleans* were thus consecrated, *Oxylus* restored the Olympic games: and after they had been again intermitted, *Iphitus* their King[37] restored them, and made them quadrennial. *Iphitus* is by some reckoned the son of *Hæmon*, by others the son of *Praxonidas*, the son of *Hæmon*: but *Hæmon* being the father of *Oxylus*, I would reckon *Iphitus* the son of *Praxonidas*, the son of *Oxylus*, the son of *Hæmon*. And by this reckoning the Return of the *Heraclides* into *Peloponnesus* will be two Generations by the eldest sons, or about 52 years, before the Olympiads.

Pausanias[38] represents that *Melas* the son of *Antissus*, of the posterity of *Gonussa* the daughter of *Sicyon*, was not above six Generations older than *Cypselus* King of *Corinth*; and that he was contemporary to *Aletes*, who returned with the *Heraclides* into *Peloponnesus*. The Reign of *Cypselus* began *An.* 2, Olymp. 31, according to Chronologers; and six Generations, at about 30 years to a Generation, amount unto 180 years. Count those years backwards from *An.* 2, Olymp. 31, and they will place the Return of the *Heraclides* into *Peloponnesus* 58 years before the first Olympiad. But it might not be so early, if the Reign of *Cypselus* began three or four Olympiads later; for he reigned before the *Persian* Empire began.

Hercules the *Argonaut* was the father of *Hyllus*; the father of *Cleodius*; the father of *Aristomachus*; the father of *Temenus*, *Cresphontes*, and *Aristodemus*, who led the *Heraclides* into *Peloponnesus* and *Eurystheus*, who was of the same age with *Hercules*, was slain in the first attempt of the *Heraclides* to return: *Hyllus* was slain in the second attempt, *Cleodius* in the third attempt, *Aristomachus* in the fourth attempt, and *Aristodemus* died as soon as they were returned, and left the Kingdom of *Sparta* to his sons *Eurysthenes* and *Procles*. Whence their Return was four Generations later than the *Argonautic* expedition: And these Generations were short ones, being by the chief of the family, and suit with the reckoning of *Thucydides* and the Ancients, that the taking of *Troy* was about 75 or eighty years before the return of the *Heraclides* into *Peloponnesus*; and the *Argonautic* expedition one Generation earlier than the taking of *Troy*. Count therefore eighty years backward from the Return of the *Heraclides* into *Peloponnesus* to the *Trojan* war, and the taking of *Troy* will be about 76 years after the death of *Solomon*. And the *Argonautic* expedition, which was one Generation earlier, will be about 43 years after it. From the taking of *Troy* to the Return of the *Heraclides*, could scarce be more than eighty years, because *Orestes* the son of *Agamemnon* was a youth at the taking of *Troy*, and his sons *Penthilus* and *Tisamenus* lived till the Return of the *Heraclides*.

Æsculapius and *Hercules* were *Argonauts*, and *Hippocrates* was the eighteenth inclusively by the father's side from *Æsculapius*, and the nineteenth from *Hercules* by the mother's side: and because these Generations, being taken notice of by writers, were most probably by the principal of the family, and so for the most part by the eldest sons; we may reckon about 28 or at the most about 30 years to a Generation. And thus the seventeen intervals by the father's side, and eighteen by the mother's, will at a middle reckoning amount unto about 507 years: which counted backwards from the beginning of the *Peloponnesian* war, at which time *Hippocrates* began to flourish, will reach up to the 43d year after the death of *Solomon*, and there place the *Argonautic* expedition.

When the *Romans* conquered the *Carthaginians*, the Archives of *Carthage* came into their hands: And thence *Appian*, in his history of the *Punic* wars, tells in round numbers that *Carthage* stood seven hundred years: and[39] *Solinus* adds the odd number of years in these words: *Adrymeto atque Carthagini author est a Tyro populus. Urbem istam, ut Cato in Oratione Senatoria autumat; cum rex Hiarbas rerum in Libya potiretur, Elissa mulier extruxit, domo Phoenix & Carthadam dixit, quod Phoenicum ore exprimit civitatem novam; mox sermone verso Carthago dicta est, quæ post annos septingentos triginta septem exciditur quam fuerat extructa.* *Elissa* was *Dido*, and *Carthage* was destroyed in the Consulship of *Lentulus* and *Mummius*, in the year of the *Julian Period* 4568; from whence count backwards 737 years, and the *Encænia* or Dedication of the City, will fall upon the 16th year of *Pygmalion*, the brother of *Dido*, and King of *Tyre*. She fled in the seventh year of *Pygmalion*, but the *Æra* of the City began with its *Encænia*. Now *Virgil*, and his Scholiast *Servius*, who might have some things from the archives of *Tyre* and *Cyprus*, as well as from those of *Carthage*, relate that *Teucer* came from the war of *Troy* to *Cyprus*, in the days of *Dido*, a little before the Reign of her brother *Pygmalion*; and, in conjunction with her father, seized *Cyprus*, and ejected *Cinyras*: and the Marbles say that *Teucer* came to *Cyprus* seven years after the destruction of *Troy*, and built *Salamis*; and *Apollodorus*, that *Cinyras* married *Metharme* the daughter of *Pygmalion*, and built *Paphos*. Therefore, if the *Romans*, in the days of *Augustus*, followed not altogether the artificial Chronology of *Eratosthenes*, but had these things from the records of *Carthage*, *Cyprus*, or *Tyre*; the arrival of *Teucer* at *Cyprus* will be in the Reign of the predecessor of *Pygmalion*: and by consequence the destruction of *Troy*, about 76 years later than the death of *Solomon*.

Dionysius Halicarnassensis[40] tells us, that in the time of the *Trojan* war, *Latinus* was King of the *Aborigines* in *Italy*, and that in the sixteenth Age after that war, *Romulus* built *Rome*. By Ages he means Reigns of Kings: for after *Latinus* he names sixteen Kings of the *Latines*, the last of which was *Numitor*, in whose days *Romulus* built *Rome*: for *Romulus* was contemporary to *Numitor*, and after him *Dionysius* and others reckon six Kings more over *Rome*, to the beginning of the Consuls. Now these twenty and two Reigns, at about 18 years to a Reign one with another, for many of these Kings were slain, took up 396 years; which counted back from the consulship of *Junius Brutus* and *Valerius Publicola*, the two first Consuls, place the *Trojan* war about 78 years after the death of *Solomon*.

The expedition of *Sesostris* was one Generation earlier than the *Argonautic* expedition: for in his return back into *Egypt* he left *Æetes* in *Colchis*, and *Æetes* reigned there 'till the *Argonautic* expedition; and *Prometheus* was left by *Sesostris* with a body of men at *Mount Caucasus*, to guard that pass, and after thirty years was released by *Hercules* the *Argonaut*: and *Phlyas* and *Eumedon*, the sons of the great *Bacchus*, so the Poets call *Sesostris*, and of *Ariadne* the daughter of *Minos*, were *Argonauts*. At the return of *Sesostris* into *Egypt*, his brother *Danaus* fled from him into *Greece* with his fifty daughters, in a long ship; after the pattern of which the ship *Argo* was built: and *Argus*, the son of *Danaus*, was the master-builder thereof. *Nauplius* the *Argonaut* was born in *Greece*, of *Amymone*, one of the daughters of *Danaus*, and of *Neptune*, the brother and admiral of *Sesostris*. And two others of the daughters of *Danaus* married *Archander* and *Archilites*, the sons of *Achæus*, the son of *Creusa*, the daughter of *Erechtheus* King of *Athens*: and therefore the daughters of *Danaus* were three Generations younger than *Erechtheus*; and by consequence contemporary to *Theseus* the son of *Ægeus*, the adopted son of *Pandion*, the son of *Erechtheus*. *Theseus*, in the time of the *Argonautic* expedition, was of about 50 years of age, and so was born about the 33d year of *Solomon*: for he stole *Helena*[41] just before that expedition, being then 50 years old, and she but seven, or as some say ten. *Pirithous* the son of *Ixion* helped *Theseus* to steal *Helena*, and then[42] *Theseus* went with *Pirithous* to steal *Persephone*, the daughter of *Aidoneus*, or *Orcus*, King of the *Molossians*, and was taken in the action: and whilst he lay in prison, *Castor* and *Pollux* returning from the *Argonautic* expedition, released their sister *Helena*, and captivated *Æthra* the mother of *Theseus*. Now the daughters of *Danaus* being contemporary to *Theseus*, and some of their sons being *Argonauts*, *Danaus* with his daughters fled from his brother *Sesostris* into *Greece* about one Generation before the *Argonautic* expedition; and therefore *Sesostris* returned into *Egypt* in the Reign of *Rehoboam*. He came out of *Egypt* in the fifth year of *Rehoboam*,[43] and spent nine years in that expedition, against the Eastern Nations and *Greece*; and therefore returned back into *Egypt*, in the fourteenth year of *Rehoboam*. *Sesac* and *Sesostris* were therefore Kings of all *Egypt*, at one and the same time: and they agree not only in the time, but also in their actions and conquests. God gave *Sesac* [Hebrew: mmlkvt h'rtsvt] *the Kingdoms of the lands*, 2 Chron. xii. Where *Herodotus* describes the expedition of *Sesostris*, *Josephus*[44] tells us that he described the expedition of *Sesac*, and attributed his actions to *Sesostris*, erring only in the name of the King. Corruptions of names are frequent in history; *Sesostris* was otherwise called *Sesochris*, *Sesochis*, *Sesoosis*, *Sethosis*, *Sesonchis*, *Sesonchosis*. Take away the *Greek* termination, and the names become *Sesost*, *Sesoch*, *Sesoos*, *Sethos*, *Sesonch*: which names differ very little from *Sesach*. *Sesonchis* and *Sesach* differ no more than *Memphis* and *Moph*, two names of the same city. *Josephus*[45] tells us also, from *Manetho*, that *Sethosis* was the brother of *Armais*, and that these brothers were otherwise called *Ægyptus* and *Danaus*; and that upon the return of *Sethosis* or *Ægyptus*, from his great conquests into *Egypt*, *Armais* or *Danaus* fled from him into *Greece*.

Egypt was at first divided into many small Kingdoms, like other nations; and grew into one monarchy by degrees: and the father of *Solomon's* Queen, was the first King of *Egypt*, who came into *Phoenicia* with an Army: but he only took *Gezir*, and gave it to his daughter. *Sesac*, the next King, came out of *Egypt* with an army of *Libyans*, *Troglodites* and *Ethiopians*, 2 Chron. xii. 3. and therefore was then King of all those countries; and we do not read in Scripture, that any former King of *Egypt*; who Reigned over all those nations, came out of *Egypt* with a great army to conquer other countries. The sacred history of the *Israelites*, from the days of *Abraham* to the days of *Solomon*, admits of no such conqueror. *Sesostris* reigned over all the same nations of the *Libyans*, *Troglodites* and *Ethiopians*, and came out of *Egypt* with a great army to conquer other Kingdoms. The Shepherds reigned long in the lower part of *Egypt*, and were expelled thence, just before the building of *Jerusalem* and the Temple; according to *Manetho*; and whilst they Reigned in the lower part of *Egypt*, the upper part thereof was under other Kings: and while *Egypt* was divided into several Kingdoms, there was no room for any such King of all *Egypt* as *Sesostris*; and no historian makes him later than *Sesac*: and therefore he was one and the same King of *Egypt* with *Sesac*. This is no new opinion: *Josephus* discovered it when he affirmed that *Herodotus* erred, in ascribing the actions of *Sesac* to *Sesostris*, and that the error was only in the name of the King: for this is as much as to say, that the true name of him who did those things described by *Herodotus*, was *Sesac*; and that *Herodotus* erred only in calling him *Sesostris*; or that he was called *Sesostris* by a corruption of his name. Our great Chronologer, *Sir John Marsham*, was also of opinion that *Sesostris* was *Sesac*: and if this be granted, it is then most certain, that *Sesostris* came out of *Egypt* in the fifth year of *Rehoboam* to invade the nations, and returned back into *Egypt* in the 14th year of that King; and that *Danaus* then flying from his brother, came into *Greece* within a year or two after: and the *Argonautic* expedition being one Generation later than that invasion, and than the coming of *Danaus* into *Greece*, was certainly about 40 or 45 years later than the death of *Solomon*. *Prometheus* stay'd on *Mount Caucasus*[46] thirty years, and then was released by *Hercules*: and therefore the *Argonautic* expedition was thirty years after *Prometheus* had been left on *Mount Caucasus* by *Sesostris*, that is, about 44 years after the death of *Solomon*.

All nations, before the just length of the Solar year was known, reckoned months by the course of the moon; and years by the[47] returns of winter and summer, spring and autumn: and in making Calendars for their Festivals, reckoned thirty days to a Lunar month, and twelve Lunar months to a year; taking the nearest round numbers: whence came the division of the Ecliptic into 360 degrees. So in the time of *Noah*'s flood, when the Moon could not be seen, *Noah* reckoned thirty days to a month: but if the Moon appeared a day or two before the end of the month,[48] they began the next month with the first day of her appearing: and this was done generally, 'till the *Egyptians* of *Thebais* found the length of the Solar year. So[49] *Diodorus* tells us that *the* Egyptians *of* Thebais *use no intercalary months, nor subduct any days* [from the month] *as is done by most of the* Greeks. And[50] *Cicero, est consuetudo Siculorum cæterorumque Græcorum, quod suos dies mensesque congruere volunt cum Solis Lunæque ratione, ut nonnumquam siquid discrepet, eximant unum aliquem diem aut summum biduum ex mense* [civili dierum triginta] *quos illi* [Greek: exairesimous] *dies nominant.* And *Proclus*, upon *Hesiod*'s [Greek: triakas] mentions the same thing. And[51] *Geminus*: [Greek: Prothesis gar ên tois archaiois, tous men mênas agein kata selênên, tous de eniautous kath' hêlion. To gar hypo tôn nomôn, kai tôn chrêsmôn parangellomenon, to thyein kata g', êgoun ta patria, mênas, hêmeras, eniautous: touto dielabon apantes hoi Hellênes tôi tous men heniautous symphônôs agein tôi hêliôi; tas de hêmeras kai tous mênas têi selênê. esti de to men kath' hêlion agein tous eniautous, to peri tas autas hôras tou eniautou tas autas thysias tois theois epiteleithai, kai tên men earinên thysian dia pantos kata to ear synteleithai; tên de therinên, kata to theros; homoiôs de kai kata tous loipous kairous tou etous tas autas thysias piptein. Touto gar hypelabon prosênes, kai kecharismenon einai tois theois. Touto d' allôs ouk an dynaito genesthai, ei mê hai tropai, kai hai isêmeriai peri tous autous topous gignointo. To de kata selênên agein tas hêmeras, toiouton esti; to akolouthôs tois tês selênês phôtismois tas prosêgorias tôn hêmerôn ginesthai. apo gar tôn tês selênês phôtismôn hai prosêgoriai tôn hêmerôn katônomasthêsan. En hêi men gar hêmerai nea hê selênê phainetai, kata synaloiphên neomênia prosêgoreuthê; en hêi de hêmerai tên deuteran phasin poieitai, deuteran prosêgoreusan; tên de kata meson tou mênos ginomenên phasin tês selênês, apo autou tou symbainontos dichomênian ekalesan. kai katholou de pasas tas hêmeras apo tôn tês selênês phôtismatôn prosônomasan. hothen kai tên triakostên tou mênos hêmeran eschatên ousan apo autou tou symbainontos triakada ekalesan.]

Propositum enim fuit veteribus, menses quidem agere secundum Lunam, annos vero secundum Solem. Quod enim a legibus & Oraculis præcipiebatur, ut sacrificarent secundum tria, videlicet patria, menses, dies, annos; hoc ita distincte faciebant universi Græci, ut annos agerent congruenter cum Sole, dies vero & menses cum Luna. Porro secundum Solem annos agere, est circa easdem tempestates anni eadem sacrificia Diis perfici, & vernum sacrificium semper in vere consummari, æstivum autem in æstate: similiter & in reliquis anni temporibus eadem sacrificia cadere. Hoc enim putabant acceptum & gratum esse Diis. Hoc autem aliter fieri non posset nisi conversiones solstitiales & æquinoctia in iisdem Zodiaci locis fierent. Secundum Lunam vero dies agere est tale ut congruant cum Lunæ illuminationibus appellationes dierum. Nam a Lunæ illuminationibus appellationes dierum sunt denominatæ. In qua enim die Luna apparet nova, ea per Synaloephen, seu compositionem [Greek: neomênia] id est, Novilunium appellatur. In qua vero die secundam facit apparitionem, eam secundam Lunam vocarunt. Apparitionem Lunæ quæ circa medium mensis fit, ab ipso eventu [Greek: dichomênian], id est medietatem mensis nominarunt. Ac summatim, omnes dies a Lunæ illuminationibus denominarunt. Unde etiam tricesimam mensis diem, cum ultima sit, ab ipso eventu [Greek: triakada] vocarunt.

The ancient Calendar year of the *Greeks* consisted therefore of twelve Lunar months, and every month of thirty days: and these years and months they corrected from time to time, by the courses of the Sun and Moon, omitting a day or two in the month, as often as they found the month too long for the course of the Moon; and adding a month to the year, as often as they found the twelve Lunar months too short for the return of the four seasons. *Cleobulus*,[52] one of the seven wise men of *Greece*, alluded to this year of the *Greeks*, in his Parable of one father who had twelve sons, each of which had thirty daughters half white and half black: and *Thales*[53] called the last day of the month [Greek: triakada], the thirtieth: and *Solon* counted the ten last days of the month backward from the thirtieth, calling that day [Greek: enên kai nean], the old and the new, or the last day of the old month and the first day of the new: for he introduced months of 29 and 30 days alternately, making the thirtieth day of every other month to be the first day of the next month.

To the twelve Lunar months[54] the ancient *Greeks* added a thirteenth, every other year, which made their *Dieteris*; and because this reckoning made their year too long by a month in eight years, they omitted an intercalary month once in eight years, which made their *Octaeteris*, one half of which was their *Tetraeteris*: And these Periods seem to have been almost as old as the religions of *Greece*, being used in divers of their *Sacra*. The[55] *Octaeteris* was the *Annus magnus* of *Cadmus* and *Minos*, and seems to have been brought into *Greece* and *Crete* by the *Phoenicians*, who came thither with *Cadmus* and *Europa*, and to have continued 'till after the days of *Herodotus*: for in counting the length of seventy years[56], he reckons thirty days to a Lunar month, and twelve such months, or 360 days, to the ordinary year, without the intercalary months, and 25 such months to the *Dieteris*: and according to the number of days in the Calendar year of the *Greeks*, *Demetrius Phalereus* had 360 Statues erected to him by the *Athenians*. But the *Greeks*, *Cleostratus*, *Harpalus*, and others, to make their months agree better with the course of the Moon, in the times of the *Persian* Empire, varied the manner of intercaling the three months in the *Octaeteris*; and *Meton* found out the Cycle of intercaling seven months in nineteen years.

The Ancient year of the *Latines* was also Luni-solar; for *Plutarch*[57] tells us, that the year of *Numa* consisted of twelve Lunar months, with intercalary months to make up what the twelve Lunar months wanted of the Solar year. The Ancient year of the *Egyptians* was also Luni-solar, and continued to be so 'till the days of *Hyperion*, or *Osiris*, a King of *Egypt*, the father of *Helius* and *Selene*, or *Orus* and *Bubaste*: For the *Israelites* brought this year out of *Egypt*; and *Diodorus* tells[58] us that *Ouranus* the father of *Hyperion* used this year, and[59] that in the Temple of *Osiris* the Priests appointed thereunto filled 360 Milk Bowls every day: I think he means one Bowl every day, in all 360, to count the number of days in the Calendar year, and thereby to find out the difference between this and the true Solar year: for the year of 360 days was the year, to the end of which they added five days.

That the *Israelites* used the Luni-solar year is beyond question. Their months began with their new Moons. Their first month was called *Abib*, from the earing of Corn in that month. Their Passover was kept upon the fourteenth day of the first month, the Moon being then in the full: and if the Corn was not then ripe enough for offering the first Fruits, the Festival was put off, by adding an intercalary month to the end of the year; and the harvest was got in before the Pentecost, and the other Fruits gathered before the Feast of the seventh month.

Simplicius in his commentary[60] on the first of *Aristotle*'s *Physical Acroasis*, tells us, that *some begin the year upon the Summer Solstice, as the People of* Attica; *or upon the Autumnal Equinox, as the People of* Asia; *or in Winter, as the* Romans; *or about the Vernal Equinox, as the* Arabians *and People of* Damascus: *and the month began, according to some, upon the Full Moon, or upon the New.* The years of all these Nations were therefore Luni-solar, and kept to the four Seasons: and the *Roman* year began at first in Spring, as I seem to gather from the Names of their Months, *Quintilis, Sextilis, September, October, November, December*: and the beginning was afterwards removed to Winter. The ancient civil year of the *Assyrians* and *Babylonians* was also Luni-solar: for this year was also used by the *Samaritans*, who came from several parts of the *Assyrian* Empire; and the *Jews* who came from *Babylon* called the months of their Luni-solar year after the Names of the months of the *Babylonian* year: and *Berosus*[61] tells us that the *Babylonians* celebrated the Feast *Sacæa* upon the 16th day of the month *Lous*, which was a Lunar month of the *Macedonians*, and kept to one and the same Season of the year: and the *Arabians*, a Nation who peopled *Babylon*, use Lunar months to this day. *Suidas*[62] tells us, that the *Sarus* of the *Chaldeans* contains 222 Lunar months, which are eighteen years, consisting each of twelve Lunar months, besides six intercalary months: and when[63] *Cyrus* cut the River *Gindus* into 360 Channels, he seems to have alluded unto the number of days in the Calendar year of the *Medes* and *Persians*: and the Emperor *Julian*[64] writes, *For when all other People, that I may say it in one word, accommodate their months to the course of the Moon, we alone with the* Egyptians *measure the days of the year by the course of the Sun.*

At length the *Egyptians*, for the sake of Navigation, applied themselves to observe the Stars; and by their Heliacal Risings and Settings found the true Solar year to be five days longer than the Calendar year, and therefore added five days to the twelve Calendar months; making the Solar year to consist of twelve months and five days. *Strabo*[65] and[66] *Diodorus* ascribe this invention to the *Egyptians* of *Thebes*. The Theban Priests, saith *Strabo*, *are above others said to be Astronomers and Philosophers. They invented the reckoning of days not by the course of the Moon, but by the course of the Sun. To twelve months each of thirty days they add yearly five days.* In memory of this Emendation of the year they dedicated the[67] five additional days to *Osiris, Isis, Orus* senior, *Typhon*, and *Nephthe* the wife of *Typhon*, feigning that those days were added to the year when these five Princes were born, that is, in the Reign of *Ouranus*, or *Ammon*, the father of *Sesac*: and in[68] the Sepulchre of *Amenophis*, who Reigned soon after, they placed a Golden Circle of 365 cubits in compass, and divided it into 365 equal parts, to represent all the days in the year, and noted upon each part the Heliacal Risings and Settings of the Stars on that day; which Circle remained there 'till the invasion of *Egypt* by *Cambyses* King of *Persia*. 'Till the Reign of *Ouranus*, the father of *Hyperion*, and grandfather of *Helius* and *Selene*, the *Egyptians* used the old Lunisolar year: but in his Reign, that is, in the Reign of *Ammon*, the father of *Osiris* or *Sesac*, and grandfather of *Orus* and *Bubaste*, the *Thebans* began to apply themselves to Navigation and Astronomy, and by the Heliacal Risings and Settings of the Stars determined the length of the Solar year; and to the old Calendar year added five days, and dedicated them to his five children above mentioned, as their birth days: and in the Reign of *Amenophis*, when by further Observations they had sufficiently determined the time of the Solstices, they might place the beginning of this new year upon the Vernal Equinox. This year being at length propagated into *Chaldæa*, gave occasion to the year of *Nabonassar*; for the years of *Nabonassar* and those of *Egypt* began on one and the same day, called by them *Thoth*, and were equal and in all respects the same: and the first year of *Nabonassar* began on the 26th day of *February* of the old *Roman* year, seven hundred forty and seven years before the Vulgar Æra of *Christ*, and thirty and three days and five hours before the Vernal Equinox, according to the Sun's mean motion; for it is not likely that the Equation of the Sun's motion should be known in the infancy of Astronomy. Now reckoning that the year of 365 days wants five hours and 49 minutes of the Equinoctial year; the beginning of this year will move backwards thirty and three days and five hours in 137 years: and by consequence this year began at first in *Egypt* upon the Vernal Equinox, according to the Sun's mean motion, 137 years before the *Æra* of *Nabonassar* began; that is, in the year of the *Julian* Period 3830, or 96 years after the death of *Solomon*: and if it began upon the next day after the Vernal Equinox, it might begin four years earlier; and about that time ended the Reign of *Amenophis*: for he came not from *Susa* to the *Trojan* war, but died afterwards in *Egypt*. This year was received by the *Persian* Empire from the *Babylonian*; and the *Greeks* also used it in the *Æra Philippæa*, dated from the Death of *Alexander* the great; and *Julius Cæsar* corrected it, by adding a day in every four years, and made it the year of the *Romans*.

Syncellus tells us, that the five days were added to the old year by the last King of the Shepherds: and the difference in time between the Reign of this King, and that of *Ammon*, is but small; for the Reign of the Shepherds ended but one Generation, or two, before *Ammon* began to add those days. But the Shepherds minded not Arts and Sciences.

The first month of the Luni-solar year, by reason of the Intercalary month, began sometimes a week or a fortnight before the Equinox or Solstice, and sometimes as much after it. And this year gave occasion to the first Astronomers, who formed the *Asterisms*, to place the Equinoxes and Solstices in the middles of the Constellations of *Aries, Cancer, Chelæ,* and *Capricorn. Achilles Tatius*[69] tells us, that *some antiently placed the Solstice in the beginning of Cancer, others in the eighth degree of Cancer, others about the twelfth degree, and others about the fifteenth degree thereof.* This variety of opinions proceeded from the precession of the Equinox, then not known to the *Greeks*. When the Sphere was first formed, the Solstice was in the fifteenth degree or middle of the Constellation of *Cancer*: then it came into the twelfth, eighth, fourth, and first degree successively. *Eudoxus,* who flourished about sixty years after *Meton*, and an hundred years before *Aratus*, in describing the Sphere of the Ancients, placed the Solstices and Equinoxes in the middles of the Constellations of *Aries, Cancer, Chelæ,* and *Capricorn,* as is affirmed by[70] *Hipparchus Bithynus*; and appears also by the Description of the Equinoctial and Tropical Circles in *Aratus*,[71] who copied after *Eudoxus*; and by the positions of the *Colures* of the Equinoxes and Solstices, which in the Sphere of *Eudoxus*, described by *Hipparchus*, went through the middles of those Constellations. For *Hipparchus* tells us, that *Eudoxus* drew the *Colure* of the Solstices, through the middle of the *great Bear*, and the middle of *Cancer*, and the neck of *Hydrus*, and the Star between the Poop and Mast of *Argo*, and the Tayl of the *South Fish*, and through the middle of *Capricorn*, and of *Sagitta*, and through the neck and right wing of the *Swan*, and the left hand of *Cepheus*; and that he drew the Equinoctial *Colure*, through the left hand of *Arctophylax*, and along the middle of his Body, and cross the middle of *Chelæ*, and through the right hand and fore-knee of the *Centaur*, and through the flexure of *Eridanus* and head of *Cetus*, and the back of *Aries* a-cross, and through the head and right hand of *Perseus*.

Now *Chiron* delineated [Greek: schêmata olympou] the *Asterisms*, as the ancient Author of *Gigantomachia*, cited by[72] *Clemens Alexandrinus* informs us: for *Chiron* was a practical Astronomer, as may be there understood also of his daughter *Hippo*: and *Musæus*, the son of *Eumolpus* and master of *Orpheus*, and one of the *Argonauts*,[73] made a Sphere, and is reputed the first among the *Greeks* who made one: and the Sphere it self shews that it was delineated in the time of the *Argonautic* expedition; for that expedition is delineated in the *Asterisms*, together with several other ancienter Histories of the *Greeks*, and without any thing later. There's the golden *RAM*, the ensign of the Vessel in which *Phryxus* fled to *Colchis*; the *BULL* with brazen hoofs tamed by *Jason*; and the *TWINS*, *CASTOR* and *POLLUX*, two of the *Argonauts*, with the *SWAN* of *Leda* their mother. There's the Ship *ARGO*, and *HYDRUS* the watchful Dragon; with *Medea*'s *CUP*, and a *RAVEN* upon its Carcass, the Symbol of Death. There's *CHIRON* the master of *Jason*, with his *ALTAR* and *SACRIFICE*. There's the *Argonaut HERCULES* with his *DART* and *VULTURE* falling down; and the *DRAGON*, *CRAB* and *LION*, whom he slew; and the *HARP* of the *Argonaut Orpheus*. All these relate to the *Argonauts*. There's *ORION* the son of *Neptune*, or as some say, the grandson of *Minos*, with his *DOGS*, and *HARE*, and *RIVER*, and *SCORPION*. There's the story of *Perseus* in the Constellations of *PERSEUS*, *ANDROMEDA*, *CEPHEUS*, *CASSIOPEA* and *CETUS*: That of *Callisto*, and her son *Arcas*, in *URSA MAJOR* and *ARCTOPHYLAX*: That of *Icareus* and his daughter *Erigone* in *BOOTES*, *PLAUSTRUM* and *VIRGO*. *URSA MINOR* relates to one of the Nurses of *Jupiter*, *AURIGA* to *Erechthonius*, *OPHIUCHUS* to *Phorbas*, *SAGITTARIUS* to *Crolus* the son of the Nurse of the Muses, *CAPRICORN* to *Pan*, and *AQUARIUS* to *Ganimede*. There's *Ariadne*'s *CROWN*, *Bellerophon*'s *HORSE*, *Neptune*'s *DOLPHIN*, *Ganimede*'s *EAGLE*, *Jupiter*'s *GOAT* with her *KIDS*, *Bacchus*'s *ASSES*, and the *FISHES* of *Venus* and *Cupid*, and their Parent the *SOUTH FISH*. These with *DELTOTON*, are the old Constellations mentioned by *Aratus*: and they all relate to the *Argonauts* and their Contemporaries, and to Persons one or two Generations older: and nothing later than that Expedition was delineated there Originally. *ANTINOUS* and *COMA BERENICES* are novel. The Sphere seems therefore to have been formed by *Chiron* and *Musæus*, for the use of the *Argonauts*: for the Ship *Argo* was the first long ship built by the *Greeks*. Hitherto they had used round vessels of burden, and kept within sight of the shore; and now, upon an Embassy to several Princes upon the coasts of the *Euxine* and *Mediterranean* Seas,[74] by the dictates of the Oracle, and consent of the Princes of *Greece*, the Flower of *Greece* were to sail with Expedition through the deep, in a long Ship with Sails, and guide their Ship by the Stars. The People of the Island *Corcyra*[75] attributed the invention of the Sphere to *Nausicaa*, the daughter of *Alcinous*, King of the *Pheaces* in that Island: and it's most probable that she had it from the *Argonauts*, who[76] in their return home sailed to that Island, and made some stay there with her father. So then in the time of the *Argonautic* Expedition, the Cardinal points of the Equinoxes and Solstices were in the middles of the Constellations of *Aries*, *Cancer*, *Chelæ*, and *Capricorn*.

In the end of the year of our Lord 1689 the Star called *Prima Arietis* was in [Aries]. 28°. 51'. 00", with North Latitude 7°. 8'. 58". And the Star called *ultima caudæ Arietis* was in [Taurus]. 19°. 3'. 42", with North Latitude 2°. 34'. 5". And the *Colurus Æquinoctiorum* passing through the point in the middle between those two Stars did then cut the Ecliptic in [Taurus]. 6°. 44': and by this reckoning the Equinox in the end of the year 1689 was gone back 36°. 44'. since the *Argonautic* Expedition: Supposing that the said *Colure* passed through the middle of the Constellation of *Aries*, according to the delineation of the Ancients. The Equinox goes back fifty seconds in one year, and one degree in seventy and two years, and by consequence 36°. 44'. in 2645 years, which counted back from the end of the year of our Lord 1689, or beginning of the year 1690, will place the *Argonautic* Expedition about 25 years after the Death of *Solomon*: but it is not necessary that the middle of the Constellation of *Aries* should be exactly in the middle between the two Stars called *prima Arietis* and *ultima Caudæ*. and it may be better to fix the Cardinal points by the Stars, through which the *Colures* passed in the primitive Sphere, according to the description of *Eudoxus* above recited. By the *Colure* of the Equinoxes, I mean a great Circle passing through the Poles of the Equator, and cutting the Ecliptic in the Equinoxes in an Angle of 66½ degrees, the complement of the Sun's greatest Declination; and by the *Colure* of the Solstices I mean a great Circle passing through the same Poles, and cutting the Ecliptic at right Angles in the Solstices: and by the Primitive Sphere, that which was in use before the motions of the Equinoxes and Solstices were known: now the *Colures* passed through the following Stars according to *Eudoxus*.

In the back of *Aries* is a Star of the sixth magnitude, marked [nu] by *Bayer*. in the end of the year 1689, and beginning of the year 1690, its Longitude was [Taurus]. 9°. 38'. 45", and North Latitude 6°. 7'. 56": and the *Colurus Æquinoctiorum* drawn though it, according to *Eudoxus*, cuts the Ecliptic in [Taurus]. 6°. 58'. 57". In the head of *Cetus* are two Stars of the fourth Magnitude, called [nu] and [xi] by *Bayer*. in the end of the year 1689 their Longitudes were [Taurus]. 4°. 3'. 9". and [Taurus]. 3°. 7'. 37", and their South Latitudes 9°. 12'. 26". and 5°. 53'. 7"; and the *Colurus Æquinoctiorum* passing in the mid way between them, cuts the Ecliptic in [Taurus]. 6°. 58'. 51". In the extreme flexure of *Eridanus*, rightly delineated, is a Star of the fourth Magnitude, of late referred to the breast of *Cetus*, and called [rho] by *Bayer*; it is the only Star in *Eridanus* through which this *Colure* can pass; its Longitude, in the end of the year 1689, was [Aries]. 25°. 22'. 10". and South Latitude 25°. 15'. 50". and the *Colurus Æquinoctiorum* passing through it, cuts the Ecliptic in [Taurus]. 7°. 12'. 40". In the head of *Perseus*, rightly delineated, is a Star of the fourth Magnitude, called [tau] by *Bayer*; the Longitude of this Star, in the end of the year 1689, was [Taurus]. 23°. 25'. 30", and North Latitude 34°. 20'. 12": and the *Colurus Æquinoctiorum* passing through it, cuts the Ecliptic in [Taurus]. 6°. 18'. 57". In the right hand of *Perseus*, rightly delineated, is a Star of the fourth Magnitude, called [eta] by *Bayer*; its Longitude in the end of the year 1689, was [Taurus]. 24°. 25'. 27", and North Latitude 37°. 26'. 50": and the *Colurus Æquinoctiorum* passing through it cuts the Ecliptic in [Taurus]. 4°. 56'. 40": and the fifth part of the summ of the places in which these five *Colures* cut the Ecliptic, is [Taurus]. 6°. 29'. 15": and therefore the Great Circle which in the Primitive Sphere according to *Eudoxus*, and by consequence in the time of the *Argonautic* Expedition, was the *Colurus Æquinoctiorum* passing through the Stars above described; did in the end of the year 1689, cut the Ecliptic in [Taurus]. 6°. 29'. 15": as nearly as we have been able to determin by the Observations of the Ancients, which were but coarse.

In the middle of *Cancer* is the *South Asellus*, a Star of the fourth Magnitude, called by *Bayer* [delta]; its Longitude in the end of the year 1689, was [Leo]. 4°. 23'. 40". In the neck of *Hydrus*, rightly delineated, is a Star of the fourth Magnitude, called [delta] by *Bayer*; its Longitude in the end of the year 1689, was [Leo]. 5°. 59'. 3". Between the poop and mast of the Ship *Argo* is a Star of the third Magnitude, called [iota] by *Bayer*; its Longitude in the end of that year, was [Leo]. 7°. 5'. 31". In *Sagitta* is a Star of the sixth Magnitude, called [theta] by *Bayer*; its Longitude in the end of the same year 1689, was [Aquarius]. 6°. 29'. 53". In the middle of *Capricorn* is a Star of the fifth Magnitude, called [eta] by *Bayer*; its Longitude in the end of the same year was [Aquarius]. 8°. 25'. 55": and the fifth part of the summ of the three first Longitudes, and of the complements of the two last to 180 Degrees; is [Leo]. 6°. 28'. 46". This is the new Longitude of the old *Colurus Solstitiorum* passing through these Stars. The same *Colurus* passes also in the middle between the Stars [eta] and [kappa], of the fourth and fifth Magnitudes, in the neck of the *Swan*; being distant from each about a Degree: it passeth also by the Star [kappa], of the fourth Magnitude, in the right wing of the *Swan*; and by the Star [omicron], of the fifth Magnitude, in the left hand of *Cepheus*, rightly delineated; and by the Stars in the tail of the *South-Fish*; and is at right angles with the *Colurus Æquinoctiorum* found above: and so it hath all the characters, of the *Colurus Solstitiorum* rightly drawn.

The two *Colures* therefore, which in the time of the *Argonautic* Expedition cut the Ecliptic in the Cardinal Points, did in the end of the year 1689 cut it in [Taurus]. 6°. 29'; [Leo]. 6°. 29'; [Scorpio]. 6°. 29'; and [Aquarius]. 6°. 29'; that is, at the distance of 1 Sign, 6 Degrees and 29 Minutes from the Cardinal Points of *Chiron*; as nearly as we have been able to determin from the coarse observations of the Ancients: and therefore the Cardinal Points, in the time between that Expedition and the end of the year 1689, have gone back from those *Colures* one Sign, 6 Degrees and 29 Minutes; which, after the rate of 72 years to a Degree, answers to 2627 years. Count those years backwards from the end of the year 1689, or beginning of the year 1690, and the reckoning will place the *Argonautic* Expedition, about 43 years after the death of *Solomon*.

By the same method the place of any Star in the Primitive Sphere may readily be found, counting backwards one Sign, 6°. 29'. from the Longitude which it had in the end of the year of our Lord 1689. So the Longitude of the first Star of *Aries* in the end of the year 1689 was [Aries]. 28°. 51'. as above: count backward 1 Sign, 6°. 29'. and its Longitude, counted from the Equinox in the middle of the Constellation of *Aries*, in the time of the *Argonautic* expedition, will be [Pisces]. 22°. 22': and by the same way of arguing, the Longitude of the *Lucida Pleiadum* in the time of the *Argonautic* Expedition will be [Aries]. 19°. 26'. 8": and the Longitude of *Arcturus* [Virgo]. 13°. 24'. 52": and so of any other Stars.

After the *Argonautic* Expedition we hear no more of Astronomy 'till the days of *Thales*: He[77] revived Astronomy, and wrote a book of the Tropics and Equinoxes, and predicted Eclipses; and *Pliny*[78] tells us, that he determined the *Occasus Matutinus* of the *Pleiades* to be upon the 25th day after the Autumnal Equinox: and thence[79] *Petavius* computes the Longitude of the *Pleiades* in [Aries]. 23°. 53': and by consequence the *Lucida Pleiadum* had, since the *Argonautic* Expedition, moved from the Equinox 4°. 26'. 52": and this motion, after the rate of 72 years to a Degree, answers to 320 years: count these years back from the time in which *Thales* was a young man fit to apply himself to Astronomical Studies, that is from about the 41st Olympiad, and the reckoning will place the *Argonautic* Expedition about 44 years after the death of *Solomon*, as above: and in the days of *Thales*, the Solstices and Equinoxes, by this reckoning, will have been in the middle of the eleventh Degrees of the Signs. But *Thales*, in publishing his book about the Tropics and Equinoxes, might lean a little to the opinion of former Astronomers, so as to place them in the twelfth Degrees of the Signs.

Meton and *Euctemon*,[80] in order to publish the Lunar Cycle of nineteen years, observed the Summer Solstice in the year of *Nabonassar* 316, the year before the *Peloponnesian* war began; and *Columella*[81] tells us that they placed it in the eighth Degree of *Cancer*, which is at least seven Degrees backwarder than at first. Now the Equinox, after the rate of a Degree in Seventy and two years, goes backwards seven Degrees in 504 years: count backwards those years from the 316th year of *Nabonassar*, and the *Argonautic* Expedition will fall upon the 44th year after the death of *Solomon*, or thereabout, as above. And thus you see the truth of what we cited above out of *Achilles Tatius*; viz. that some anciently placed the Solstice in the eighth Degree of *Cancer*, others about the twelfth Degree, and others about the fifteenth Degree thereof.

Hipparchus the great Astronomer, comparing his own Observations with those of former Astronomers, concluded first of any man, that the Equinoxes had a motion backwards in respect of the fixt Stars: and his opinion was, that they went backwards one Degree in about an hundred years. He made his observations of the Equinoxes between the years of *Nabonassar* 586 and 618: the middle year is 602, which is 286 years after the aforesaid observation of *Meton* and *Euctemon*; and in these years the Equinox must have gone backwards four degrees, and so have been in the fourth Degree of *Aries* in the days of *Hipparchus*, and by consequence have then gone back eleven Degrees since the *Argonautic* Expedition; that is, in 1090 years, according to the Chronology of the ancient *Greeks* then in use: and this is after the rate of about 99 years, or in the next round number an hundred years to a Degree, as was then stated by *Hipparchus*. But it really went back a Degree in seventy and two years, and eleven Degrees in 792 years: count these 792 years backward from the year of *Nabonassar*, 602, the year from which we counted the 286 years, and the reckoning will place the *Argonautic* Expedition about 43 years after the death of *Solomon*. The *Greeks* have therefore made the *Argonautic* Expedition about three hundred years ancienter than the truth, and thereby given occasion to the opinion of the great *Hipparchus*, that the Equinox went backward after the rate of only a Degree in an hundred years.

Hesiod tells us that sixty days after the winter Solstice the Star *Arcturus* rose just at Sunset: and thence it follows that *Hesiod* flourished about an hundred years after the death of *Solomon*, or in the Generation or Age next after the *Trojan* war, as *Hesiod* himself declares.

From all these circumstances, grounded upon the coarse observations of the ancient Astronomers, we may reckon it certain that the *Argonautic* Expedition was not earlier than the Reign of *Solomon*: and if these Astronomical arguments be added to the former arguments taken from the mean length of the Reigns of Kings, according to the course of nature; from them all we may safely conclude that the *Argonautic* Expedition was after the death of *Solomon*, and most probably that it was about 43 years after it.

The *Trojan* War was one Generation later than that Expedition, as was said above, several Captains of the *Greeks* in that war being sons of the *Argonauts*: and the ancient *Greeks* reckoned *Memnon* or *Amenophis*, King of *Egypt*, to have Reigned in the times of that war, feigning him to be the son of *Tithonus* the elder brother of *Priam*, and in the end of that war to have come from *Susa* to the assistance of *Priam*. *Amenophis* was therefore of the same age with the elder children of *Priam*, and was with his army at *Susa* in the last year of that war: and after he had there finished the *Memnonia*, he might return into *Egypt*, and adorn it with Buildings, and Obelisks, and Statues, and die there about 90 or 95 years after the death of *Solomon*; when he had determined and settled the beginning of the new *Egyptian* year of 365 days upon the Vernal Equinox, so as to deserve the Monument above-mentioned in memory thereof.

Rehoboam was born in the last year of King *David*, being 41 years old at the Death of *Solomon*, 1 *Kings* xiv. 21. and therefore his father *Solomon* was probably born in the 18th year of King *David's* Reign, or before: and two or three years before his Birth, *David* besieged *Rabbah* the Metropolis of the *Ammonites*, and committed adultery with *Bathsheba*: and the year before this siege began, *David* vanquished the *Ammonites*, and their Confederates the *Syrians* of *Zobah*, and *Rehob*, and *Ishtob*, and *Maacah*, and *Damascus*, and extended his Dominion over all these Nations as far as to the entring in of *Hamath* and the River *Euphrates*: and before this war began he smote *Moab*, and *Ammon*, and *Edom*, and made the *Edomites* fly, some of them into *Egypt* with their King *Hadad*, then a little child; and others to the *Philistims*, where they fortified *Azoth* against *Israel*; and others, I think, to the *Persian Gulph*, and other places whither they could escape: and before this he had several Battles with the *Philistims*: and all this was after the eighth year of his Reign, in which he came from *Hebron* to *Jerusalem*. We cannot err therefore above two or three years, if we place this Victory over *Edom* in the eleventh or twelfth year of his Reign; and that over *Ammon* and the *Syrians* in the fourteenth. After the flight of *Edom*, the King of *Edom* grew up, and married *Tahaphenes* or *Daphnis*, the sister of *Pharaoh's* Queen, and before the Death of *David* had by her a son called *Genubah*, and this son was brought up among the children of *Pharaoh*: and among these children was the chief or *first born of her mother's children*, whom *Solomon* married in the beginning of his Reign; and her *little sister who* at that time *had no breasts*, and her *brother who* then *sucked the breasts of his mother*, *Cant.* vi. 9. and viii. 1, 8: and of about the same Age with these children was *Sesac* or *Sesostris*; for he became King of *Egypt* in the Reign of *Solomon*, 1 *Kings* xi. 40; and before he began to Reign he warred under his father, and whilst he was very young, conquered *Arabia*, *Troglodytica* and *Libya*, and then invaded *Ethiopia*; and succeeding his father Reigned 'till the fifth year of *Asa*: and therefore he was of about the same age with the children of *Pharaoh* above-mentioned; and might be one of them, and be born near the end of *David*'s Reign, and be about 46 years old when he came out of *Egypt* with a great Army to invade the East: and by reason of his great Conquests, he was celebrated in several Nations by several Names. The *Chaldæans* called him *Belus*, which in their Language signified *the Lord*: the *Arabians* called him *Bacchus*, which in their Language signified *the great*: the *Phrygians* and *Thracians* called him *Ma-fors*, *Mavors*, *Mars*, which signified *the valiant*: and thence the *Amazons*, whom he carried from *Thrace* and left at *Thermodon*, called themselves the daughters of *Mars*. The *Egyptians* before his Reign called him their *Hero* or *Hercules*; and after his death, by reason of his great works done to the River *Nile*, dedicated that River to him, and Deified him by its names *Sihor*, *Nilus* and *Ægyptus*; and the *Greeks* hearing them lament *0 Sihor*, *Bou Sihor*, called him *Osiris* and *Busiris*. *Arrian*[82] tells us that the *Arabians* worshipped, only two Gods, *Coelus* and *Dionysus*; and that they worshipped *Dionysus* for the glory of leading his Army into *India*. The *Dionysus* of the *Arabians* was *Bacchus*, and all agree that *Bacchus* was the same King of *Egypt* with *Osiris*: and the *Coelus*, or *Uranus*, or *Jupiter Uranius* of the *Arabians*, I take to be the same King of *Egypt* with His father *Ammon*, according to the Poet:

Quamvis Æthiopum populis, Arabumque beatis
Gentibus, atque Indis unus sit Jupiter Ammon.

I place the end of the Reign of *Sesac* upon the fifth year of *Asa*, because in that year *Asa* became free from the Dominion of *Egypt*, so as to be able to fortify *Judæa*, and raise that great Army with which he met *Zerah*, and routed him. *Osiris* was therefore slain in the fifth year of *Asa*, by his brother *Japetus*, whom the *Egyptians* called *Typhon*, *Python*, and *Neptune*: and then the *Libyans*, under *Japetus* and his son *Atlas*, invaded *Egypt*, and raised that famous war between the Gods and Giants, from whence the *Nile* had the name of *Eridanus*: but *Orus* the son of *Osiris*, by the assistance of the *Ethiopians*, prevailed, and Reigned 'till the 15th year of *Asa*: and then the *Ethiopians* under *Zerah* invaded *Egypt*, drowned *Orus* in *Eridanus*, and were routed by *Asa*, so that *Zerah* could not recover himself. *Zerah* was succeeded by *Amenophis*, a youth of the Royal Family of the *Ethiopians*, and I think the son of *Zerah*: but the People of the lower *Egypt* revolted from him, and set up *Osarsiphus* over them, and called to their assistance a great body of men from *Phoenicia*, I think a part of the Army of *Asa*; and thereupon *Amenophis*, with the remains of his father's Army of *Ethiopians*, retired from the lower *Egypt* to *Memphis*, and there turned the River *Nile* into a new channel, under a new bridge which he built between two Mountains; and at the same time he built and fortified that City against *Osarsiphus*, calling it by his own name, *Amenoph* or *Memphis*: and then he retired into *Ethiopia*, and stayed there thirteen years; and then came back with a great Army, and subdued the lower *Egypt*, expelling the People which had been called in from *Phoenicia*: and this I take to be the second expulsion of the Shepherds. Dr. *Castel*[83] tells us, that in *Coptic*+ this City is called *Manphtha*; whence by contraction came its Names *Moph*, *Noph*.

While *Amenophis* staid in *Ethiopia*, *Egypt* was in its greatest distraction: and then it was, as I conceive, that the *Greeks* hearing thereof contrived the *Argonautic* Expedition, and sent the flower of *Greece* in the Ship *Argo* to persuade the Nations upon the Sea Coasts of the *Euxine* and *Mediterranean Seas* to revolt from *Egypt*, and set up for themselves, as the *Libyans*, *Ethiopians* and *Jews* had done before. And this is a further argument for placing that Expedition about 43 years after the Death of *Solomon*; this Period being in the middle of the distraction of *Egypt*. *Amenophis* might return from *Ethiopia*, and conquer the lower *Egypt* about eight years after that Expedition, and having settled his Government over it, he might, for putting a stop to the revolting of the eastern Nations, lead his Army into *Persia*, and leave *Proteus* at *Memphis* to govern *Egypt* in his absence, and stay some time at *Susa*, and build the *Memnonia*, fortifying that City, as the Metropolis of his Dominion in those parts.

Androgeus the son of *Minos*, upon his overcoming in the *Athenæa*, or quadrennial Games at *Athens* in his youth, was perfidiously slain out of envy: and *Minos* thereupon made war upon the *Athenians*, and compelled them to send every eighth year to *Crete* seven beardless Youths, and as many young Virgins, to be given as a reward to him that should get the Victory in the like Games instituted in *Crete* in honour of *Androgeus*. These Games seem to have been celebrated in the beginning of the *Octaeteris*, and the *Athenæa* in the beginning of the *Tetraeteris*, then brought into *Crete* and *Greece* by the *Phoenicians* and upon the third payment of the tribute of children, that is, about seventeen years after the said war was at an end, and about nineteen or twenty years after the death of *Androgeus*, *Theseus* became Victor, and returned from *Crete* with *Ariadne* the daughter of *Minos*; and coming to the Island *Naxus* or *Dia*,[84] *Ariadne* was there relinquished by him, and taken up by *Glaucus*, an *Egyptian* Commander at Sea, and became the mistress of the great *Bacchus*, who at that time returned from *India* in Triumph; and[85] by him she had two sons, *Phlyas* and *Eumedon*, who were *Argonauts*. This *Bacchus* was caught in bed in *Phrygia* with *Venus* the mother of *Æneas*, according[86] to *Homer*; just before he came over the *Hellespont*, and invaded *Thrace*; and he married *Ariadne* the daughter of *Minos*, according to *Hesiod* [87]: and therefore by the Testimony of both *Homer* and *Hesiod*, who wrote before the *Greeks* and *Egyptians* corrupted their Antiquities, this *Bacchus* was one Generation older than the *Argonauts*; and so being King of *Egypt* at the same time with *Sesostris*, they must be one and the same King: for they agree also in their actions; *Bacchus* invaded *India* and *Greece*, and after he was routed by the Army of *Perseus*, and the war was composed, the *Greeks* did him great honours, and built a Temple to him at *Argos*, and called it the Temple of the *Cresian Bacchus*, because *Ariadne* was buried in it, as *Pausanias*[88] relates. *Ariadne* therefore died in the end of the war, just before the return of *Sesostris* into *Egypt*, that is, in the 14th year of *Rehoboam*: She was taken from *Naxus* upon the return of *Bacchus* from *India*, and then became the Mistress of *Bacchus*, and accompanied him in his Triumphs; and therefore the expedition of *Theseus* to *Crete*, and the death of his father *Ægeus*, was about nine or ten years after the death of *Solomon*. *Theseus* was then a beardless young man, suppose about 19 or 20 years old, and *Androgeus* was slain about twenty years before, being then about 20 or 22 years old; and his father *Minos* might be about 25 years older, and so be born about the middle of *David's* Reign, and be about 70 years old when he pursued *Dædalus* into *Sicily*: and *Europa* and her brother *Cadmus* might come into *Europe*, two or three years before the birth of *Minos*.

Justin, in his 18th book, tells us: *A rege Ascaloniorum expugnati Sidonii navibus appulsi Tyron urbem ante annum * * Trojanæ cladis condiderunt* And *Strabo*,[89] that *Aradus was built by the men who fled from* Zidon. Hence[90] *Isaiah* calls *Tyre the daughter of* Zidon, *the inhabitants of the Isle whom the Merchants of* Zidon *have replenished*: and[91] *Solomon* in the beginning of his Reign calls the People of *Tyre Zidonians. My Servants*, saith he, in a Message to *Hiram* King of *Tyre, shall be with thy Servants, and unto thee will I give hire for thy Servants according to all that thou desirest: for thou knowest that there is not among us any that can skill to hew timber like the* Zidonians. The new Inhabitants of *Tyre* had not yet lost the name of *Zidonians*, nor had the old Inhabitants, if there were any considerable number of them, gained the reputation of the new ones for skill in hewing of timber, as they would have done had navigation been long in use at *Tyre*. The Artificers who came from *Zidon* were not dead, and the flight of the *Zidonians* was in the Reign of *David*, and by consequence in the beginning of the Reign of *Abibalus* the father of *Hiram*, and the first King of *Tyre* mentioned in History. *David* in the twelfth year of his Reign conquered *Edom*, as above, and made some of the *Edomites*, and chiefly the Merchants and Seamen, fly from the *Red Sea* to the *Philistims* upon the *Mediterranean*, where they fortified *Azoth*. For[92] *Stephanus* tells us: [Greek: Tautên ektisen heis tôn epanelthontôn ap' Erythras thalassês Pheugadôn]: *One of the Fugitives from the Red Sea built* Azoth: that is, a Prince of *Edom*, who fled from *David*, fortified *Azoth* for the *Philistims* against him. The *Philistims* were now grown very strong, by the access of the *Edomites* and Shepherds, and by their assistance invaded and took *Zidon*, that being a town very convenient for the Merchants who fled from the *Red Sea*: and then did the *Zidonians* fly by Sea to *Tyre* and *Aradus*, and to other havens in *Asia Minor*, *Greece*, and *Libya*, with which, by means of their trade, they had been acquainted before; the great wars and victories of *David* their enemy, prompting them to fly by Sea: for[93] they went with a great multitude, not to seek *Europa* as was pretended, but to seek new Seats, and therefore fled from their enemies: and when some of them fled under *Cadmus* and his brothers to *Cilicia*, *Asia minor*, and *Greece*; others fled under other Commanders to seek new Seats in *Libya*, and there built many walled towns, as *Nonnus*[94] affirms: and their leader was also there called *Cadmus*, which word signifies an eastern man, and his wife was called *Sithonis* a *Zidonian*. Many from those Cities went afterwards with the great *Bacchus* in his Armies: and by these things, the taking of *Zidon*, and the flight of the *Zidonians* under *Abibalus, Cadmus, Cilix, Thasus, Membliarius, Atymnus*, and other Captains, to *Tyre, Aradus, Cilicia, Rhodes, Caria, Bithynia, Phrygia, Calliste, Thasus, Samothrace, Crete, Greece* and *Libya*, and the building of *Tyre* and *Thebes*, and beginning of the Reigns of *Abibalus* and *Cadmus* over those Cities, are fixed upon the fifteenth or sixteenth year of *David's* Reign, or thereabout. By means of these Colonies of *Phoenicians*, the people of *Caria* learnt sea-affairs, in such small vessels with oars as were then in use, and began to frequent the *Greek Seas*, and people some of the Islands therein, before the Reign of *Minos*: for *Cadmus*, in coming to *Greece*, arrived first at *Rhodes*, an Island upon the borders of *Caria*, and left there a Colony of *Phoenicians*, who sacrificed men to *Saturn*, and the *Telchines* being repulsed by *Phoroneus*, retired from *Argos* to *Rhodes* with *Phorbas*, who purged the Island from Serpents; and *Triopas*, the son of *Phorbas*, carried a Colony from *Rhodes* to *Caria*, and there possessed himself of a promontory, thence called *Triopium*: and by this and such like Colonies *Caria* was furnished with Shipping and Seamen, and called[95] *Phoenice*. *Strabo* and *Herodotus*[96] tell us, that the *Cares* were called *Leleges*, and became subject to *Minos*, and lived first in the Islands of the *Greek Seas*, and went thence into *Caria*, a country possest before by some of the *Leleges* and *Pelasgi*: whence it's probable that when *Lelex* and *Pelasgus* came first into *Greece* to seek new Seats, they left part of their Colonies in *Caria* and the neighbouring Islands.

The *Zidonians* being still possessed of the trade of the *Mediterranean*, as far westward as *Greece* and *Libya*, and the trade of the *Red Sea* being richer; the *Tyrians* traded on the *Red Sea* in conjunction with *Solomon* and the Kings of *Judah*, 'till after the *Trojan* war; and so also did the Merchants of *Aradus, Arvad*, or *Arpad*: for in the *Persian Gulph*[97] were two Islands called *Tyre* and *Aradus*, which had Temples like the *Phoenician*; and therefore the *Tyrians* and *Aradians* sailed thither, and beyond, to the Coasts of *India*, while the *Zidonians* frequented the *Mediterranean*: and hence it is that *Homer* celebrates *Zidon*, and makes no mention of *Tyre*. But at length,[98] in the Reign of *Jehoram* King of *Judah*, *Edom* revolted from the Dominion of *Judah*, and made themselves a King; and the trade of *Judah* and *Tyre* upon the *Red Sea* being thereby interrupted, the *Tyrians* built ships for merchandise upon the *Mediterranean*, and began there to make long Voyages to places not yet frequented by the *Zidonians*; some of them going to the coasts of *Afric* beyond the *Syrtes*, and building *Adrymetum, Carthage, Leptis, Utica*, and *Capsa*; and others going to the Coasts of *Spain*, and building *Carteia, Gades* and *Tartessus*; and others going further to the *Fortunate Islands*, and to *Britain* and *Thule. Jehoram* Reigned eight years, and the two last years was sick in his bowels, and before that sickness *Edom* revolted, because of *Jehoram's* wicked Reign: if we place that revolt about the middle of the first six years, it will fall upon the fifth year of *Pygmalion* King of *Tyre*, and so was about twelve or fifteen years after the taking of *Troy*: and then, by reason of this revolt, the *Tyrians* retired from the *Red Sea*, and began long Voyages upon the *Mediterranean*; for in the seventh year of *Pygmalion*, his Sister *Dido* sailed to the Coast of *Afric* beyond the *Syrtes*, and there built *Carthage*. This retiring of the *Tyrians* from the *Red Sea* to make long Voyages on the *Mediterranean*, together with the flight of the *Edomites* from *David* to the

Philistims, gave occasion to the tradition both of the ancient *Persians*, and of the *Phoenicians* themselves, that the *Phoenicians* came originally from the *Red Sea* to the coasts of the *Mediterranean*, and presently undertook long Voyages, as *Herodotus*[99] relates: for *Herodotus*, in the beginning of his first book, relates that the *Phoenicians* coming from the *Red Sea* to the *Mediterranean*, and beginning to make long Voyages with *Egyptian* and *Assyrian* wares, among other places came to *Argos*, and having sold their wares, seized and carried away into *Egypt* some of the *Grecian* women who came to buy them; and amongst those women was *Io* the daughter of *Inachus*. The *Phoenicians* therefore came from the *Red Sea*, in the days of *Io* and her brother *Phoroneus* King of *Argos*, and by consequence at that time when *David* conquered the *Edomites*, and made them fly every way from the *Red Sea*; some into *Egypt* with their young King, and others to the *Philistims* their next neighbours and the enemies of *David*. And this flight gave occasion to the *Philistims* to call many places *Erythra*, in memory of their being *Erythreans* or *Edomites*, and of their coming from the *Erythrean* Sea; for *Erythra* was the name of a City in *Ionia*, of another in *Libya*, of another in *Locris*, of another in *Boeotia*, of another in *Cyprus*, of another in *Ætolia*, of another in *Asia* near *Chius*; and *Erythia Acra* was a promontory in *Libya*, and *Erythræum* a promontory in *Crete*, and *Erythros* a place near *Tybur*, and *Erythini* a City or Country in *Paphlagonia*: and the name *Erythea* or *Erythræ* was given to the Island *Gades*, peopled by *Phoenicians*. So *Solinus*,[100] *In capite Bæticæ insula a continenti septingentis passibus memoratur quam Tyrii a rubro mari profecti Erytheam, Poeni sua lingua Gadir, id est sepem nominarunt.* And *Pliny*,[101] concerning a little Island near it; *Erythia dicta est quoniam Tyrii Aborigines eorum, orti ab Erythræo mari ferebantur.* Among the *Phoenicians* who came with *Cadmus* into *Greece*, there were[102] *Arabians*, and[103] *Erythreans* or Inhabitants of the *Red Sea*, that is *Edomites*; and in *Thrace* there settled a People who were circumcised and called *Odomantes*, that is, as some think, *Edomites*. *Edom*, *Erythra* and *Phoenicia* are names of the same signification, the words denoting a red colour: which makes it probable that the *Erythreans* who fled from *David*, settled in great numbers in *Phoenicia*, that is, in all the Sea-coasts of *Syria* from *Egypt* to *Zidon*; and by calling themselves *Phoenicians* in the language of *Syria*, instead of *Erythreans*, gave the name of *Phoenicia* to all that Sea-coast, and to that only. So *Strabo*:[104] [Greek: Hoi men gar kai tous Phoinikas, kai tous Sidonious tous kath' hêmas apoikous einai tôn en tôi Ôkeanôi phasi, prostithentes kai dia ti Phoinikes ekalounto, hoti kai hê thalatta erythra.] *Alii referunt Phoenices & Sidonios nostros esse colonos eorum qui sunt in Oceano, addentes illos ideo vocari Phoenices* [puniceos] *quod mare rubrum sit.*

Strabo[105] mentioning the first men who left the Sea-coasts, and ventured out into the deep, and undertook long Voyages, names *Bacchus*, *Hercules*, *Jason*, *Ulysses* and *Menelaus*; and saith that the Dominion of *Minos* over the Sea was celebrated, and the Navigation of the *Phoenicians* who went beyond the Pillars of *Hercules*, and built Cities there, and in the middle of the Sea-coasts of *Afric*, presently after the war of *Troy*. These *Phoenicians*[106] were the *Tyrians*, who at that time built *Carthage* in *Afric*, and *Carteia* in *Spain*, and *Gades* in the Island of that name without the *Straights*; and gave the name of *Hercules* to their chief Leader, because of his labours and success, and that of *Heraclea* to the city *Carteia* which he built. So *Strabo*:[107] [Greek: Ekpleousin oun ek tês hêmeteras thalattês eis tên exô, dexion esti touto; kai pros auto Kalpê [Kartêia]][108] [Greek: polis en tettarakonta stadiois axiologos kai palaia, naustathmon pote genomenê tôn Ibêrôn; enioi de kai Êrakleous ktisma legousin autên, hôn esti kai Timosthenês; hos Phêsi kai Êrakleian onomazesthai to palaion; deiknysthai te megan peribolon, kai neôsoikous.] *Mons Calpe ad dextram est e nostro mari foras navigantibus, & ad quadraginta inde stadia urbs Carteia vetusta ac memorabilis, olim statio navibus Hispanorum. Hanc ab Hercule quidam conditam aiunt, inter quos est Timosthenes, qui eam antiquitus Heracleam fuisse appellatam refert, ostendique adhuc magnum murorum circuitum & navalia.* This *Hercules*, in memory of his building and Reigning over the City *Carteia*, they called also *Melcartus*, the King of *Carteia*. *Bochart*[109] writes, that *Carteia* was at first called *Melcarteia*, from its founder *Melcartus*, and by an *Aphæresis*, *Carteia*; and that *Melcartus* signifies *Melec Kartha*, the King of the city, that is, saith he, of the city *Tyre*: but considering that no ancient Author tells us, that *Carteia* was ever called *Melcarteia*, or that *Melcartus* was King of *Tyre*; I had rather say that *Melcartus*, or *Melecartus*, had his name from being the Founder and Governor or Prince of the city *Carteia*. Under *Melcartus* the *Tyrians* sailed as far as *Tartessus* or *Tarshish*, a place in the Western part of *Spain*, between the two mouths of the river *Boetis*, and there they[110] met with much silver, which they purchased for trifles: they sailed also as far as *Britain* before the death of *Melcartus*; for[111] *Pliny* tells us, *Plumbum ex Cassiteride insula primus apportavit Midacritus*. And *Bochart*[112] observes that *Midacritus* is a *Greek* name corruptly written for *Melcartus*; *Britain* being unknown to the *Greeks* long after it was discovered by the *Phoenicians*. After the death of *Melcartus*, they[113] built a Temple to him in the Island *Gades*, and adorned it with the sculptures of the labours of *Hercules*, and of his *Hydra*, and the Horses to whom he threw *Diomedes*, King of the *Bistones* in *Thrace*, to be devoured. In this Temple was the golden Belt of *Teucer*, and the golden Olive of *Pygmalion* bearing *Smaragdine* fruit: and by these consecrated gifts of *Teucer* and *Pygmalion*, you may know that it was built in their days. *Pomponius* derives it from the times of the *Trojan* war; for *Teucer*, seven years after that war, according to the Marbles, arrived at *Cyprus*, being banished from home by his father *Telamon*, and there built *Salamis*: and he and his Posterity Reigned there 'till *Evagoras*, the last of them, was conquered by the *Persians*, in the twelfth year of *Artaxerxes Mnemon*. Certainly this *Tyrian Hercules* could be no older than the *Trojan* war, because the *Tyrians* did not begin to navigate the *Mediterranean* 'till after that war: for *Homer* and *Hesiod* knew nothing of this navigation, and the *Tyrian Hercules* went to the coasts of *Spain*, and was buried in *Gades*: so *Arnobius*[114]; *Tyrius Hercules sepultus in finibus Hispaniæ*: and *Mela*, speaking of the Temple of *Hercules* in *Gades*, saith, *Cur sanctum sit ossa ejus ibi sepulta efficiunt. Carthage*[115] paid tenths to this *Hercules*, and sent their payments yearly to *Tyre*: and thence it's probable that this *Hercules* went to the coast of *Afric*, as well as to that of *Spain*, and by his discoveries prepared the way to *Dido*: *Orosius*[116] and others tell us that he built *Capsa* there. *Josephus* tells of an earlier *Hercules*, to whom *Hiram* built a Temple at

Tyre: and perhaps there might be also an earlier *Hercules* of *Tyre*, who set on foot their trade on the *Red Sea* in the days of *David* or *Solomon*.

Tatian, in his book against the *Greeks*, relates, that amongst the *Phoenicians* flourished three ancient Historians, *Theodotus*, *Hysicrates* and *Mochus*, *who all of them delivered in their histories, translated into* Greek *by* Latus, *under which of the Kings happened the rapture of* Europa; *the voyage of* Menelaus *into* Phoenicia; *and the league and friendship between* Solomon *and* Hiram, *when* Hiram *gave his daughter to* Solomon, *and furnished him with timber for building the Temple: and that the same is affirmed by* Menander *of* Pergamus. *Josephus*[117] lets us know that the Annals of the *Tyrians*, from the days of *Abibalus* and *Hiram*, Kings of *Tyre*, were extant in his days; and that *Menander* of *Pergamus* translated them into *Greek*, and that *Hiram*'s friendship to *Solomon*, and assistance in building the Temple, was mentioned in them; and that the Temple was founded in the eleventh year of *Hiram*: and by the testimony of *Menander* and the ancient *Phoenician* historians, the rapture of *Europa*, and by consequence the coming of her brother *Cadmus* into *Greece*, happened within the time of the Reigns of the Kings of *Tyre* delivered in these histories; and therefore not before the Reign of *Abibalus*, the first of them, nor before the Reign of King *David* his contemporary. The voyage of *Menelaus* might be after the destruction of *Troy*. *Solomon* therefore Reigned in the times between the raptures of *Europa* and *Helena*, and *Europa* and her brother *Cadmus* flourished in the days or *David*. *Minos*, the son of *Europa*, flourished in the Reign of *Solomon*, and part of the Reign of *Rehoboam*: and the children of *Minos*, namely *Androgeus* his eldest son, *Deucalion* his youngest son and one of the *Argonauts*, *Ariadne* the mistress of *Theseus* and *Bacchus*, and *Phædra* the wife of *Theseus*; flourished in the latter end of *Solomon*, and in the Reigns of *Rehoboam*, *Abijah* and *Asa*: and *Idomeneus*, the grandson of *Minos*, was at the war of *Troy*: and *Hiram* succeeded his father *Abibalus*, in the three and twentieth year of *David*: and *Abibalus* might found the Kingdom of *Tyre* about sixteen or eighteen years before, when *Zidon* was taken by the *Philistims*; and the *Zidonians* fled from thence, under the conduct of *Cadmus* and other commanders, to seek new seats. Thus by the Annals of *Tyre*, and the ancient *Phoenician* Historians who followed them, *Abibalus*, *Alymnus*, *Cadmus*, and *Europa* fled from *Zidon* about the sixteenth year of *David*'s Reign: and the *Argonautic* Expedition being later by about three Generations, will be about three hundred years later than where the *Greeks* have placed it.

After Navigation in long ships with sails, and one order of oars, had been propagated from *Egypt* to *Phoenicia* and *Greece*, and thereby the *Zidonians* had extended their trade to *Greece*, and carried it on about an hundred and fifty years; and then the *Tyrians* being driven from the *Red Sea* by the *Edomites*, had begun a new trade on the *Mediterranean* with *Spain*, *Afric*, *Britain*, and other remote nations; they carried it on about an hundred and sixty years; and then the *Corinthians* began to improve Navigation, by building bigger ships with three orders of oars, called *Triremes*. For[118] *Thucydides* tells us that the *Corinthians* were the first of the *Greeks* who built such ships, and that a ship-carpenter of *Corinth* went thence to *Samos*, about 300 years before the end of the *Peloponnesian* war, and built also four ships for the *Samians*; and that 260 years before the end of that war, that is, about the 29th Olympiad, there was a fight at sea between the *Corinthians* and the *Corcyreans* which was the oldest sea-fight mentioned in history. *Thucydides* tells us further, that the first colony which the *Greeks* sent into *Sicily*, came from *Chalcis* in *Euboea*, under the conduct of *Thucles*, and built *Naxus*; and the next year *Archias* came from *Corinth* with a colony, and built *Syracuse*; and that *Lamis* came about the same time into *Sicily*, with a colony from *Megara* in *Achaia*, and lived first at *Trotilum*, and then at *Leontini*, and died at *Thapsus* near *Syracuse*; and that after his death, this colony was invited by *Hyblo* to *Megara* in *Sicily*, and lived there 245 years, and was then expelled by *Gelo* King of *Sicily*. Now *Gelo* flourished about 78 years before the end of the *Peloponnesian* war: count backwards the 78 and the 245 years, and about 12 years more for the Reign of *Lamis* in *Sicily*, and the reckoning will place the building of *Syracuse* about 335 years before the end of the *Peloponnesian* war, or in the tenth Olympiad; and about that time *Eusebius* and others place it: but it might be twenty or thirty years later, the antiquities of those days having been raised more or less by the *Greeks*. From the colonies henceforward sent into *Italy* and *Sicily* came the name of *Græcia magna*.

Thucydide[119] tells us further, that the *Greeks* began to come into *Sicily* almost three hundred years after the *Siculi* had invaded that Island with an army out of *Italy*: suppose it 280 years after, and the building of *Syracuse* 310 years before the end of the *Peloponnesian* war; and that invasion of *Sicily* by the *Siculi* will be 590 years before the end of that war, that is, in the 27th year of *Solomon*'s Reign, or thereabout. *Hellanicus*[120] tells us, that it was in the third Generation before the *Trojan* war; and in the 26th year of the Priesthood of *Alcinoe*, Priestess of *Juno Argiva*: and *Philistius* of *Syracuse*, that it was 80 years before the *Trojan* war: whence it follows that the *Trojan* war and *Argonautic* Expedition were later than the days of *Solomon* and *Rehoboam*, and could not be much earlier than where we have placed them.

The Kingdom of *Macedon*[121] was founded by *Caranus* and *Perdiccas*, who being of the Race of *Temenus* King of *Argos*, fled from *Argos* in the Reign of *Phidon* the brother of *Caranus*. *Temenus* was one of the three brothers who led the *Heraclides* into *Peloponnesus*, and shared the conquest among themselves: he obtained *Argos*; and after him, and his son *Cisus*, the Kingdom of *Argos* became divided among the posterity of *Temenus*, until *Phidon* reunited it, expelling his kindred. *Phidon* grew potent, appointed weights and measures in *Peloponnesus*, and coined silver money; and removing the *Pisæans* and *Eleans*, presided in the Olympic games; but was soon after subdued by the *Eleans* and *Spartans*. *Herodotus*[122] reckons that *Perdiccas* was the first King of *Macedon*; later writers, as *Livy*, *Pausanias* and *Suidas*, make *Caranus* the first King: *Justin* calls *Perdiccas* the Sucessor of *Caranus*; and *Solinus* saith that *Perdiccas* succeeded *Caranus*; and was the first that obtained the name of King. It's probable that *Caranus* and *Perdiccas* were contemporaries, and fled about the same time from *Phidon*, and at first erected small principalities in *Macedonia*, which, after the death of *Caranus*, became one under *Perdiccas*. *Herodotus*[123] tells us, that after *Perdiccas* Reigned *Aræus*, or *Argæus*, *Philip*, *Æropus*, *Alcetas*, *Amyntas*, and *Alexander*, successively. *Alexander* was contemporary to

Xerxes King of *Persia*, and died *An.* 4. Olymp. 79, and was succeeded by *Perdiccas*, and he by his son *Archelaus*: and *Thucydides*[124] tells us that there were eight Kings of *Macedon* before this *Archelaus*: now by reckoning above forty years a-piece to these Kings, Chronologers have made *Phidon* and *Caranus* older than the Olympiads; whereas if we should reckon their Reigns at about 18 or 20 years a-piece one with another, the first seven Reigns counted backwards from the death of this *Alexander*, will place the dominion of *Phidon*, and the beginning of the Kingdom of *Macedon* under *Perdiccas* and *Caranus*, upon the 46th or 47th Olympiad, or thereabout. It could scarce be earlier, because *Leocides* the son of *Phidon*, and *Megacles* the son of *Alcmæon*, at one and the same time courted *Agarista*, the daughter of *Clisthenes* King of *Sicyon*, as *Herodotus*[125] tells us; and the *Amphictyons*, by the advice of *Solon*, made *Alcmæon*, and *Clisthenes*, and *Eurolycus* King of *Thessaly*, commanders of their army, in their war against *Cirrha*; and the *Cirrheans* were conquered *An.* 2. Olymp. 47. according to the Marbles. *Phidon* therefore and his brother *Caranus* were contemporary to *Solon*, *Alcmæon*, *Clisthenes*, and *Eurolycus*, and flourished about the 48th and 49th Olympiads. They were also contemporary in their later days to *Croesus*; for *Solon* conversed with *Croesus*, and *Alcmæon* entertained and conducted the messengers whom *Croesus* sent to consult the Oracle at *Delphi*, *An.* 1. Olymp. 56. according to the Marbles, and was sent for by *Croesus*, and rewarded with much riches.

But the times set down in the Marbles before the *Persian* Empire began, being collected by reckoning the Reigns of Kings equipollent to Generations, and three Generations to an hundred years or above; and the Reigns of Kings, one with another, being shorter in the proportion of about four to seven; the Chronology set down in the Marbles, until the Conquest of *Media* by *Cyrus*, *An.* 4, Olymp. 60, will approach the truth much nearer, by shortening the times before that Conquest in the proportion of four to seven. So the *Cirrheans* were conquered *An.* 2, Olymp. 47, according to the Marbles, that is 54 years before the Conquest of *Media*; and these years being shortened in the proportion of four to seven, become 31 years; which subducted from *An.* 4, Olymp. 60, place the Conquest of *Cirrha* upon *An.* 1, Olymp. 53: and, by the like correction of the Marbles, *Alcmæon* entertained and conducted the messengers whom *Croesus* sent to consult the Oracle at *Delphi*, *An.* 1, Olymp. 58; that is, four years before the Conquest of *Sardes* by *Cyrus*: and the Tyranny of *Pisistratus*, which by the Marbles began at *Athens*, *An.* 4, Olymp. 54, by the like correction began *An.* 3, Olymp. 57; and by consequence *Solon* died *An.* 4, Olymp. 57. This method may be used alone, where other arguments are wanting; but where they are not wanting, the best arguments are to be preferred.

Iphitus[126] presided both in the Temple of *Jupiter Olympius*, and in the Olympic Games, and so did his Successors 'till the 26th Olympiad; and so long the victors were rewarded with a *Tripos*: but then the *Pisæans* getting above the *Eleans*, began to preside, and rewarded the victors with a Crown, and instituted the *Carnea* to *Apollo*; and continued to preside 'till *Phidon* interrupted them, that is, 'till about the time of the 49th Olympiad: for[127] in the 48th Olympiad the *Eleans* entered the country of the *Pisæans*, suspecting their designs, but were prevailed upon to return home quietly; afterwards the *Pisæans* confederated with several other *Greek* nations, and made war upon the *Eleans*, and in the end were beaten: in this war I conceive it was that *Phidon* presided, suppose in the 49th Olympiad; for[128] in the 50th Olympiad, for putting an end to the contentions between the Kings about presiding, two men were chosen by lot out of the city *Elis* to preside, and their number in the 65th Olympiad was increased to nine, and afterwards to ten; and these judges were called *Hellenodicæ*, judges for or in the name of *Greece*. *Pausanias* tells us, that the *Eleans* called in *Phidon* and together with him celebrated the 8th Olympiad; he should have said the 49th Olympiad; but *Herodotus* tells us, that *Phidon* removed the *Eleans*; and both might be true: the *Eleans* might call in *Phidon* against the *Pisæans*, and upon overcoming be refused presiding in the Olympic games by *Phidon*, and confederate with the *Spartans*, and by their assistance overthrow the Kingdom of *Phidon*, and recover their ancient right of presiding in the games.

Strabo[129] tells us that *Phidon* was the tenth from *Temenus*; not the tenth King, for between *Cisus* and *Phidon* they Reigned not, but the tenth from father to son, including *Temenus*. If 27 years be reckoned to a Generation by the eldest sons, the nine intervals will amount unto 243 years, which counted back from the 48th Olympiad, in which *Phidon* flourished, will place the Return of the *Heraclides* about fifty years before the beginning of the Olympiads, as above. But Chronologers reckon about 515 years from the Return of the *Heraclides* to the 48th Olympiad, and account *Phidon* the seventh from *Temenus*; which is after the rate of 85 years to a Generation, and therefore not to be admitted.

Cyrus took *Babylon*, according to *Ptolomy*'s Canon, nine years before his death, *An. Nabonass.* 209, *An.* 2, Olymp. 60: and he took *Sardes* a little before, namely *An.* 1, Olymp. 59, as *Scaliger* collects from *Sosicrates*. *Croesus* was then King of *Sardes*, and Reigned fourteen years, and therefore began to Reign *An.* 3, Olymp. 55. After *Solon* had made laws for the *Athenians*, he obliged them upon oath to observe those laws 'till he returned from his travels; and then travelled ten years, going to *Egypt* and *Cyprus*, and visiting *Thales* of *Miletus*: and upon His Return to *Athens*, *Pisistratus* began to affect the Tyranny of that city, which made *Solon* travel a second time; and now he was invited by *Croesus* to *Sardes*; and *Croesus*, before *Solon* visited him, had subdued all *Asia Minor*, as far as to the River *Halys*; and therefore he received that visit towards the latter part of his Reign; and we may place it upon the ninth year thereof, *An.* 3, Olymp. 57: and the legislature of *Solon* twelve years earlier, *An.* 3, Olymp. 54: and that of *Draco* still ten years earlier, *An.* 1, Olymp. 52. After *Solon* had visited *Croesus*, he went into *Cilicia* and some other places, and died[130] in his travels: and this was in the second year of the Tyranny of *Pisistratus*. *Comias* was Archon when *Solon* returned from his first travels to *Athens*; and the next year *Hegestratus* was Archon, and *Solon* died before the end of the year, *An.* 3, Olymp. 57, as above: and by this reckoning the objection of *Plutarch* above mentioned is removed.

We have now shewed that the *Phoenicians* of *Zidon*, under the conduct of *Cadmus* and other captains, flying from their enemies, came into *Greece*, with letters and other arts, about the sixteenth year of King *David*'s Reign; that *Europa* the sister of *Cadmus*, fled some days before him from *Zidon* and came to *Crete*, and there became the mother of *Minos*, about the 18th or 20th year of *David's* Reign; that *Sesostris* and the great *Bacchus*, and by consequence also *Osiris*, were one and the same King of *Egypt* with *Sesac*, and came out of *Egypt* in the fifth year of *Rehoboam* to invade the nations, and died 25 years after *Solomon*; that the *Argonautic* expedition was about 43 years after the death of *Solomon*; that *Troy* was taken about 76 or 78 years after the death of *Solomon*; that the *Phoenicians* of *Tyre* were driven from the *Red Sea* by the *Edomites*, about 87 years after the death of *Solomon*, and within two or three years began to make long voyages upon the *Mediterranean*, sailing to *Spain*, and beyond, under a commander whom for his industry, conduct, and discoveries, they honoured with the names of *Melcartus* and *Hercules*; that the return of the *Heraclides* into *Peloponnesus* was about 158 years after the death of *Solomon*; that *Lycurgus* the Legislator Reigned at *Sparta*, and gave the three Discs to the Olympic treasury, *An.* 1, Olymp. 18, or 273 years after the death of *Solomon*, the *Quinquertium* being at that time added to the Olympic Games; that the *Greeks* began soon after to build *Triremes*, and to send Colonies into *Sicily* and *Italy*, which gave the name of *Græcia magna* to those countries; that the first *Messenian* war ended about 350 years after the death of *Solomon*, *An.* 1, Olymp. 37; that *Phidon* was contemporary to *Solon*, and presided in the Olympic Games in the 49th Olympiad, that is, 397 years after the death of *Solomon*; that *Draco* was Archon, and made his laws, *An.* 1, Olymp. 52; and *Solon*, *An.* 3, Olymp. 54; and that *Solon* visited *Croesus* Ann. 3, Olymp. 57, or 433 years after the death of *Solomon*; and *Sardes* was taken by *Cyrus* 438 years, and *Babylon* by *Cyrus* 443 years, and *Echatane* by *Cyrus* 445 years after the death of *Solomon*: and these periods being settled, they become a foundation for building the Chronology of the antient times upon them; and nothing more remains for settling such a Chronology, than to make these Periods a little exacter, if it can be, and to shew how the rest of the Antiquities of *Greece*, *Egypt*, *Assyria*, *Chaldæa*, and *Media* may suit therewith.

Whilst *Bacchus* made his expedition into *India*, *Theseus* left *Ariadne* in the Island *Naxus* or *Dia*, as above, and succeeded his father *Ægeus* at *Athens*; and upon the Return of *Bacchus* from *India*, *Ariadne* became his mistress, and accompanied him in his triumphs; and this was about ten years after the death of *Solomon*: and from that time reigned eight Kings in *Athens*, viz. *Theseus, Menestheus, Demophoon, Oxyntes, Aphidas, Thymætes, Melanthus,* and *Codrus*; these Kings, at 19 years a-piece one with another, might take up about 152 years, and end about 44 years before the Olympiads: then Reigned twelve Archons for life, which at 14 or 15 years a-piece, the State being unstable, might take up about 174 years, and end *An.* 2, Olymp. 33: then reigned seven decennial Archons, which are usually reckoned at seventy years; but some of them dying in their Regency, they might not take up above forty years, and so end about *An.* 2, Olymp. 43, about which time began the Second *Messenian* war: these decennial Archons were followed by the annual Archons, amongst whom were the Legislators *Draco* and *Solon*. Soon after the death of *Codrus*, his second Son *Neleus*, not bearing the Reign of his lame brother *Medon* at *Athens*, retired into *Asia*, and was followed by his younger brothers *Androcles* and *Cyaretus*, and many others: these had the name of *Ionians*, from *Ion* the son of *Xuthus*, who commanded the army of the *Athenians* at the death of *Erechtheus*, and gave the name of *Ionia* to the country which they invaded: and about 20 or 25 years after the death of *Codrus*, these new Colonies, being now Lords of *Ionia*, set up over themselves a common Council called *Panionium*, and composed of Counsellors sent from twelve of their cities, *Miletus*, *Myus*, *Priene*, *Ephesus*, *Colophon*, *Lebedus*, *Teos*, *Clazomenæ*, *Phocæa*, *Samos*, *Chios*, and *Erythræa*: and this was the *Ionic* Migration.

[131]When the *Greeks* and *Latines* were forming their Technical Chronology, there were great disputes about the Antiquity of *Rome*: the *Greeks* made it much older than the Olympiads: some of them said it was built by *Æneas*; others, by *Romus*, the son or grandson of *Æneas*; others, by *Romus*, the son or grandson of *Latinus* King of the *Aborigines*; others, by *Romus* the son of *Ulysses*, or of *Ascanius*, or of *Italus*: and some of the *Latines* at first fell in with the opinion of the *Greeks*, saying that it was built by *Romulus*, the son or grandson of *Æneas*. *Timæus Siculus* represented it built by *Romulus*, the grandson of *Æneas*, above an hundred years before the Olympiads; and so did *Nævius* the Poet, who was twenty years older than *Ennius*, and served in the first *Punic* war, and wrote the history of that war. Hitherto nothing certain was agreed upon, but about 140 or 150 years after the death of *Alexander the Great*, they began to say that *Rome* was built a second time by *Romulus*, in the fifteenth Age after the destruction of *Troy*: by Ages they meant Reigns of the Kings of the *Latines* at *Alba*, and reckoned the first fourteen Reigns at about 432 years, and the following Reigns of the seven Kings of *Rome* at 244 years, both which numbers made up the time of about 676 years from the taking of *Troy*, according to these Chronologers; but are much too long for the course of nature: and by this reckoning they placed the building of *Rome* upon the sixth or seventh Olympiad; *Varro* placed it on the first year of the Seventh Olympiad, and was therein generally followed by the *Romans*; but this can scarce be reconciled to the course of nature: for I do not meet with any instance in all history, since Chronology was certain, wherein seven Kings, most of whom were slain, Reigned 244 years in continual Succession. The fourteen Reigns of the Kings of the *Latines*, at twenty years a-piece one with another, amount unto 280 years, and these years counted from the taking of *Troy* end in the 38th Olympiad: and the Seven Reigns of the Kings of *Rome*, four or five of them being slain and one deposed, may at a moderate reckoning amount to fifteen or sixteen years a-piece one with another: let them be reckoned at seventeen years a-piece, and they will amount unto 119 years; which being counted backwards from the Regifuge, end also in the 38th Olympiad: and by these two reckonings *Rome* was built in the 38th Olympiad, or thereabout. The 280 years and the 119 years together make up 399 years; and the same number of years arises by counting the twenty and one Reigns at nineteen years a-piece: and this being the whole time between the taking of *Troy* and the Regifuge, let these years be counted backward from the Regifuge, *An.* 1, Olymp. 68, and they will place the taking of *Troy* about 74 years after the death of *Solomon*.

When *Sesostris* returned from *Thrace* into *Egypt*, he left *Æetes* with part of his army in *Colchis*, to guard that pass; and *Phryxus* and his sister *Helle* fled from *Ino*, the daughter of *Cadmus*, to *Æetes* soon after, in a ship whose ensign was a golden ram: *Ino* was therefore alive in the fourteenth year of *Rehoboam*, the year in which *Sesostris* returned into *Egypt*; and by consequence her father *Cadmus* flourished in the Reign of *David*, and not before. *Cadmus* was the father of *Polydorus*, the father of *Labdacus*, the father of *Laius*, the father of *Oedipus*, the father of *Eteocles* and *Polynices* who slew one another in their youth, in the war of the seven Captains at *Thebes*, about ten or twelve years after the *Argonautic* Expedition: and *Thersander*, the son of *Polynices*, warred at *Troy*. These Generations being by the eldest sons who married young, if they be reckoned at about twenty and four years to a Generation, will place the birth of *Polydorus* upon the 18th year of *David*'s Reign, or thereabout: and thus *Cadmus* might be a young man, not yet married, when he came first into *Greece*. At his first coming he sail'd to *Rhodes*, and thence to *Samothrace*, an Island near *Thrace* on the north side of *Lemnos*, and there married *Harmonia*, the sister of *Jasius* and *Dardanus*, which gave occasion to the *Samothracian* mysteries: and *Polydorus* might be their son, born a year or two after their coming; and his sister *Europa* might be then a young woman, in the flower of her age. These Generations cannot well be shorter; and therefore *Cadmus*, and his son *Polydorus*, were not younger than we have reckoned them: nor can they be much longer, without making *Polydorus* too old to be born in *Europe*, and to be the son of *Harmonia* the sister of *Jasius*. *Labdacus* was therefore born in the end of *David*'s Reign, *Laius* in the 24th year of *Solomon*'s, and *Oedipus* in the seventh of *Rehoboam*'s, or thereabout: unless you had rather say, that *Polydorus* was born at *Zidon*, before his father came into *Europe*; but his name *Polydorus* is in the language of *Greece*.

Polydorus married *Nycteis*, the daughter of *Nycteus* a native of *Greece*, and dying young, left his Kingdom and young son *Labdacus* under the administration of *Nycteus*. Then *Epopeus* King of *Ægialus*, afterwards called *Sicyon*, stole *Antiope* the daughter of *Nycteus*,[132] and *Nycteus* thereupon made war upon him, and in a battle wherein *Nycteus* overcame, both were wounded and died soon after. *Nycteus* left the tuition of *Labdacus*, and administration of the Kingdom, to his brother *Lycus*; and *Epopeus* or, as *Hyginus*[133] calls him, *Epaphus* the *Sicyonian*, left his Kingdom to *Lamedon*, who presently ended the war, by sending home *Antiope*: and she, in returning home, brought forth *Amphion* and *Zethus*. *Labdacus* being grown up received the Kingdom from *Lycus*, and soon after dying left it again to his administration, for his young son *Laius*. When *Amphion* and *Zethus* were about twenty years old, at the instigation of their mother *Antiope*, they killed *Lycus*, and made *Laius* flee to *Pelops*, and seized the city *Thebes*, and compassed it with a wall; and *Amphion* married *Niobe* the sister of *Pelops*, and by her had several children, amongst whom was *Chloris*, the mother of *Periclymenus* the *Argonaut*. *Pelops* was the father of *Plisthenes*, *Atreus*, and *Thyestes*; and *Agamemnon* and *Menelaus*, the adopted sons of *Atreus*, warred at *Troy*. *Ægisthus*, the son of *Thyestes*, slew *Agamemnon* the year after the taking of *Troy*; and *Atreus* died just before *Paris* stole *Helena*, which, according to[134] *Homer*, was twenty years before the taking of

Troy. *Deucalion* the son of *Minos*,[135] was an *Argonaut*; and *Talus* another son of *Minos*, was slain by the *Argonauts*; and *Idomeneus* and *Meriones* the grandsons of *Minos* were at the *Trojan* war. All these things confirm the ages of *Cadmus* and *Europa*, and their posterity, above assigned, and place the death of *Epopeus* or *Epaphus* King of *Sicyon*, and birth of *Amphion* and *Zethus*, upon the tenth year of *Solomon*; and the taking of *Thebes* by *Amphion* and *Zethus*, and the flight of *Laius* to *Pelops*, upon the thirtieth year of that King, or thereabout. *Amphion* might marry the sister of *Pelops*, the same year, and *Pelops* come into *Greece* three or four years before that flight, or about the 26th year of *Solomon*.

[Sidenode p: Hygin. Fab. 14.]

In the days of *Erechtheus* King of *Athens*, and *Celeus* King of *Eleusis*, *Ceres* came into *Attica*; and educated *Triptolemus* the son of *Celeus*, and taught him to sow corn. She[136] lay with *Jasion*, or *Jasius*, the brother of *Harmonia* the wife of *Cadmus*; and presently after her death *Erechtheus* was slain, in a war between the *Athenians* and *Eleusinians*; and, for the benefaction of bringing tillage into *Greece*, the *Eleusinia Sacra* were instituted to her[137] with *Egyptian* ceremonies, by *Celeus* and *Eumolpus*; and a Sepulchre or Temple was erected to her in *Eleusine*, and in this Temple the families of *Celeus* and *Eumolpus* became her Priests: and this Temple, and that which *Eurydice* erected to her daughter *Danae*, by the name of *Juno Argiva*, are the first instances that I meet with in *Greece* of Deifying the dead, with Temples, and Sacred Rites, and Sacrifices, and Initiations, and a succession of Priests to perform them. Now by this history it is manifest that *Erechtheus*, *Celeus*, *Eumolpus*, *Ceres*, *Jasius*, *Cadmus*, *Harmonia*, *Asterius*, and *Dardanus* the brother of *Jasius*, and one of the founders of the Kingdom of *Troy*, were all contemporary to one another, and flourished in their youth, when *Cadmus* came first into *Europe*. *Erechtheus* could not be much older, because his daughter *Procris* convers'd with *Minos* King of *Crete*; and his grandson *Thespis* had fifty daughters, who lay with *Hercules*; and his daughter *Orithyia* was the mother of *Calais* and *Zetes*, two of the *Argonauts* in their youth; and his son *Orneus*[138] was the father of *Peteos* the father of *Menestheus*, who warred at *Troy*: nor much younger, because his second son *Pandion*, who with the *Metionides* deposed his elder brother *Cecrops*, was the father of *Ægeus*, the father of *Theseus*; and *Metion*, another of his sons, was the father of *Eupalamus*, the father of *Dædalus*, who was older than *Theseus*; and his daughter *Creusa* married *Xuthus*, the son of *Hellen*, and by him had two sons, *Achæus* and *Ion*; and *Ion* commanded the army of the *Athenians* against the *Eleusinians*, in the battle in which his grandfather *Erechtheus* was slain: and this was just before the institution of the *Eleusinia Sacra*, and before the Reign of *Pandion* the father of *Ægeus*. *Erechtheus* being an *Egyptian* procured corn from *Egypt*, and for that benefaction was made King of *Athens*; and near the beginning of his Reign *Ceres* came into *Attica* from *Sicily*, in quest of her daughter *Proserpina*. We cannot err much if we make *Hellen* contemporary to the Reign of *Saul*, and to that of *David* at *Hebron*; and place the beginning of the Reign of *Erechtheus* in the 25th year, the coming of *Ceres* into *Attica* in the 30th year, and the dispersion of corn by *Triptolemus* about the 40th year of *David's* Reign; and the death of *Ceres* and *Erechtheus*, and institution of the *Eleusinia Sacra*, between the tenth and fifteenth year of *Solomon*.

Teucer, Dardanus, Erichthonius, Tros, Ilus, Laomedon, and *Priamus* Reigned successively at *Troy*; and their Reigns, at about twenty years a-piece one with another, amount unto an hundred and forty years: which counted back from the taking of *Troy*, place the beginning of the Reign of *Teucer* about the fifteenth year of the Reign of King *David*; and that of *Dardanus*, in the days of *Ceres*, who lay with *Jasius* the brother of *Dardanus*: whereas Chronologers reckon that the six last of these Kings Reigned 296 years, which is after the rate of 49-1/3 years a-piece one with another; and that they began their Reign in the days of *Moses*. *Dardanus* married the daughter of *Teucer*, the Son of *Scamander*, and succeeded him: whence *Teucer* was of about the same age with *David*.

Upon the return of *Sesostris* into *Egypt*, his brother *Danaus* not only attempted his life, as above, but also commanded his daughters, who were fifty in number and had married the sons of *Sesostris*, to slay their husbands; and then fled with his daughters from *Egypt*, in a long ship of fifty oars. This Flight was in the fourteenth year of *Rehoboam*. *Danaus* came first to *Lindus*, a town in *Rhodes*, and there built a Temple, and erected a Statue to *Minerva*, and lost three of his daughters by a plague which raged there; and then sailed thence with the rest of his daughters to *Argos*. He came to *Argos* therefore in the fifteenth or sixteenth year of *Rehoboam*: and at length contending there with *Gelanor* the brother of *Eurystheus* for the crown of *Argos*, was chosen by the people, and Reigned at *Argos*, while *Eurystheus* Reigned at *Mycenæ*; and *Eurystheus* was born[139] the same year with *Hercules*. *Gelanor* and *Eurystheus* were the sons of *Sthenelus*, by *Nicippe* the daughter of *Pelops*; and *Sthenelus* was the son of *Perseus*, and Reigned at *Argos*, and *Danaus*, who succeeded him at *Argos*, was succeeded there by his son in law *Lynceus*, and he by his son *Abas*; that *Abas* who is commonly, but erroneously, reputed the father of *Acrisius* and *Prœtus*. In the time of the *Argonautic* expedition *Castor* and *Pollux* were beardless young men, and their sisters *Helena* and *Clytemnestra* were children, and their wives *Phoebe* and *Ilaira* were also very young: all these, with the *Argonauts Lynceus* and *Idas*, were the grandchildren of *Gorgophone*, the daughter of *Perseus*, the son of *Danae*, the daughter of *Acrisius* and *Eurydice*; and *Perieres* and *Oebalus*, the husbands of *Gorgophone*, were the sons of *Cynortes*, the son of *Amyclas*, the brother of *Eurydice*. *Mestor* or *Mastor*, the brother of *Sthenelus*, married *Lysidice*, another of the daughters of *Pelops*: and *Pelops* married *Hippodamia*, the daughter of *Evarete*, the daughter of *Acrisius*. *Alcmena*, the mother of *Hercules*, was the daughter of *Electryo*; and *Sthenelus, Mestor* and *Electryo* were brothers of *Gorgophone*, and sons of *Perseus* and *Andromeda*: and the *Argonaut Æsculapius* was the grandson of *Leucippus* and *Phlegia*, and *Leucippus* was the son of *Perieres*, the grandson of *Amyclas* the brother of *Eurydice*, and *Amyclas* and *Eurydice* were the children of *Lacedæmon* and *Sparta*: and *Capaneus*, one of the seven Captains against *Thebes*, was the husband of *Euadne* the daughter of *Iphis*, the son of *Elector*, the son of *Anaxagoras*, the son of *Megapenthes*, the son of *Prœtus* the brother of *Acrisius*. Now from these Generations it may be gathered that *Perseus, Perieres* and *Anaxagoras* were of about the same age with *Minos, Pelops, Ægeus* and *Sesac*; and that *Acrisius, Prœtus, Eurydice,* and *Amyclas*, being two little Generations older, were of about the same age with King *David* and *Erechtheus*;

and that the Temple of *Juno Argiva* was built about the same time with the Temple of *Solomon*; the same being built by *Eurydice* to her daughter *Danae*, as above; or as some say, by *Pirasus* or *Piranthus*, the son or successor of *Argus*, and great grandson of *Phoroneus*: for the first Priestess of that Goddess was *Callithea* the daughter of *Piranthus*; *Callithea* was succeeded by *Alcinoe*, about three Generations before the taking of *Troy*, that is about the middle of *Solomon*'s Reign: in her Priesthood the *Siculi* passed out of *Italy* into *Sicily*: afterwards *Hypermnestra* the daughter of *Danaus* became Priestess of this Goddess, and she flourished in the times next before the *Argonautic* expedition: and *Admeta*, the daughter of *Eurystheus*, was Priestess of this *Juno* about the times of the *Trojan* war. *Andromeda* the wife of *Perseus*, was the daughter of *Cepheus* an *Egyptian*, the son of *Belus*, according to[140] *Herodotus*; and the *Egyptian Belus* was *Ammon*. *Perseus* took her from *Joppa*, where *Cepheus*, I think a kinsman of *Solomon*'s Queen, resided in the days of *Solomon*. *Acrisius* and *Prætus* were the sons of *Abas*: but this *Abas* was not the same man with *Abas* the grandson of *Danaus*, but a much older Prince, who built *Abæa* in *Phocis*, and might be the Prince from whom the island *Euboea*[141] was anciently called *Abantis*, and the people thereof *Abantes*: for *Apollonius Rhodius*[142] tells us, that the *Argonaut Canthus* was the son of *Canethus*, and that *Canethus* was of the posterity of *Abas*; and the Commentator upon *Apollonius* tells us further, that from this *Abas* the inhabitants of *Euboea* were anciently called *Abantes*. This *Abas* therefore flourished three or four Generations before the *Argonautic* expedition, and so might be the father of *Acrisius*: the ancestors of *Acrisius* were accounted *Egyptians* by the *Greeks*, and they might come from *Egypt* under *Abas* into *Euboea*, and from thence into *Peloponnesus*. I do not reckon *Phorbas* and his son *Triopas* among the Kings of *Argos*, because they fled from that Kingdom to the Island *Rhodes*; nor do I reckon *Crotopus* among them, because because he went from *Argos*, and built a new city for himself in *Megaris*, as[143] *Conon* relates.

We said that *Pelops* came into *Greece* about the 26th year of *Solomon*: he[144] came thither in the days of *Acrisius*, and in those of *Endymion*, and of his sons, and took *Ætolia* from *Aetolus*. *Endymion* was the son of *Aëthlius*, the son of *Protogenia*, the sister of *Hellen*, and daughter of *Deucalion*: *Phrixus* and *Helle*, the children of *Athamas*, the brother of *Sisyphus* and Son of *Æolus*, the son of *Hellen*, fled from their stepmother *Ino*, the daughter of *Cadmus*, to *Æetes* in *Colchis*, presently after the return of *Sesostris* into *Egypt*: and *Jason* the *Argonaut* was the son of *Æson*, the son of *Cretheus*, the son of *Æolus*, the son of *Hellen*: and *Calyce* was the wife of *Aëthlius*, and mother of *Endymion*, and daughter of *Æolus*, and sister of *Cretheus*, *Sisyphus* and *Athamas*: and by these circumstances *Cretheus*, *Sisyphus* and *Athamas* flourished in the latter part of the Reign of *Solomon*, and in the Reign of *Rehoboam*. *Aëthlius*, *Æolus*, *Xuthus*, *Dorus*, *Tantalus*, and *Danae* were contemporary to *Erechtheus*, *Jasius* and *Cadmus*; and *Hellen* was about one, and *Deucalion* about two Generations older than *Erechtheus*. They could not be much older, because *Xuthus* the youngest son of *Hellen*[145] married *Creusa* the daughter of *Erechtheus*; nor could they be much younger, because *Cephalus* the son of *Deioneus*, the son of *Æolus*, the eldest son of *Hellen*,[146] married *Procris* the daughter of *Erechtheus*; and *Procris* fled from her husband to *Minos*. Upon the death of *Hellen*, his youngest son *Xuthus*[147] was expelled *Thessaly* by his brothers *Æolus* and *Dorus*, and fled to *Erechtheus*, and married *Creusa* the daughter of *Erechtheus*; by whom he had two sons, *Achæus* and *Ion*, the youngest of which grew up before the death of *Erechtheus*, and commanded the army of the *Athenians*, in the war in which *Erechtheus* was slain: and therefore *Hellen* died about one Generation before *Erechtheus*.

Sisyphus therefore built *Corinth* about the latter end of the Reign of *Solomon*, or the beginning of the Reign of *Rehoboam*. Upon the flight of *Phrixus* and *Helle*, their father *Athamas*, a little King in *Boeotia*, went distracted and slew his son *Learchus*; and his wife *Ino* threw her self into the sea, together with her other son *Melicertus*; and thereupon *Sisyphus* instituted the *Isthmia* at *Corinth* to his nephew *Melicertus*. This was presently after *Sesostris* had left *Æetes* in *Colchis*, I think in the fifteenth or sixteenth year of *Rehoboam*: so that *Athamas*, the son of *Æolus* and grandson of *Hellen*, and *Ino* the daughter of *Cadmus*, flourished 'till about the sixteenth year of *Rehoboam*. *Sisyphus* and his successors *Ornytion*, *Thoas*, *Demophon*, *Propodas*, *Doridas*, and *Hyanthidas* Reigned successively at *Corinth*, 'till the return of the *Heraclides* into *Peloponnesus*: then Reigned the *Heraclides*, *Aletes*, *Ixion*, *Agelas*, *Prumnis*, *Bacchis*, *Agelas II*, *Eudamus*, *Aristodemus*, and *Telestes* successively about 170 years, and then *Corinth* was governed by *Prytanes* or annual Archons about 42 years, and after them by *Cypselus* and *Periander* about 48 years more.

Celeus King of *Eleusis*, who was contemporary to *Erechtheus*,[148] was the son of *Rharus*, the son of *Cranaus*, the successor of *Cecrops*; and in the Reign of *Cranaus*, *Deucalion* fled with his sons *Hellen* and *Amphictyon* from the flood which then overflowed *Thessaly*, and was called *Deucalion*'s flood: they fled into *Attica*, and there *Deucalion* died soon after; and *Pausanias* tells us that his Sepulchre was to be seen near *Athens*. His eldest son *Hellen* succeeded him in *Thessaly*, and his other son *Amphictyon* married the daughter of *Cranaus*, and Reigning at *Thermopylæ*, erected there the *Amphictyonic* Council; and *Acrisius* soon after erected the like Council at *Delphi*. This I conceive was done when *Amphictyon* and *Acrisius* were aged, and fit to be Counsellors; suppose in the latter half of the Reign of *David*, and beginning of the Reign of *Solomon*; and soon after, suppose about the middle of the Reign of *Solomon*, did *Phemonoë* become the first Priestess of *Apollo* at *Delphi*, and gave Oracles in hexameter verse: and then was *Acrisius* slain accidentally by his grandson *Perseus*. The Council of *Thermopylæ* included twelve nations of the *Greeks*, without *Attica*, and therefore *Amphictyon* did not then Reign at *Athens*: he might endeavour to succeed *Cranaus*, his wife's father, and be prevented by *Erechtheus*.

Between the Reigns of *Cranaus* and *Erechtheus*, Chronologers place also *Erichthonius*, and his son *Pandion*; but I take this *Erichthonius* and this his son *Pandion*, to be the same with *Erechtheus* and his son and successor *Pandion*, the names being only repeated with a little variation in the list of the Kings of *Attica*: for *Erichthonius*, he that was the son of the Earth, nursed up by *Minerva*, is by *Homer* called *Erechtheus*; and *Themistius*[149] tells us, that it was *Erechtheus* that first joyned a chariot to horses; and *Plato*[150] alluding to the story of *Erichthonius* in a basket, saith, *The people of magnanimous* Erechtheus *is beautiful, but it behoves us to behold him taken out*. Erechtheus therefore immediately succeeded *Cranaus*, while *Amphictyon* Reigned at *Thermopylæ*. In the Reign of *Cranaus* the Poets place the flood of *Deucalion*, and therefore the death of *Deucalion*, and the Reign of his sons *Hellen* and *Amphictyon*, in *Thessaly* and *Thermpolyæ*, was but a few years, suppose eight or ten, before the Reign of *Erechtheus*.

The first Kings of *Arcadia* were successively *Pelasgus*, *Lycaon*, *Nyctimus*, *Arcas*, *Clitor*, *Æpytus*, *Aleus*, *Lycurgus*, *Echemus*, *Agapenor*, *Hippothous*, *Æpytus* II, *Cypselus*, *Olæas*, &c. Under *Cypselus* the *Heraclides* returned into *Peloponnesus*, as above: *Agapenor* was one of those who courted *Helena*; he courted her before he reigned, and afterwards he went to the war at *Troy*, and thence to *Cyprus*, and there built *Paphos*. *Echemus* slew *Hyllus* the son of *Hercules*. *Lycurgus*, *Cepheus*, and *Auge*, were[151] the children of *Aleus*, the son of *Aphidas*, the son of *Arcas*, the son of *Callisto*, the daughter of *Lycaon*. *Auge* lay with *Hercules*, and *Ancæus* the son of *Lycurgus* was an *Argonaut*, and his uncle *Cepheus* was his Governour in that Expedition; and *Lycurgus* stay'd at home, to look after his aged father *Aleus*, who might be born about 75 years before that Expedition; and his grandfather *Arcas* might be born about the end of the Reign of *Saul*, and *Lycaon* the grandfather of *Arcas* might be then alive, and dye before the middle of *David*'s Reign; and His youngest son *Oenotrus*, the *Janus* of the *Latines*, might grow up, and lead a colony into *Italy* before the Reign of *Solomon*. *Arcas* received[152] bread-corn from *Triptolemus*, and taught his people to make bread of it; and so did *Eumelus*, the first King of a region afterwards called *Achaia*: and therefore *Arcas* and *Eumelus* were contemporary to *Triptolemus*, and to his old father *Celeus*, and to *Erechtheus* King of *Athens*; and *Callisto* to *Rharus*, and her father *Lycaon* to *Cranaus*: but *Lycaon* died before *Cranaus*, so as to leave room for *Deucalion*'s flood between their deaths. The eleven Kings of *Arcadia*, between this Flood and the Return of the *Heraclides* into *Peloponnesus*, that is, between the Reigns of *Lycaon* and *Cypselus*, after the rate of about twenty years to a Reign one with another, took up about 220 years; and these years counted back from the Return of the *Heraclides*, place the Flood of *Deucalion* upon the fourteenth year of *David*'s Reign, or thereabout.

Herodotus[153] tells us, that the *Phoenicians* who came with *Cadmus* brought many doctrines into *Greece*: for amongst those *Phoenicians* were a sort of men called *Curetes*, who were skilled in the Arts and Sciences of *Phoenicia*, above other men, and[154] settled some in *Phrygia*, where they were called *Corybantes*; some in *Crete*, where they were called *Idæi Dactyli*; some in *Rhodes*, where they were called *Telchines*; some in *Samothrace*, where they were called *Cabiri*; some in *Euboea*, where, before the invention of iron, they wrought in copper, in a city thence called *Chalcis* some in *Lemnos*, where they assisted *Vulcan*; and some in *Imbrus*, and other places: and a considerable number of them settled in *Ætolia*, which was thence called the country of the *Curetes*; until *Ætolus* the son of *Endymion*, having slain *Apis* King of *Sicyon*, fled thither, and by the assistance of his father invaded it, and from his own name called it *Ætolia*: and by the assistance of these artificers, *Cadmus* found out gold in the mountain *Pangæus* in *Thrace*, and copper at *Thebes*; whence copper ore is still called *Cadmia*. Where they settled they wrought first in copper, 'till iron was invented, and then in iron; and when they had made themselves armour, they danced in it at the sacrifices with tumult and clamour, and bells, and pipes, and drums, and swords, with which they struck upon one another's armour, in musical times, appearing seized with a divine fury; and this is reckoned the original of music in *Greece:* so *Solinus*[155] *Studium musicum inde coeptum cum Idæi Dactyli modulos crepitu & tinnitu æris deprehensos in versificum ordinem transtulissent*: and[156] *Isidorus, Studium musicum ab Idæis Dactylis coeptum. Apollo* and the Muses were two Generations later. *Clemens*[157] calls the *Idæi Dactyli* barbarous, that is strangers; and saith, that they reputed the first wise men, to whom both the letters which they call *Ephesian*, and the invention of musical rhymes are referred: it seems that when the *Phoenician* letters, ascribed to *Cadmus*, were brought into *Greece*, they were at the same time brought into *Phrygia* and *Crete*, by the *Curetes*; who settled in those countries, and called them *Ephesian*, from the city *Ephesus*, where they were first taught. The *Curetes*, by their manufacturing copper and iron, and making swords, and armour, and edged tools for hewing and carving of wood, brought into *Europe* a new way of fighting; and gave *Minos* an opportunity of building a Fleet, and gaining the dominion of the seas; and set on foot the trades of Smiths and Carpenters in *Greece*, which are the foundation of manual trades: the[158] fleet of *Minos* was without sails, and *Dædalus* fled from him by adding sails to his vessel; and therefore ships with sails were not used by the *Greeks* before the flight of *Dædalus*, and death of *Minos*, who was slain in pursuing him to *Sicily*, in the Reign of *Rehoboam. Dædalus* and his nephew *Talus*, in the latter part of the Reign of *Solomon*, invented the chip-ax, and saw, and wimble, and perpendicular, and compass, and turning-lath, and glew, and the potter's wheel; and his father *Eupalamus* invented the anchor: and these things gave a beginning to manual Arts and Trades in *Europe.*

The[159] *Curetes*, who thus introduced Letters, and Music, and Poetry, and Dancing, and Arts, and attended on the Sacrifices, were no less active about religious institutions, and for their skill and knowledge and mystical practices, were accounted wise men and conjurers by the vulgar. In *Phrygia* their mysteries were about *Rhea*, called *Magna Mater*, and from the places where she was worshipped, *Cybele, Berecynthia, Pessinuntia, Dindymene, Mygdonia*, and *Idæa Phrygia*: and in *Crete*, and the *Terra Curetum*, they were about *Jupiter Olympius*, the son of the *Cretan Rhea*: they represented,[160] that when *Jupiter* was born in *Crete*, his mother *Rhea* caused him to be educated in a cave in mount *Ida*, under their care and tuition; and[161] that they danced about him in armour, with great noise, that his father *Saturn* might not hear him cry; and when he was grown up, assisted him in conquering his father, and his father's friends; and in memory of these things instituted their mysteries. *Bochart*[162] brings them from *Palestine*, and thinks that they had the name of *Curetes* from the people among the *Philistims* called *Crethim*, or *Cerethites*: *Ezek*. xxv. 16. *Zeph*. ii. 5. 1 *Sam*. xxx. 14, for the *Philistims* conquered *Zidon*, and mixed with the *Zidonians.*

The two first Kings of *Crete*, who reigned after the coming of the *Curetes*, were *Asterius* and *Minos*; and *Europa* was the Queen of *Asterius*, and mother of

Minos; and the *Idæan Curetes* were her countrymen, and came with her and her brother *Alymnus* into *Crete*, and dwelt in the *Idæan* cave in her Reign, and there educated *Jupiter*, and found out iron, and made armour: and therefore these three, *Asterius*, *Europa*, and *Minos*, must be the *Saturn*, *Rhea* and *Jupiter* of the *Cretans. Minos* is usually called the son of *Jupiter*; but this is in relation to the fable, that *Jupiter* in the shape of a bull, the Ensign of the Ship, carried away *Europa* from *Zidon*: for the *Phoenicians*, upon their first coming into *Greece*, gave the name of *Jao-pater*, *Jupiter*, to every King: and thus both *Minos* and his father were *Jupiters. Echemenes*, an ancient author cited by *Athenæus*,[163] said that *Minos* was that *Jupiter* who committed the rape upon *Ganimede*; though others said more truly that it was *Tantalus. Minos* alone was that *Jupiter* who was most famous among the *Greeks* for Dominion and Justice, being the greatest King in all *Greece* in those days, and the only legislator. *Plutarch*[164] tells us, that the people of *Naxus*, contrary to what others write, pretended that there were two *Minos's*, and two *Ariadnes*; and that the first *Ariadne* married *Bacchus*, and the last was carried away by *Theseus*: but[165] *Homer*, *Hesiod*, *Thucydides*, *Herodotus*, and *Strabo*, knew but of one *Minos*; and *Homer* describes him to be the son of *Jupiter* and *Europa*, and the brother of *Rhadamanthus* and *Sarpedon*, and the father of *Deucalion* the *Argonaut*, and grandfather of *Idomeneus* who warred at *Troy*, and that he was the legislator of Hell: *Herodotus*[166] makes *Minos* and *Rhadamanthus* the sons of *Europa*, contemporary to *Ægeus*: and[167] *Apollodorus* and *Hyginus* say, that *Minos*, the father of *Androgeus*, *Ariadne* and *Phædra*, was the son of *Jupiter* and *Europa*, and brother of *Rhadamanthus* and *Sarpedon*.

Lucian[168] lets us know that *Europa* the mother of *Minos* was worshipped by the name of *Rhea*, the form of a woman sitting in a chariot drawn by lions, with a drum in her hand, and a *Corona turrita* on her head, like *Astarte* and *Isis*; and the *Cretans*[169] anciently shewed the house where this *Rhea* lived: and[170] *Apollonius Rhodius* tells us, that *Saturn*, while he Reigned over the *Titans* in *Olympus*, a mountain in *Crete*, and *Jupiter* was educated by the *Curetes* in the *Cretan* cave, deceived *Rhea*, and of *Philyra* begot *Chiron*: and therefore the *Cretan Saturn* and *Rhea*, were but one Generation older than *Chiron*, and by consequence not older than *Asterius* and *Europa*, the parents of *Minos*; for *Chiron* lived 'till after the *Argonautic* Expedition, and had two grandsons in that Expedition, and *Europa* came into *Crete* above an hundred years before that Expedition: *Lucian*[171] tells us, that the *Cretans* did not only relate, that *Jupiter* was born and buried among them, but also shewed his sepulchre: and *Porphyry*[172] tells us, that *Pythagoras* went down into the *Idæan* cave, to see sepulchre: and *Cicero*,[173] in numbering three *Jupiters*, saith, that the third was the *Cretan Jupiter*, *Saturn's* son, whose sepulchre was shewed in *Crete*: and the Scholiast upon *Callimachus*[174] lets us know, that this was the sepulchre of *Minos*. his words are, [Greek: En Krêtê epi tôi taphôi tou Minôos epegegrapto, MINÔOS TOU DIOS TAPHOS. tôi chronôi de tou Minôos apêleiphthê, hôste perileiphthênai, DIOS TAPHOS. ek toutou oun echein legousi Krêtes ton taphon tou Dios.] *In* Crete *upon the Sepulchre of* Minos *was written* Minois Jovis sepulchrum: *but in time* Minois *wore out so that there remained only,* Jovis sepulchrum, *and thence the* Cretans *called it the Sepulchre of* Jupiter. By

Saturn, *Cicero*, who was a *Latine*, understood the *Saturn* so called by the *Latines*: for when *Saturn* was expelled his Kingdom he fled from *Crete* by sea, to *Italy*; and this the Poets exprest by saying, that *Jupiter* cast him down to *Tartarus*, that is, into the Sea: and because he lay hid in *Italy*, the *Latines* called him *Saturn*; and *Italy*, *Saturnia*, and *Latium*, and themselves *Latines*: so[175] *Cyprian*; *Antrum Jovis in Creta visitur, & sepulchrum ejus ostenditur: & ab eo Saturnum fugatum esse manifestum est: unde Latium de latebra ejus nomen accepit: hic literas imprimere, hic signare nummos in Italia primus instituit, unde ærarium Saturni vocatur; & rusticitatis hic cultor fuit, inde falcem ferens senex pingitur.* and *Minutius Felix*; *Saturnus Creta profugus, Italiam metu filii sævientis accesserat, & Jani susceptus hospitio, rudes illos homines & agrestes multa docuit, ut Græculus & politus, literas imprimere, nummos signare, instrumenta conficere: itaque latebram suam, quod tuto latuisset, vocari maluit Latium, & urbem Saturniam de suo nomine. * * Ejus filius Jupiter Cretæ excluso parente regnavit, illic obiit, illic filios habuit; adhuc antrum Jovis visitur, & sepulchrum ejus ostenditur, & ipsis sacris suis humanitatis arguitur.* and *Tertullian*;[176] *Quantum rerum argumenta docent, nusquam invenio fideliora quam apud ipsam Italiam, in qua Saturnus post multas expeditiones, postque Attica hospitia consedit, exceptus ab Jano, vel Jane ut Salii volunt. Mons quem incoluerat Saturnius dictus: civitas quam depalaverat Saturnia usque nunc est. Tota denique Italia post Oenotriam Saturnia cognominabatur. Ab ipso primum tabulæ, & imagine signatus nummus, & inde ærario præsidet.* By *Saturn*'s carrying letters into *Italy*, and coyning money, and teaching agriculture, and making instruments, and building a town, you may know that he fled from *Crete*, after letters, and the coyning of money, and manual arts were brought into *Europe* by the *Phoenicians*; and from *Attica*, after agriculture was brought into *Greece* by *Ceres*; and so could not be older than *Asterius*, and *Europa*, and her brother *Cadmus*: and by *Italy*'s being called *Oenotria*, before it was called *Saturnia*, you may know that he came into *Italy* after *Oenotrus*, and so was not older than the sons of *Lycaon*. *Oenotrus* carried the first colony of the *Greeks* into *Italy*, *Saturn* the second, and *Evander* the third; and the *Latines* know nothing older in *Italy* than *Janus* and *Saturn*: and therefore *Oenotrus* was the *Janus* of the *Latines*, and *Saturn* was contemporary to the sons of *Lycaon*, and by consequence also to *Celeus*, *Erechtheus*, *Ceres*, and *Asterius*: for *Ceres* educated *Triptolemus* the son of *Celeus*, in the Reign of *Erechtheus*, and then taught him to plow and sow corn: *Arcas* the son of *Callisto*, and grandson of *Lycaon*, received corn from *Triptolemus*, and taught his people to make bread of it; and *Procris*, the daughter of *Erechtheus*, fled to *Minos* the son of *Asterius*. In memory of *Saturn*'s coming into *Italy* by sea, the *Latines* coined their first money with his head on one side, and a ship on the other. *Macrobius*[177] tells us, that when *Saturn* was dead, *Janus* erected an Altar to him, with sacred rites as to a God, and instituted the *Saturnalia*, and that humane sacrifices were offered to him; 'till *Hercules* driving the cattle of *Geryon* through *Italy*, abolished that custom: by the human sacrifices you may know that *Janus* was of the race of *Lycaon*; which character agrees to *Oenotrus*. *Dionysius Halicarnassensis* tells us further, that *Oenotrus* having found in the western parts of *Italy* a large region fit for pasturage and tillage, but yet for the most part uninhabited, and where it was inhabited, peopled but thinly; in a certain part of it, purged from the *Barbarians*, he built towns little and numerous, in the mountains; which manner of building was familiar to the ancients: and this was the Original of Towns in *Italy.*

Pausanias[178] tells us that *the people of* Elis, *who were best skilled in Antiquities, related this to have been the Original of the Olympic Games: that* Saturn *Reigned first and had a Temple built to him in* Olympia *by the men of the Golden Age; and that when* Jupiter *was newly born, his mother* Rhea *recommended him to the care of the* Idæi Dactyli, *who were also called* Curetes: *that afterwards five of them, called* Hercules, Poeonius, Epimedes, Jasius, *and* Ida, *came from* Ida, *a mountain in* Crete, *into* Elis*; and* Hercules, *called also* Hercules Idæus, *being the oldest of them, in memory of the war between* Saturn *and* Jupiter, *instituted the game of racing, and that the victor should be rewarded with a crown of olive*; and there erected an altar to *Jupiter Olympius,* and called these games Olympic: and that some of the *Eleans* said, *that* Jupiter *contended here with* Saturn *for the Kingdom; others that* Hercules Idæus *instituted these games in memory of their victory over the* Titans: for the people of *Arcadia*[179] had a tradition, that the Giants fought with the Gods in the valley of *Bathos,* near the river *Alpheus* and the fountain *Olympias*[180] Before the Reign of *Asterius,* his father *Teutamus* came into *Crete* with a colony from *Olympia*; and upon the flight of *Asterius,* some of his friends might retire with him into their own country, and be pursued and beaten there by the *Idæan Hercules*: the *Eleans* said also that *Clymenus* the grandson of the *Idæan Hercules,* about fifty years after *Deucalion's* flood, coming from *Crete,* celebrated these games again in *Olympia,* and erected there an altar to *Juno Olympia,* that is, to *Europa,* and another to this *Hercules* and the rest of the *Curetes*; and Reigned in *Elis* 'till he was expelled by *Endymion,*[181] who thereupon celebrated these games again: and so did *Pelops,* who expelled *Ætolus* the son of *Endymion*; and so also did *Hercules* the son of *Alcmena,* and *Atreus* the son of *Pelops,* and *Oxylus*: they might be celebrated originally in triumph for victories, first by *Hercules Idæus,* upon the conquest of *Saturn* and the *Titans,* and then by *Clymenus,* upon his coming to Reign in the *Terra Curetum*; then by *Endymion,* upon his conquering *Clymenus*; and afterwards by *Pelops,* upon his conquering *Ætolus*; and by *Hercules,* upon his killing *Augeas*; and by *Atreus,* upon his repelling the *Heraclides*; and by *Oxylus,* upon the return of the *Heraclides* into *Peloponnesus.* This *Jupiter,* to whom they were instituted, had a Temple and Altar erected to him in *Olympia,* where the games were celebrated, and from the place was called *Jupiter Olympius*: *Olympia* was a place upon the confines of *Pisa,* near the river *Alpheus.*

In the[182] Island *Thasus,* where *Cadmus* left his brother *Thasus,* the *Phoenicians* built a Temple to *Hercules Olympius,* that *Hercules,* whom *Cicero*[183] calls *ex Idæis Dactylis; cui inferias afferunt.* When the mysteries of *Ceres* were instituted in *Eleusis,* there were other mysteries instituted to her and her daughter and daughter's husband, in the Island *Samothrace,* by the *Phoenician* names of *Dii Cabiri Axieros, Axiokersa,* and *Axiokerses,* that is, the great Gods *Ceres, Proserpina* and *Pluto*: for[184] *Jasius* a *Samothracian,* whose sister married *Cadmus,* was familiar with *Ceres*; and *Cadmus* and *Jasius* were both of them instituted in these mysteries. *Jasius* was the brother of *Dardanus,* and married *Cybele* the daughter of *Meones* King of *Phrygia,* and by her had *Corybas*; and after his death, *Dardanus, Cybele* and *Corybas* went into *Phrygia*, and carried thither the mysteries of the mother of the Gods, and *Cybele* called the goddess after her own name, and *Corybas* called her priests *Corybantes*: thus *Diodorus*; but *Dionysius* saith[185] that *Dardanus* instituted the *Samothracian* mysteries, and that his wife *Chryses* learnt them in *Arcadia*, and that *Idæus* the son of *Dardanus* instituted afterwards the mysteries of the mother of the gods in *Phrygia*: this *Phrygian* Goddess was drawn in a chariot by lions, and had a *corona turrita* on her head, and a drum in her hand, like the *Phoenician* Goddess *Astarte*, and the *Corybantes* danced in armour at her sacrifices in a furious manner, like the *Idæi Dactyli*; and *Lucian*[186] tells us that she was the *Cretan Rhea*, that is, *Europa* the mother of *Minos*: and thus the *Phoenicians* introduced the practice of Deifying dead men and women among the *Greeks* and *Phrygians*; for I meet with no instance of Deifying dead men and women in *Greece*, before the coming of *Cadmus* and *Europa* from *Zidon*.

From these originals it came into fashion among the *Greeks*, [Greek: kterizein], *parentare*, to celebrate the funerals of dead parents with festivals and invocations and sacrifices offered to their ghosts, and to erect magnificent sepulchres in the form of temples, with altars and statues, to persons of renown; and there to honour them publickly with sacrifices and invocations: every man might do it to his ancestors; and the cities of *Greece* did it to all the eminent *Greeks*: as to *Europa* the sister, to *Alymnus* the brother, and to *Minos* and *Rhadamanthus* the nephews of *Cadmus*; to his daughter *Ino*, and her son *Melicertus*; to *Bacchus* the son of his daughter *Semele*, *Aristarchus* the husband of his daughter *Autonoe*, and *Jasius* the brother of his wife *Harmonia*; to *Hercules* a *Theban*, and his mother *Alcmena*; to *Danae* the daughter of *Acrisius*; to *Æsculapius* and *Polemocrates* the son of *Machaon*, to *Pandion* and *Theseus* Kings of *Athens*, *Hippolytus* the son of *Theseus*, *Pan* the son of *Penelope*, *Proserpina*, *Triptolemus*, *Celeus*, *Trophonius*, *Castor*, *Pollux*, *Helena*, *Menelaus*, *Agamemnon*, *Amphiaraus* and his son *Amphilochus*, *Hector* and *Alexandra* the son and daughter of *Priam*, *Phoroneus*, *Orpheus*, *Protesilaus*, *Achilles* and his mother *Thetis*, *Ajax*, *Arcas*, *Idomeneus*, *Meriones*, *Æacus*, *Melampus*, *Britomartis*, *Adrastus*, *Iolaus*, and divers others. They Deified their dead in divers manners, according to their abilities and circumstances, and the merits of the person; some only in private families, as houshold Gods or *Dii Pænates*; others by erecting gravestones to them in publick, to be used as altars for annual sacrifices; others, by building also to them sepulchres in the form of houses or temples; and some by appointing mysteries, and ceremonies, and set sacrifices, and festivals, and initiations, and a succession of priests for performing those institutions in the temples, and handing them down to posterity. Altars might begin to be erected in *Europe* a little before the days of *Cadmus*, for sacrificing to the old God or Gods of the Colonies, but Temples began in the days of *Solomon*; for[187] *Æacus* the son of *Ægina*, who was two Generations older than the *Trojan* war, is by some reputed one of the first who built a Temple in *Greece*. Oracles came first from *Egypt* into *Greece* about the same time, as also did the custom of forming the images of the Gods with their legs bound up in the shape of the *Egyptian* mummies: for Idolatry began in *Chaldæa* and *Egypt*, and spread thence into *Phoenicia* and the neighbouring countries, long before it came into *Europe*;

and the *Pelasgians* propagated it in *Greece*, by the dictates of the Oracles. The countries upon the *Tigris* and the *Nile* being exceeding fertile, were first frequented by mankind, and grew first into Kingdoms, and therefore began first to adore their dead Kings and Queens: hence came the Gods of *Laban*, the Gods and Goddesses called *Baalim* and *Ashtaroth* by the *Canaanites*, the Dæmons or Ghosts to whom they sacrificed, and the *Moloch* to whom they offered their children in the days of *Moses* and the Judges. Every City set up the worship of its own Founder and Kings, and by alliances and conquests they spread this worship, and at length the *Phoenicians* and *Egyptians* brought into *Europe* the practice of Deifying the dead. The Kingdom of the lower *Egypt* began to worship their Kings before the days of *Moses*; and to this worship the second commandment is opposed: when the Shepherds invaded the lower *Egypt*, they checked this worship of the old *Egyptians*, and spread that of their own Kings: and at length the *Egyptians* of *Coptos* and *Thebais*, under *Misphragmuthosis* and *Amosis*, expelling the Shepherds, checked the worship of the Gods of the Shepherds, and Deifying their own Kings and Princes, propagated the worship of twelve of them into their conquests; and made them more universal than the false Gods of any other nation had been before, so as to be called, *Dii magni majorum gentium*. *Sesostris* conquered *Thrace*, and *Amphictyon* the son of *Prometheus* brought the twelve Gods from *Thrace* into *Greece*. *Herodotus*[188] tells us that they came from *Egypt*; and by the names of the cities of *Egypt* dedicated to many of these Gods, you may know that they were of an *Egyptian* original: and the *Egyptians*, according to *Diodorus*,[189] usually represented, that after their *Saturn* and *Rhea*, Reigned *Jupiter* and *Juno*, the parents of *Osiris* and *Isis*, the parents of *Orus* and *Bubaste*.

By all this it may be understood, that as the *Egyptians* who Deified their Kings, began their monarchy with the Reign of their Gods and Heroes, reckoning *Menes* the first man who reigned after their Gods; so the *Cretans* had the Ages of their Gods and Heroes, calling the first four Ages of their Deified Kings and Princes, the Golden, Silver, Brazen, and Iron Ages. *Hesiod*[190] describing these four Ages of the Gods and Demi-Gods of *Greece*, represents them to be four Generations of men, each of which ended when the men then living grew old and dropt into the grave, and tells us that the fourth ended with the wars of *Thebes* and *Troy*: and so many Generations there were, from the coming of the *Phoenicians* and *Curetes* with *Cadmus* and *Europa* into *Greece* unto the destruction of *Troy*. *Apollonius Rhodius* saith that when the *Argonauts* came to *Crete*, they slew *Talus* a brazen man, who remained of those that were of the Brazen Age, and guarded that pass: *Talus* was reputed[191] the son of *Minos*, and therefore the sons of *Minos* lived in the Brazen Age, and *Minos* Reigned in the Silver Age: it was the Silver Age of the *Greeks* in which they began to plow and sow Corn, and *Ceres*, that taught them to do it, flourished in the Reign of *Celeus* and *Erechtheus* and *Minos*. Mythologists tell us that the last woman with whom *Jupiter* lay, was *Alcmena*; and thereby they seem to put an end to the Reign of *Jupiter* among mortals, that is to the Silver Age, when *Alcmena* was with child of *Hercules*; who therefore was born about the eighth or tenth year of *Rehoboam's*

Reign, and was about 34 years old at the time of the *Argonautic* expedition. *Chiron* was begot by *Saturn* of *Philyra* in the Golden Age, when *Jupiter* was a child in the *Cretan* cave, as above; and this was in the Reign of *Asterius* King of *Crete*: and therefore *Asterius* Reigned in *Crete* in the Golden Age; and the Silver Age began when *Chiron* was a child: if *Chiron* was born about the 35th year of *David's* Reign, he will be born in the Reign of *Asterius*, when *Jupiter* was a child in the *Cretan* cave, and be about 88 years old in the time of the *Argonautic* expedition, when he invented the Asterisms; and this is within the reach of nature. The Golden Age therefore falls in with the Reign of *Asterius*, and the Silver Age with that of *Minos*; and to make these Ages much longer than ordinary generations, is to make *Chiron* live much longer than according to the course of nature. This fable of the four Ages seems to have been made by the *Curetes* in the fourth Age, in memory of the first four Ages of their coming into *Europe*, as into a new world; and in honour of their country-woman *Europa*, and her husband *Asterius* the *Saturn* of the *Latines*, and of her son *Minos* the *Cretan Jupiter* and grandson *Deucalion*, who Reigned 'till the *Argonautic* expedition, and is sometimes reckoned among the *Argonauts*, and of their great grandson *Idomeneus* who warred at *Troy*. *Hesiod* tells us that he himself lived in the fifth Age, the Age next after the taking of *Troy*, and therefore he flourished within thirty or thirty five years after it: and *Homer* was of about the same Age; for he[192] lived sometime with *Mentor* in *Ithaca*, and there learnt of him many things concerning *Ulysses*, with whom *Mentor* had been personally acquainted: now *Herodotus*, the oldest Historian of the *Greeks* now extant,[193] tells us that *Hesiod* and *Homer* were not above four hundred years older than himself, and therefore they flourished within 110 or 120 years after the death of *Solomon*; and according to my reckoning the taking of *Troy* was but one Generation earlier.

Mythologists tell us, that *Niobe* the daughter of *Phoroneus* was the first woman with whom *Jupiter* lay, and that of her he begat *Argus*, who succeeded *Phoroneus* in the Kingdom of *Argos*, and gave his name to that city; and therefore *Argus* was born in the beginning of the Silver Age: unless you had rather say that by *Jupiter* they might here mean *Asterius*; for the *Phoenicians* gave the name of *Jupiter* to every King, from the time of their first coming into *Greece* with *Cadmus* and *Europa*, until the invasion of *Greece* by *Sesostris*, and the birth of *Hercules*, and particularly to the fathers of *Minos*, *Pelops*, *Lacedæmon*, *Æacus*, and *Perseus*.

The four first Ages succeeded the flood of *Deucalion*; and some tell us that *Deucalion* was the son of *Prometheus*, the son of *Japetus*, and brother of *Atlas*: but this was another *Deucalion*; for *Japetus* the father of *Prometheus*, *Epimetheus*, and *Atlas*, was an *Egyptian*, the brother of *Osiris*, and flourished two generations after the flood of *Deucalion*.

I have now carried up the Chronology of the *Greeks* as high as to the first use of letters, the first plowing and sowing of corn, the first manufacturing of copper and iron, the beginning of the trades of Smiths, Carpenters, Joyners, Turners, Brick-makers, Stone-cutters, and Potters, in *Europe*; the first walling of cities about, the first building of Temples, and the original of Oracles in *Greece*; the beginning of navigation by the Stars in long ships with sails; the erecting of the *Amphictyonic* Council; the first Ages of *Greece*, called the Golden, Silver, Brazen and Iron Ages, and the flood of *Deucalion* which immediately preceded them. Those Ages could not be earlier than the invention and use of the four metals in *Greece*, from whence they had their names; and the flood of *Ogyges* could not be much above two or three ages earlier than that of *Deucalion*: for among such wandering people as were then in *Europe*, there could be no memory of things done above three or four ages before the first use of letters: and the expulsion of the Shepherds out of *Egypt*, which gave the first occasion to the coming of people from *Egypt* into *Greece*, and to the building of houses and villages in *Greece*, was scarce earlier than the days of *Eli* and *Samuel*; for *Manetho* tells us, that when they were forced to quit *Abaris* and retire out of *Egypt*, they went through the wilderness into *Judæa* and built *Jerusalem*: I do not think, with *Manetho*, that they were the *Israelites* under *Moses*, but rather believe that they were *Canaanites*; and upon leaving *Abaris* mingled with the *Philistims* their next neighbours: though some of them might assist *David* and *Solomon* in building *Jerusalem* and the Temple.

Saul was made King[194], that he might rescue *Israel* out of the hand of the *Philistims*, who opressed them; and in the second year of his Reign, the *Philistims* brought into the field against him *thirty thousand chariots, and six thousand horsemen, and people as the sand which is on the sea shore for multitude*: the *Canaanites* had their horses from *Egypt*; and yet in the days of *Moses* all the chariots of *Egypt*, with which *Pharaoh* pursued *Israel* were but six hundred, *Exod.* xiv. 7. From the great army of the *Philistims* against *Saul*, and the great number of their horses, I seem to gather that the Shepherds had newly relinquished *Egypt*, and joyned them: the Shepherds might be beaten and driven out of the greatest part of *Egypt*, and shut up in *Abaris* by *Misphragmuthosis* in the latter end of the days of *Eli*; and some of them fly to the *Philistims*, and strengthen them against *Israel*, in the last year of *Eli*; and from the *Philistims* some of the Shepherds might go to *Zidon*, and from *Zidon*, by sea to *Asia minor* and *Greece*: and afterwards, in the beginning of the Reign of *Saul*, the Shepherds who still remained in *Egypt* might be forced by *Tethmosis* or *Amosis* the son of *Misphragmuthosis*, to leave *Abaris*, and retire in very great numbers to the *Philistims*; and upon these occasions several of them, as *Pelasgus, Inachus, Lelex, Cecrops,* and *Abas*, might come with their people by sea from *Egypt* to *Zidon* and *Cyprus*, and thence to *Asia minor* and *Greece*, in the days of *Eli, Samuel* and *Saul*, and thereby begin to open a commerce by sea between *Zidon* and *Greece*, before the revolt of *Edom* from *Judæa*, and the final coming of the *Phoenicians* from the *Red Sea*.

Pelasgus Reigned in *Arcadia*, and was the father of *Lycaon*, according to *Pherecydes Atheniensis*, and *Lycaon* died just before the flood of *Deucalion*; and therefore his father *Pelasgus* might come into *Greece* about two Generations before *Cadmus*, or in the latter end of the days of *Eli*: *Lycaon* sacrificed children, and therefore his father might come with his people from the Shepherds in *Egypt*, and perhaps from the regions of *Heliopolis*, where they sacrificed men, 'till *Amosis* abolished that custom. *Misphragmuthosis* the father of *Amosis*, drove the Shepherds out of a great part of *Egypt*, and shut the remainder up in *Abaris*: and then great numbers might escape to *Greece*; some from the regions of *Heliopolis* under *Pelasgus*, and others from *Memphis* and other places, under other Captains: and hence it might come to pass that the *Pelasgians* were at the first very numerous in *Greece*, and spake a different language from the *Greek*, and were the ringleaders in bringing into *Greece* the worship of the dead.

Inachus is called the son of *Oceanus*, perhaps because he came to *Greece* by sea: he might come with his people to *Argos* from *Egypt* in the days of *Eli*, and seat himself upon the river *Inachus*, so named from him, and leave his territories to his sons *Phoroneus*, *Ægialeus*, and *Phegeus*, in the days of *Samuel*: for *Car* the son of *Phoroneus* built a Temple to *Ceres* in *Megara*, and therefore was contemporary to *Erechtheus*. *Phoroneus* Reigned at *Argos*, and *Aegialeus* at *Sicyon*, and founded those Kingdoms; and yet *Ægialeus* is made above five hundred years older than *Phoroneus* by some Chronologers: but[195] *Acusilaus*,[196] *Anticlides* and[197] *Plato*, accounted *Phoroneus* the oldest King in *Greece*, and[198] *Apollodorus* tells us, *Ægialeus* was the brother of *Phoroneus*. *Ægialeus* died without issue, and after him Reigned *Europs*, *Telchin*, *Apis*, *Lamedon*, *Sicyon*, *Polybus*, *Adrastus*, and *Agamemnon*, *&c.* and *Sicyon* gave his name to the Kingdom: *Herodotus*[199] saith that *Apis* in the *Greek* Tongue is *Epaphus*; and *Hyginus*,[200] that *Epaphus* the *Sicyonian* got *Antiopa* with child: but the later *Greeks* have made two men of the two names *Apis* and *Epaphus* or *Epopeus*, and between them inserted twelve feigned Kings of *Sicyon*, who made no wars, nor did any thing memorable, and yet Reigned five hundred and twenty years, which is, one with another, above forty and three years a-piece. If these feigned Kings be rejected, and the two Kings *Apis* and *Epopeus* be reunited; *Ægialeus* will become contemporary to his brother *Phoroneus*, as he ought to be; for *Apis* or *Epopeus*, and *Nycteus* the guardian of *Labdacus*, were slain in battle about the tenth year of *Solomon*, as above; and the first four Kings of *Sicyon*, *Ægialeus*, *Europs*, *Telchin*, *Apis*, after the rate of about twenty years to a Reign, take up about eighty years; and these years counted upwards from the tenth year of *Solomon*, place the beginning of the Reign of *Ægialeus* upon the twelfth year of *Samuel*, or thereabout: and about that time began the Reign of *Phoroneus* at *Argos*; *Apollodorus*[201] calls *Adrastus* King of *Argos*; but *Homer* [202] tells us, that he Reigned first at *Sicyon*: he was in the first war against *Thebes*. Some place *Janiscus* and *Phæstus* between *Polybus* and *Adrastus*, but without any certainty.

Lelex might come with his people into *Laconia* in the days of *Eli*, and leave his territories to his sons *Myles*, *Eurotas*, *Cleson*, and *Polycaon* in the days of *Samuel*. *Myles* set up a quern, or handmill to grind corn, and is reputed the first among the *Greeks* who did so: but he flourished before *Triptolemus*, and seems to have had his corn and artificers from *Egypt*. *Eurotas* the brother, or as some say the son of *Myles*, built *Sparta*, and called it after the name of his daughter *Sparta*, the wife of *Lacedæmon*, and mother of *Eurydice*. *Cleson* was the father of *Pylas* the father of *Sciron*, who married the daughter of *Pandion* the son of *Erechtheus*, and contended with *Nisus* the son of *Pandion* and brother of *Ægeus*, for the Kingdom; and *Æacus* adjudged it to *Nisus*. *Polycaon* invaded *Messene*, then peopled only by villages, called it *Messene* after the name of his wife, and built cities therein.

Cecrops came from *Sais* in *Egypt* to *Cyprus*, and thence into *Attica*: and he might do this in the days of *Samuel*, and marry *Agraule* the daughter of *Actæus*, and succeed him in *Attica* soon after, and leave his Kingdom to *Cranaus* in the Reign of *Saul*, or in the beginning of the Reign of *David*: for the flood of *Deucalion* happened in the Reign of *Cranaus*.

Of about the same age with *Pelasgus*, *Inachus*, *Lelex*, and *Actæus*, was *Ogyges*: he Reigned in *Boeotia*, and some of his people were *Leleges*: and either he or his son *Eleusis* built the city *Eleusis* in *Attica*, that is, they built a few houses of clay, which in time grew into a city. *Acusilaus* wrote that *Phoroneus* was older than *Ogyges*, and that *Ogyges* flourished 1020 years before the first Olympiad, as above; but *Acusilaus* was an *Argive*, and feigned these things in honour of his country: to call things *Ogygian* has been a phrase among the ancient *Greeks*, to signify that they are as old as the first memory of things; and so high we have now carried up the Chronology of the *Greeks*. *Inachus* might be as old as *Ogyges*, but *Acusilaus* and his followers made them seven hundred years older than the truth; and Chronologers, to make out this reckoning, have lengthened the races of the Kings of *Argos* and *Sicyon*, and changed several contemporary Princes of *Argos* into successive Kings, and inserted many feigned Kings into the race of the Kings of *Sicyon*.

Inachus had several sons, who Reigned in several parts of *Peloponnesus*, and there built Towns; as *Phoroneus*, who built *Phoronicum*, afterwards called *Argos*, from *Argus* his grandson; *Ægialeus*, who built *Ægialea*, afterwards called *Sicyon*, from *Sicyon* the grandson of *Erechtheus*; *Phegeus*, who built *Phegea*, afterwards called *Psophis*, from *Psophis* the daughter of *Lycaon*: and these were the oldest towns in *Peloponnesus* then *Sisyphus*, the son of *Æolus* and grandson of *Hellen*, built *Ephyra*, afterwards called *Corinth*; and *Aëthlius*, the son of *Æolus*, built *Elis*: and before them *Cecrops* built *Cecropia*, the cittadel of *Athens*; and *Lycaon* built *Lycosura*, reckoned by some the oldest town in *Arcadia*; and his sons, who were at least four and twenty in number, built each of them a town; except the youngest, called *Oenotrus*, who grew up after his father's death, and sailed into *Italy* with his people, and there set on foot the building of towns, and became the *Janus* of the *Latines*. *Phoroneus* had also several children and grand-children, who Reigned in several places, and built new towns, as *Car*, *Apis*, &c. and *Hæmon*, the son of *Pelasgus*, Reigned in *Hæmonia*, afterwards called *Thessaly*, and built towns there. This division and subdivision has made great confusion in the history of the first Kingdoms of *Peloponnesus*, and thereby given occasion to the vain-glorious *Greeks*, to make those kingdoms much older than they really were: but by all the reckonings abovementioned, the first civilizing of the *Greeks*, and teaching them to dwell in houses and towns, and the oldest towns in *Europe*, could scarce be above two or three Generations older than the coming of *Cadmus* from *Zidon* into *Greece*; and might most probably be occasioned by the expulsion of the Shepherds out of *Egypt* in the days of *Eli* and *Samuel*, and their flying into *Greece* in considerable numbers: but it's difficult to set right the Genealogies and Chronology of the Fabulous Ages of the *Greeks*, and I leave these things to be further examined.

Before the *Phoenicians* introduced the Deifying of dead men, the *Greeks* had a Council of Elders in every town for the government thereof, and a place where the elders and people worshipped their God with Sacrifices: and when many of those towns, for their common safety, united under a common Council, they erected a *Prytaneum* or Court in one of the towns, where the Council and People met at certain times, to consult their common safety, and worship their common God with sacrifices, and to buy and sell: the towns where these Councils met, the *Greeks* called [Greek: dêmoi], peoples or communities, or Corporation Towns: and at length, when many of these [Greek: dêmoi] for their common safety united by consent under one common Council, they erected a *Prytaneum* in one of the [Greek: dêmoi] for the common Council and People to meet in, and to consult and worship in, and feast, and buy, and sell; and this [Greek: dêmos] they walled about for its safety, and called [Greek: tên polin] the city: and this I take to have been the original of Villages, Market-Towns, Cities, common Councils, Vestal Temples, Feasts and Fairs, in *Europe*: the *Prytaneum*, [Greek: pyros tameion], was a Court with a place of worship, and a perpetual fire kept therein upon an Altar for sacrificing: from the word [Greek: Hestia] fire, came the name *Vesta*, which at length the people turned into a Goddess, and so became fire-worshippers like the ancient *Persians*: and when these Councils made war upon their neighbours, they had a general commander to lead their armies, and he became their King.

So *Thucydides*[203] tells us, that *under* Cecrops *and the ancient Kings, untill* Theseus*; Attica was always inhabited city by city, each having Magistrates and Prytanea: neither did they consult the King, when there was no fear of danger, but each apart administred their own common-wealth, and had their own Council, and even sometimes made war, as the* Eleusinians *with* Eumolpus *did against* Erechtheus*: but when* Theseus*, a prudent and potent man obtained the Kingdom, he took away the Courts and Magistrates of the other cities, and made them all meet in one Council and* Prytaneum *at* Athens. *Polemon*, as he is cited by[204] *Strabo*, tells us, *that in this body of* Attica, *there were* 170 [Greek: dêmoi], *one of which was* Eleusis: and *Philochorus*[205] relates, *that when* Attica *was infested by sea and land by the* Cares *and* Boeoti, Cecrops *the first of any man reduced the multitude*, that is the 170 towns, *into twelve cities*, whose names were Cecropia, Tetrapolis, Epacria, Decelia, Eleusis, Aphydna, Thoricus, Brauron, Cytherus, Sphettus, Cephissia, *and* Phalerus*; and that* Theseus *contracted those twelve cities into one, which was* Athens.

The original of the Kingdom of the *Argives* was much after the same manner: for *Pausanias*[206] tells us, *that* Phoroneus *the son of* Inachus *was the first who gathered into one community the* Argives, *who 'till then were scattered, and lived every where apart, and the place where they were first assembled was called* Phoronicum, *the city of* Phoroneus: *and* Strabo[207] *observes, that* Homer *calls all the places which he reckons up in* Peloponnesus, *a few excepted, not cities but regions, because each of them consisted of a convention of many* [Greek: dêmoi], *free towns, out of which afterward noble cities were built and frequented: so the* Argives *composed* Mantinæa *in* Arcadia *out of five towns, and* Tegea *out of nine; and out of so many was* Heræa *built by* Cleombrotus, *or by* Cleonymus*: so also* Ægium *was built out of seven or eight towns*, Patræ: *out of seven, and* Dyme *out of eight; and so* Elis *was erected by the conflux of many towns into one city.*

Pausanias[208] tells us, that the *Arcadians* accounted *Pelasgus* the first man, and that he was their first King; and *taught the ignorant people to built houses, for defending themselves from heat, and cold, and rain; and to make them garments of skins; and instead of herbs and roots, which were sometimes noxious, to eat the acorns of the beech tree;* and that his son *Lycaon* built the oldest city in all *Greece*: he tells us also, that in the days of *Lelex* the *Spartans* lived in villages apart. The *Greeks* therefore began to build houses and villages in the days of *Pelasgus* the father of *Lycaon*, and in the days of *Lelex* the father of *Myles*, and by consequence about two or three Generations before the Flood of *Deucalion*, and the coming of *Cadmus*; 'till then[209] they lived in woods and caves of the earth. The first houses were of clay, 'till the brothers *Euryalus* and *Hyperbius* taught them to harden the clay into bricks, and to build therewith. In the days of *Ogyges*, *Pelasgus*, *Æzeus*, *Inachus* and *Lelex*, they began to build houses and villages of clay, *Doxius* the son of *Coelus* teaching them to do it; and in the days of *Lycaon*, *Phoroneus*, *Ægialeus*, *Phegeus*, *Eurotas*, *Myles*, *Polycaon*, and *Cecrops*, and their sons, to assemble the villages into [Greek: dêmoi], and the [Greek: dêmoi] into cities.

When *Oenotrus* the son of *Lycaon* carried a Colony into *Italy*, he[210] *found that country for the most part uninhabited; and where it was inhabited, peopled but thinly: and seizing a part of it, he built towns in the mountains, little and numerous*, as above: these towns were without walls; but after this Colony grew numerous, and began to want room, *they expelled the* Siculi, *compassed many cities with walls, and became possest of all the territory between the two rivers* Liris *and* Tibre: and it is to be understood that those cities had their Councils and *Prytanea* after the manner of the *Greeks*: for *Dionysius*[211] tells us, that the new Kingdom of *Rome*, as *Romulus* left it, consisted of thirty Courts or Councils, in thirty towns, each with the sacred fire kept in the *Prytaneum* of the Court, for the Senators who met there to perform Sacred Rites, after the manner of the *Greeks*: *but when* Numa *the successor of* Romulus *Reigned, he leaving the several fires in their own Courts, instituted one common to them all at* Rome: whence *Rome* was not a compleat city before the days of *Numa*.

When navigation was so far improved that the *Phoenicians* began to leave the sea-shore, and sail through the *Mediterranean* by the help of the stars, it may be presumed that they began to discover the islands of the *Mediterranean*, and for the sake of trafic to sail as far as *Greece*: and this was not long before they carried away *Io* the daughter of *Inachus*, from *Argos*. The *Cares* first infested the *Greek* seas with piracy, and then *Minos* the son of *Europa* got up a potent fleet, and sent out Colonies: for *Diodorus*[212] tells us, that the *Cyclades* islands, those near *Crete*, were at first desolate and uninhabited; but *Minos* having a potent fleet, sent many Colonies out of *Crete*, and peopled many of them; and particularly that the island *Carpathus* was first seized by the soldiers of *Minos*: *Syme* lay waste and desolate 'till *Triops* came thither with a Colony under *Chthonius*: *Strongyle* or *Naxus* was first inhabited by the *Thracians* in the days of *Boreas*, a little before the *Argonautic* Expedition: *Samsos* was, at first desert, and inhabited only by a great multitude of terrible wild beasts, 'till *Macareus* peopled it, as he did also the islands *Chius* and *Cos*. *Lesbos* lay waste and desolate 'till *Xanthus* sailed thither with a Colony: *Tenedos* lay desolate 'till *Tennes*, a little before the *Trojan* war, sailed thither from

Troas. Aristæus, who married *Autonoe* the daughter of *Cadmus*, carried a Colony from *Thebes* into *Cæa*, an island not inhabited before: the island *Rhodes* was at first called *Ophiusa*, being full of serpents, before *Phorbas*, a Prince of *Argos*, went thither, and made it habitable by destroying the serpents, which was about the end of *Solomon's* Reign; in memory of which he is delineated in the heavens in the Constellation of *Ophiuchus*. The discovery of this and some other islands made a report that they rose out of the Sea: *in Asia Delos emersit, & Hiera, & Anaphe, & Rhodus*, saith[213] *Ammianus*: and[214] *Pliny, claræ jampridem insulæ, Delos & Rhodos memoriæ produntur enatæ, postea minores, ultra Melon Anaphe, inter Lemnum & Hellespontum Nea, inter Lebedum & Teon Halone*, &c.

Diodorus[215] tells us also, that the seven islands called *Æolides*, between *Italy* and *Sicily*, were desert and uninhabited 'till *Lipparus* and *Æolus*, a little before the *Trojan* war, went thither from *Italy*, and peopled them: and that *Malta* and *Gaulus* or *Gaudus* on the other side of *Sicily*, were first peopled by *Phoenicians*; and so was *Madera* without the *Straits*: and *Homer* writes that *Ulysses* found the Island *Ogygia* covered with wood, and uninhabited, except by *Calypso* and her maids, who lived in a cave without houses; and it is not likely that *Great Britain* and *Ireland* could be peopled before navigation was propagated beyond the *Straits*.

The *Sicaneans* were reputed the first inhabitants of *Sicily*, they built little Villages or Towns upon hills, and every Town had its own King; and by this means they spread over the country, before they formed themselves into larger governments with a common King: *Philistus*[216] saith that *they were transplanted into* Sicily *from the River* Sicanus *in* Spain; and *Dionysius*[217], that *they were a* Spanish *people who fled from the* Ligures *in* Italy; he means the *Ligures*[218] who opposed *Hercules* when he returned from his expedition against *Geryon* in *Spain*, and endeavoured to pass the *Alps* out of *Gaul* into *Italy*. *Hercules* that year got into *Italy*, and made some conquests there, and founded the city *Croton*; and[219] after winter, upon the arrival of his fleet from *Erythra* in *Spain*, sailed to *Sicily*, and there left the *Sicani*: for *it was his custom to recruit his army with conquered people, and after they had assisted him in making new conquests to reward them with new seats*. this was the *Egyptian Hercules*, who had a potent fleet, and in the days of *Solomon* sailed to the *Straits*, and according to his custom set up pillars there, and conquered *Geryon*, and returned back by *Italy* and *Sicily* to *Egypt*, and was by the ancient *Gauls* called *Ogmius*, and by *Egyptians*[220] *Nilus*: for *Erythra* and the country of *Geryon* were without the *Straits*. *Dionysius*[221] represents this *Hercules* contemporary to *Evander*.

The first inhabitants of *Crete*, according to *Diodorus*[222] were called *Eteocretans*; but whence they were, and how they came thither, is not said in history: then sailed thither a Colony of *Pelasgians* from *Greece*; and soon after *Teutamus*, the grandfather of *Minos*, carried thither a Colony of *Dorians* from *Laconia*, and from the territory of *Olympia* in *Peloponnesus*: and these several Colonies spake several languages, and fed on the spontaeous fruits of the earth, and lived quietly in caves and huts, 'till the invention of iron tools, in the days of *Asterius* the son of *Teutamus*; and at length were reduced into one Kingdom, and one People, by *Minos*, who was their first law-giver, and built many towns and ships, and introduced plowing and sowing, and in whose days the *Curetes* conquered his father's friends in *Crete* and *Peloponnesus*. The *Curetes*[223] sacrificed children to *Saturn* and according to *Bochart*[224] were *Philistims*; and *Eusebius* faith that *Crete* had its name from *Cres*, one of the *Curetes* who nursed up *Jupiter*: but whatever was the original of the island, it seems to have been peopled by Colonies which spake different languages, 'till the days of *Asterius* and *Minos*; and might come thither two or three Generations before, and not above, for want of navigation in those seas.

The island *Cyprus* was discovered by the *Phoenicians* not long before; for *Eratosthenes*[225] tells us, *that* Cyprus *was at first so overgrown with wood that it could not be tilled, and that they first cut down the wood for the melting of copper and silver, and afterwards when they began to sail safely upon the* Mediterranean, that is, presently after the *Trojan* war, *they built ships and even navies of it: and when they could not thus destroy the wood, they gave every man leave to cut down what wood he pleased, and to possess all the ground which he cleared of wood.* So also *Europe* at first abounded very much with woods, one of which, called the *Hercinian*, took up a great part of *Germany*, being full nine days journey broad, and above forty long, in *Julius Cæsar*'s days: and yet the *Europeans* had been cutting down their woods, to make room for mankind, ever since the invention of iron tools, in the days of *Asterius* and *Minos*.

All these footsteps there are of the first peopling of *Europe*, and its Islands, by sea; before those days it seems to have been thinly peopled from the northern coast of the *Euxine-sea* by *Scythians* descended from *Japhet*, who wandered without houses, and sheltered themselves from rain and wild beasts in thickets and caves of the earth; such as were the caves in mount *Ida* in *Crete*, in which *Minos* was educated and buried; the cave of *Cacus*, and the *Catacombs* in *Italy* near *Rome* and *Naples*, afterwards turned into burying-places; the *Syringes* and many other caves in the sides of the mountains of *Egypt*; the caves of the *Troglodites* between *Egypt* and the *Red Sea*, and those of the *Phaurusii* in *Afric*, mentioned by[226] *Strabo*; and the caves, and thickets, and rocks, and high places, and pits, in which the *Israelites* hid themselves from the *Philistims* in the days of *Saul*, 1 *Sam.* xiii. 6. But of the state of mankind in *Europe* in those days there is now no history remaining.

The antiquities of *Libya* were not much older than those of *Europe*; for *Diodorus*[227] tells us, that *Uranus* the father of *Hyperion*, and grandfather of *Helius* and *Selene*, that is *Ammon* the father of *Sesac*, *was their first common King, and caused the people, who 'till then wandered up and down, to dwell in towns*: and *Herodotus*[228] tells us, that all *Media* was peopled by [Greek: dêmoi], towns without walls, 'till they revolted from the *Assyrians*, which was about 267 years after the death of *Solomon*: and that after that revolt they set up a King over them, and built *Ecbatane* with walls for his seat, the first town which they walled about; and about 72 years after the death of *Solomon*, *Benhadad* King of *Syria*[229] had two and thirty Kings in his army against *Ahab*: and when *Joshuah* conquered the land of *Canaan*, every city of the *Canaanites* had its own King, like the cities of *Europe*, before they conquered one another; and one of those Kings, *Adonibezek*, the King of *Bezek* had conquered seventy other Kings a little before, *Judg.* i. 7. and therefore towns began to be built in that land not many ages before the days of

Joshuah: for the Patriarchs wandred there in tents, and fed their flocks where-ever they pleased, the fields of *Phoenicia* not being yet fully appropriated, for want of people. The countries first inhabited by mankind, were in those days so thinly peopled, that[230] four Kings from the coasts of *Shinar* and *Elam* invaded and spoiled the *Rephaims,* and the inhabitants of the countries of *Moab, Ammon, Edom,* and the Kingdoms of *Sodom, Gomorrah, Admah* and *Zeboim;* and yet were pursued and beaten by *Abraham* with an armed force of only 318 men, the whole force which *Abraham* and the princes with him could raise: and *Egypt* was so thinly peopled before the birth of *Moses,* that *Pharaoh* said of the *Israelites;*[231] *behold the people of the children of* Israel *are more and mightier than we:* and to prevent their multiplying and growing too strong, he caused their male children to be drowned.

These footsteps there are of the first peopling of the earth by mankind, not long before the days of *Abraham;* and of the overspreading it with villages, towns and cities, and their growing into Kingdoms, first Smaller and then greater, until the rise of the Monarchies of *Egypt, Assyria, Babylon, Media, Persia, Greece,* and *Rome,* the first great Empires on this side *India. Abraham* was the fifth from *Peleg,* and all mankind lived together in *Chaldea* under the Government of *Noah* and his sons, untill the days of *Peleg:* so long they were of one language, one society, and one religion: and then they divided the earth, being perhaps, disturbed by the rebellion of *Nimrod,* and forced to leave off building the tower of *Babel:* and from thence they spread themselves into the several countries which fell to their shares, carrying along with them the laws, customs and religion, under which they had 'till those days been educated and governed, by *Noah,* and his sons and grandsons: and these laws were handed down to *Abraham, Melchizedek,* and *Job,* and their contemporaries, and for some time were observed by the judges of the eastern countries: so *Job*[232] tells us, that adultery was *an heinous crime, yea an iniquity to be punished by the judges:* and of idolatry he[233] saith, *If I beheld the sun when it shined, or the moon walking in brightness, and my heart hath been secretly inticed, or my mouth hath kissed my hand, this also were an iniquity to be punished by the judge: for I should have denied the God that is above:* and there being no dispute between *Job* and his friends about these matters, it may be presumed that they also with their countrymen were of the same religion. *Melchizedek* was a Priest of the most high God, and *Abraham* voluntarily paid tythes to him; which he would scarce have done had they not been of one and the same religion. The first inhabitants of the land of *Canaan* seem also to have been originally of the same religion, and to have continued in it 'till the death of *Noah,* and the days of *Abraham;* for *Jerusalem* was anciently[234] called *Jebus,* and its people *Jebusites,* and *Melchizedek* was their Priest and King: these nations revolted therefore after the days of *Melchizedek* to the worship of false Gods; as did also the posterity of *Ismael, Esau, Moab, Ammon,* and that of *Abraham* by *Keturah:* and the *Israelites* themselves were very apt to revolt: and one reason why *Terah* went from *Ur* of the *Chaldees* to *Haran* in his way to the land of *Canaan;* and why *Abraham* afterward left *Haran,* and went into the land of *Canaan,* might be to avoid the worship of false Gods, which in their days began in *Chaldea,* and spread every way from thence; but did not yet reach into the land of *Canaan.* Several of the laws and precepts in which this primitive religion consisted are mentioned in the book of *Job,* chap. i. ver. 5, and chap, xxxi, *viz. not to blaspheme God, nor to worship the Sun or Moon, nor to kill, nor steal, nor to commit adultery, nor trust in riches, nor oppress the poor or fatherless, nor curse your enemies, nor rejoyce at their misfortunes: but to be friendly, and hospitable and merciful, and to relieve the poor and needy, and to set up Judges.* This was the morality and religion of the first ages, still called by the *Jews, The precepts of the sons of* Noah: this was the religion of *Moses* and the Prophets, comprehended in the two great commandments, of *loving the Lord our God with all our heart and soul and mind, and our neighbour as our selves:* this was the religion enjoyned by *Moses* to the uncircumcised stranger within the gates of *Israel,* as well as to the *Israelites:* and this is the primitive religion of both *Jews* and *Christians,* and ought to be the standing religion of all nations, it being for the honour of God, and good of mankind: and *Moses* adds the precept of *being merciful even to brute beasts, so as not to suck out their blood, nor to cut off their flesh alive with the blood in it, nor to kill them for the sake of their blood, nor to strangle them; but in killing them for food, to let out their blood and spill it upon the ground,* Gen. ix. 4, and *Levit.* xvii. 12, 13. This law was ancienter than the days of *Moses,* being given to *Noah* and his sons long before the days of *Abraham:* and therefore when the Apostles and Elders in the Council at *Jerusalem* declared that the Gentiles were not obliged to be circumcised and keep the law of *Moses,* they excepted this law of *abstaining from blood, and things strangled* as being an earlier law of God, imposed not on the sons of *Abraham* only, but on all nations, while they lived together in *Shinar* under the dominion of *Noah:* and of the same kind is the law of *abstaining from meats offered to Idols or false Gods, and from fornication.* So then, *the believing that the world was framed by one supreme God, and is governed by him; and the loving and worshipping him, and honouring our parents, and loving our neighbour as our selves, and being merciful even to brute beasts,* is the oldest of all religions: and the Original of letters, agriculture, navigation, music, arts and sciences, metals, smiths and carpenters, towns and houses, was not older in *Europe* than the days of *Eli, Samuel* and *David;* and before those days the earth was so thinly peopled, and so overgrown with woods, that mankind could not be much older than is represented in Scripture.

CHAP. II

Of the Empire of Egypt.

THE *Egyptians* anciently boasted of a very great and lasting Empire under their Kings *Ammon, Osiris, Bacchus, Sesostris, Hercules, Memnon,* &c. reaching eastward to the *Indies,* and westward to the *Atlantic Ocean;* and out of vanity have made this monarchy some thousands of years older than the world: let us now try to rectify the Chronology of *Egypt;* by comparing the affairs of *Egypt* with the synchronizing affairs of the *Greeks* and *Hebrews.*

Bacchus the conqueror loved two women, *Venus* and *Ariadne: Venus* was the mistress of *Anchises* and *Cinyras,* and mother of *Æneas,* who all lived 'till the destruction of *Troy;* and the sons of *Bacchus* and *Ariadne* were *Argonauts;* as above: and therefore the great *Bacchus* flourished but one Generation before the *Argonautic* expedition. This *Bacchus*[235] was potent at sea, conquered eastward as far as *India* returned in triumph, brought his army over the *Hellespont;* conquered *Thrace,* left music, dancing and poetry there; killed *Lycurgus* King of *Thrace,* and *Pentheus* the grandson of *Cadmus;* gave the Kingdom of *Lycurgus* to *Tharops;* and one of his minstrells, called by the *Greeks Calliope,* to *Oeagrus* the son of *Tharops;* and of *Oeagrus* and *Calliope* was born *Orpheus,* who sailed with the *Argonauts:* this *Bacchus* was therefore contemporary to *Sesostris;* and both being Kings of *Egypt,* and potent at sea, and great conquerors, and carrying on their conquests into *India* and *Thrace,* they must be one and the same man.

The antient *Greeks,* who made the fables of the Gods, related that *Io* the daughter of *Inachus* was carried into *Egypt;* and there became the *Egyptian Isis;* and that *Apis* the son of *Phoroneus* after death became the God *Serapis;* and some said that *Epaphus* was the son of *Io: Serapis* and *Epaphus* are *Osiris,* and therefore *Isis* and *Osiris,* in the opinion of the ancient *Greeks* who made the fables of the Gods, were not above two or three Generations older than the *Argonautic* expedition. *Dicæarchus,* as he is cited by the scholiast upon *Apollonius,*[236] represents them two Generations older than *Sesostris,* saying that after *Orus* the son of *Osiris* and *Isis,* Reigned *Sesonchosis.* He seems to have followed the opinion of the people of *Naxus,* who made *Bacchus* two Generations older than *Theseus,* and for that end feigned two *Minos's* and two *Ariadnes;* for by the consent of all antiquity *Osiris* and *Bacchus* were one and the same King of *Egypt:* this is affirmed by the *Egyptians,* as well as by the *Greeks;* and some of the antient Mythologists, as *Eumolpus* and *Orpheus,*[237] called *Osiris* by the names of *Dionysus* and *Sirius. Osiris* was King of all *Egypt,* and a great conqueror, and came over the *Hellespont* in the days of *Triptolemus,* and subdued *Thrace,* and there killed *Lycurgus;* and therefore his expedition falls in with that of the great *Bacchus. Osiris, Bacchus* and *Sesostris* lived about the same time, and by the relation of historians were all of them Kings of all *Egypt,* and Reigned at *Thebes,* and adorned that city, and were very potent by land and sea: all three were great conquerors, and carried on their conquests by land through *Asia* as far as *India:* all three came over the *Hellespont* and were there in danger of losing their army: all three conquered *Thrace,* and there put a stop to their victories, and returned back from thence into *Egypt*: all three left pillars with inscriptions in their conquests: and therefore all three must be one and the same King of *Egypt*; and this King can be no other than *Sesac*. All *Egypt*, including *Thebais*, *Ethiopia* and *Libya*, had no common King before the expulsion of the Shepherds who Reigned in the lower *Egypt*; no Conqueror of *Syria*, *India*, *Asia minor* and *Thrace*, before *Sesac*; and the sacred history admits of no *Egyptian* conqueror of *Palestine* before this King.

Thymœtes[238] who was contemporary to *Orpheus*, and wrote a poesy called *Phrygia*, of the actions of *Bacchus* in very old language and character, said that *Bacchus* had *Libyan* women in his army, amongst whom was *Minerva* a woman born in *Libya*, near the river *Triton*, and that *Bacchus* commanded the men and *Minerva* the women. *Diodorus*[239] calls her *Myrina*, and saith that she was Queen of the *Amazons* in *Libya*, and there conquered the *Atlantides* and *Gorgons*, and then made a league with *Orus* the son of *Isis*, sent to her by his father *Osiris* or *Bacchus* for that purpose, and passing through *Egypt* subdued the *Arabians*, and *Syria* and *Cilicia*, and came through *Phrygia*, *viz*. in the army of *Bacchus* to the *Mediterranean*; but palling over into *Europe*, was slain with many of her women by the *Thracians* and *Scythians*, under the conduct of *Sipylus* a *Scythian*, and *Mopsus* a *Thracian* whom *Lycurgus* King of *Thrace* had banished. This was that *Lycurgus* who opposed the passage of *Bacchus* over the *Hellespont*, and was soon after conquered by him, and slain: but afterwards *Bacchus* met with a repulse from the *Greeks*, under the conduct of *Perseus*, who slew many of his women, as *Pausanias*[240] relates, and was assisted by the *Scythians* and *Thracians* under the conduct of *Sipylus* and *Mopsus*; which repulses, together with a revolt of his brother *Danaus* in *Egypt*; put a stop to his victories: and in returning home he left part of his men in *Colchis* and at *Mount Caucasus*, under *Æetes* and *Prometheus*; and his women upon the river *Thermodon* near *Colchis*, under their new Queens *Marthesia* and *Lampeto*: for *Diodorus*[241] speaking of the *Amazons* who were seated at *Thermodon*, saith, that they dwelt originally in *Libya*, and there Reigned over the *Atlantides*, and invading their neighbours conquered as far as *Europe*: and *Ammianus*,[242] that the ancient *Amazons* breaking through many nations, attack'd the *Athenians*, and there receiving a great slaughter retired to *Thermodon*: and *Justin*,[243] that these *Amazons* had at first, he means at their first coming to *Thermodon*, two Queens who called themselves daughters of *Mars*; and that they conquered part of *Europe*, and some cities of *Asia*, *viz*. in the Reign of *Minerva*, and then sent back part of their army with a great booty, under their said new Queens; and that *Marthesia* being afterwards slain, was succeeded by her daughter *Orithya*, and she by *Penthesilea*; and that *Theseus* captivated and married *Antiope* the sister of *Orithya*. *Hercules* made war upon the *Amazons*, and in the Reign of *Orithya* and *Penthesilea* they came to the *Trojan* war: whence the first wars of the *Amazons* in *Europe* and *Asia*, and their settling at *Thermodon*, were but one Generation before those actions of *Hercules* and *Theseus*, and but two before the *Trojan* war, and so fell in with the expedition of *Sesostris*: and since they warred in the days of *Isis* and her son *Orus*, and were a part of the army of *Bacchus* or *Osiris*, we have here a further argument for making *Osiris* and *Bacchus* contemporary to *Sesostris*, and all three one and the same King with *Sesac*.

The *Greeks* reckon *Osiris* and *Bacchus* to be sons of *Jupiter*, and the *Egyptian* name of *Jupiter* is *Ammon*. *Manetho* in his 11th and 12th *Dynasties*, as he is cited by *Africanus* and *Eusebius* names these four Kings of *Egypt*, as reigning in order; *Ammenemes, Gesongeses* or *Sesonchoris* the son of *Ammenemes, Ammenemes* who was slain by his Eunuchs, and *Sesostris* who subdued all *Asia* and part of *Europe*. *Gesongeses* and *Sesonchoris* are corruptly written for *Sesonchosis*; and the two first of these four Kings, *Ammenemes* and *Sesonchosis*, are the same with the two last, *Ammenemes* and *Sesostris*, that is, with *Ammon* and *Sesac*; for *Diodorus* saith[244] that *Osiris* built in *Thebes* a magnificent temple to his parents *Jupiter* and *Juno*, and two other temples to *Jupiter*, a larger to *Jupiter Uranius*, and a less to his father *Jupiter Ammon* who reigned in that city: and[245] *Thymætes* abovementioned, who was contemporary to *Orpheus*, wrote expresly that the father of *Bacchus* was *Ammon*, a King Reigning over part of *Libya*, that is, a King of *Egypt* Reigning over all that part of *Libya*, anciently called *Ammonia*. *Stephanus*[246] saith [Greek: Pasa hê Libyê houtôs ekaleito apo Ammônos;] *All* Libya *was anciently called* Ammonia *from* Ammon: this is that King of *Egypt* from whom *Thebes* was called *No-Ammon*, and *Ammon-no* the city of *Ammon*, and by the *Greeks Diospolis*, the city of *Jupiter Ammon*: *Sesostris* built it sumptuously, and called it by his father's name, and from the same King the[247] River called *Ammon*, the people called *Ammonii*, and the[248] promontory *Ammonium* in *Arabia fælix* had their names.

The lower part of *Egypt* being yearly overflowed by the *Nile*, was scarce inhabited before the invention of corn, which made it useful: and the King, who by this invention first peopled it and Reigned over it, perhaps the King of the city *Mesir* where *Memphis* was afterwards built, seems to have been worshipped by his subjects after death, in the ox or calf, for this benefaction: for this city stood in the most convenient place to people the lower *Egypt*, and from its being composed of two parts seated on each side of the river *Nile*, might give the name of *Mizraim* to its founder and people; unless you had rather refer the word to the double people, those above the *Delta*, and those within it: and this I take to be the state of the lower *Egypt*, 'till the Shepherds or *Phoenicians* who fled from *Joshuah* conquered it, and being afterwards conquered by the *Ethiopians*, fled into *Afric* and other places: for there was a tradition that some of them fled into *Afric*; and St. *Austin*[249] confirms this, by telling us that the common people of *Afric* being asked who they were, replied *Chanani*, that is, *Canaanites*. *Interrogati rustici nostri*, saith he, *quid sint, Punice respondentes Chanani, corrupta scilicet voce sicut in talibus solet, quid aliud respondent quam Chanaanæi? Procopius* also[250] tells us of two pillars in the west of *Afric*, with inscriptions signifying that the people were *Canaanites* who fled from *Joshuah*: and *Eusebius*[251] tells us, that these *Canaanites* flying from the sons of *Israel*, built *Tripolis* in *Afric*; and the *Jerusalem Gemara*,[252] that the *Gergesites* fled from *Joshua*, going into *Afric*: and *Procopius* relates their flight in this manner. [Greek: Epei de hêmas ho tês historias logos entauth' êgagen. epanankes eipein anôthen, hothen te ta Maurousiôn ethnê es Libyên êlthe, kai hopôs ôikêsanto. Epeidê Hebraioi ex Aigyptou anechôrêsan, kai anchi tôn Palaistinês horiôn egenonto; Môsês men sophos anêr, hos autos tês hodou hêgêsato, thnêskei. diadechetai de tên hêgemonian Iêsous ho tou Nauê pais; hos es te tên

Palaistinên ton leôn touton eisêgage; kai aretên en tôi polemôi kreissô hê kata anthrôpou physin epideixamenos, tên chôran esche; kai ta ethnê hapanta katastrepsamenos, tas poleis eupetôs parestêsato, anikêtos te pantapasin edoxen einai. tote de hê epithalassia chôra, ek Sidônos mechri tôn Aigyptou horiôn, Phoinikê xympasa ônomazeto. basileus de eis to palaion ephestêkei; hôsper hapasin hômologêtai, hoi Phoinikôn ta archaiotata anegrapsanto. entauth' ôkênto ethnê polyanthrôpotata, Gergesaioi te kai Iebousaioi, kai alla atta onomata echonta, hois dê auta hê tôn Hebraiôn historia kalei. houtos ho laos epei amachon ti chrêma ton epêlytên stratêgon eidon; ex êthôn tôn patriôn exanastantes, ep' Aigypton homorou ousês echôrêsan. entha chôron oudena sphisin hikanon enoikêsasthai heurontes, epei en Aigyptô polyanthrôpia ek palaiou ên; es Libyên mechri stêlôn tôn Hêrakleous eschon; entautha te kai es eme têi Phoinikôn phônêi chrômenoi ôikêntai]. *Quando ad Mauros nos historia deduxit, congruens nos exponere unde orta gens in Africa sedes fixerit. Quo tempore egressi Ægypto Hebræi jam prope Palestinæ fines venerant, mortuus ibi Moses, vir sapiens, dux itineris. Successor imperii factus Jesus Navæ filius intra Palæstinam duxit popularium agmen; & virtute usus supra humanum modum, terram occupavit, gentibusque excisis urbes ditionis suæ fecit, & invicti famam tulit. Maritima ora quæ a Sidone ad Ægypti limitem extenditur, nomen habet Phoenices. Rex unus [Hebræis] imperabat ut omnes qui res Phoenicias scripsere consentiunt. In eo tractatu numerosæ gentes erant, Gergesæi, Jebusæi, quosque aliis nominibus Hebræorum annales memorant. Hi homines ut impares se venienti imperatori videre, derelicto patriæ solo ad finitimam primum venere Ægyptum, sed ibi capacem tantæ multitudinis locum non reperientes, erat enim Ægyptus ab antiquo foecunda populis, in Africam profecti, multis conditis urbibus, omnem eam Herculis columnas usque, obtinuerunt: ubi ad meam ætatem sermone Phoenicio utentes habitant.* By the language and extreme poverty of the *Moors*, described also by *Procopius* and by their being unacquainted with merchandise and sea-affairs, you may know that they were *Canaanites* originally, and peopled *Afric* before the *Tyrian* merchants came thither. These *Canaanites* coming from the East, pitched their tents in great numbers in the lower *Egypt*, in the Reign of *Timaus*, as[253] *Manetho* writes, and easily seized the country, and fortifying *Pelusium*, then called *Abaris*, they erected a Kingdom there, and Reigned long under their own Kings, *Salatis, Boeon, Apachnas, Apophis, Janias, Assis*, and others successively: and in the mean time the upper part of *Egypt* called *Thebais*, and according to[254] *Herodotus, Ægyptus*, and in Scripture the land of *Pathros*, was under other Kings, Reigning perhaps at *Coptos*, and *Thebes*, and *This*, and *Syene*, and[255] *Pathros*, and *Elephantis*, and *Heracleopolis*, and *Mesir*, and other great cities, 'till they conquered one another, or were conquered by the *Ethiopians*: for cities grew great in those days, by being the seats of Kingdoms: but at length one of these Kingdoms conquered the rest, and made a lasting war upon the Shepherds, and in the Reign of its King *Misphragmuthosis*, and his son *Amosis*, called also *Tethmosis, Tuthmosis*, and *Thomosis*, drove them out of *Egypt*, and made them fly into *Afric* and *Syria*, and other places, and united all *Egypt* into one Monarchy; and under their next Kings, *Ammon* and *Sesac*, enlarged it into a great Empire. This conquering people worshipped not the Kings of the Shepherds whom they conquered and expelled, but[256] abolished their religion of sacrificing men, and after the manner of those ages Deified their own Kings, who founded their new Dominion, beginning the history of their Empire with the Reign and great acts of their Gods and Heroes: whence their Gods *Ammon* and *Rhea*, or *Uranus* and *Titæa*; *Osiris* and *Isis*; *Orus* and *Bubaste*: and their Secretary *Thoth*, and Generals *Hercules* and *Pan*; and Admiral *Japetus, Neptune,* or *Typhon*; were all of them *Thebans*, and flourished after the expulsion of the Shepherds. *Homer* places *Thebes* in *Ethiopia*, and the *Ethiopians* reported that[257] the *Egyptians* were a colony drawn out of them by *Osiris*, and that thence it came to pass that most of the laws of *Egypt* were the same with those of *Ethiopia*, and that the *Egyptians* learnt from the *Ethiopians* the custom of Deifying their Kings.

When *Joseph* entertained his brethren in *Egypt*, they did eat at a table by themselves, and he did eat at another table by himself; and the *Egyptians* who did eat with him were at another table, *because the* Egyptians *might not eat bread with the* Hebrews; *for that was an abomination to the* Egyptians, *Gen.* xliii. 32. These *Egyptians* who did eat with *Joseph* were of the Court of *Pharaoh*; and therefore *Pharaoh* and his Court were at this time not Shepherds but genuine *Egyptians*; and these *Egyptians* abominated eating bread with the *Hebrews*, at one and the same table: and of these *Egyptians* and their fellow-subjects, it is said a little after, that *every Shepherd is an abomination to the* Egyptians: *Egypt* at this time was therefore under the government of the genuine *Egyptians*, and not under that of the Shepherds.

After the descent of *Jacob* and his sons into *Egypt, Joseph* lived 70 years, and so long continued in favour with the Kings of *Egypt*: and 64 years after his death *Moses* was born: and between the death of *Joseph* and the birth of *Moses, there arose up a new King over* Egypt, *which knew not* Joseph, *Exod.* i. 8. But this King of *Egypt* was not one of the Shepherds; for he is called *Pharaoh, Exod.* i. 11, 22: and *Moses* told his successor, that if the people of *Israel* should sacrifice in the land of *Egypt, they should sacrifice the abomination of the* Egyptians *before their eyes, and the* Egyptians *would stone them, Exod.* viii. 26. that is, they should sacrifice sheep or oxen, contrary to the religion of *Egypt*. The Shepherds therefore did not Reign over *Egypt* while *Israel* was there, but either were driven out of *Egypt* before *Israel* went down thither, or did not enter into *Egypt* 'till after *Moses* had brought *Israel* from thence: and the latter must be true, if they were driven out of *Egypt* a little before the building of the temple of *Solomon*, as *Manetho* affirms.

Diodorus[258] saith in his 40th book, *that in* Egypt *there were formerly multitudes of strangers of several nations, who used foreign rites and ceremonies in worshipping the Gods, for which they were expelled* Egypt; *and under* Danaus, Cadmus, *and other skilful commanders, after great hardships, came into* Greece, *and other places; but the greatest part of them came into* Judæa, *not far from* Egypt, *a country then uninhabited and desert, being conducted thither by one* Moses, *a wise and valiant man, who after he had possest himself of the country, among other things built* Jerusalem, *and the Temple. Diodorus* here mistakes the original of the *Israelites*, as *Manetho* had done before, confounding their flight into the wilderness under the conduct of *Moses*, with the flight of the Shepherds from *Misphragmuthosis*, and his son *Amosis*, into *Phoenicia* and *Afric*; and not knowing that *Judæa* was inhabited by *Canaanites*, before the *Israelites* under *Moses* came thither: but however, he lets us know that the Shepherds were expelled

Egypt by *Amosis*, a little before the building of *Jerusalem* and the Temple, and that after several hardships several of them came into *Greece*, and other places, under the conduct of *Cadmus*, and other Captains, but the most of them Settled in *Phoenicia* next *Egypt*. We may reckon therefore that the expulsion of the Shepherds by the Kings of *Thebais*, was the occasion that the *Philistims* were so numerous in the days of *Saul*; and that so many men came in those times with colonies out of *Egypt* and *Phoenicia* into *Greece*; as *Lelex*, *Inachus*, *Pelasgus*, *Ægeus*, *Cecrops*, *Ægialeus*, *Cadmus*, *Phoenix*, *Membliarius*, *Alymnus*, *Abas*, *Erechtheus*, *Peteos*, *Phorbas*, in the days of *Eli*, *Samuel*, *Saul* and *David*: some of them fled in the days of *Eli*, from *Misphragmuthosis*, who conquered part of the lower *Egypt*; others retired from his Successor *Amosis* into *Phoenicia*, and *Arabia Petræa*, and there mixed with the old inhabitants; who not long after being conquered by *David*, fled from him and the *Philistims* by sea, under the conduct of *Cadmus* and other Captains, into *Asia Minor*, *Greece*, and *Libya*, to seek new seats, and there built towns, erected Kingdoms, and set on foot the worship of the dead: and some of those who remained in *Judæa* might assist *David* and *Solomon*, in building *Jerusalem* and the Temple. Among the foreign rites used by the strangers in *Egypt*, in worshipping the Gods, was the sacrificing of men; for *Amosis* abolished that custom at *Heliopolis*: and therefore those strangers were *Canaanites*, such as fled from *Joshua*; for the *Canaanites* gave their seed, that is, their children, to *Moloch*, *and burnt their sons and their daughters in the fire to their Gods*, Deut. xii. 31. *Manetho* calls them *Phoenician* strangers.

After *Amosis* had expelled the Shepherds, and extended his dominion over all *Egypt*, his son and Successor *Ammenemes* or *Ammon*, by much greater conquests laid the foundation of the *Egyptian* Empire: for by the assistance of his young son *Sesostris*, whom he brought up to hunting and other laborious exercises, he conquered *Arabia*, *Troglodytica*, and *Libya*: and from him all *Libya* was anciently called *Ammonia*: and after his death, in the temples erected to him at *Thebes*, and in *Ammonia* and at *Meroe* in *Ethiopia*, they set up Oracles to him, and made the people worship him as the God that acted in them: and these are the oldest Oracles mentioned in history; the *Greeks* therein imitating the *Egyptians*: for the[259] Oracle at *Dodona* was the oldest in *Greece*, and was set up by an *Egyptian* woman, after the example of the Oracle of *Jupiter Ammon* at *Thebes*.

In the days of *Ammon* a body of the *Edomites* fled from *David* into *Egypt*, with their young King *Hadad*, as above; and carried thither their skill in navigation: and this seems to have given occasion to the *Egyptians* to build a fleet on the *Red Sea* near *Coptos*, and might ingratiate *Hadad* with *Pharaoh*: for the *Midianites* and *Ishmaelites*, who bordered upon the *Red Sea*, near *Mount Horeb* on the south-side of *Edom*, were merchants from the days of *Jacob* the Patriarch, Gen. xxxvii. 28, 36. and by their merchandise the *Midianites* abounded with gold in the days of *Moses*, Numb. xxxi. 50, 51, 52. and in the days of the judges of *Israel*, *because they were* Ishmaelites, Judg. viii 24. The *Ishmaelites* therefore in those days grew rich by merchandise; they carried their merchandise on camels through *Petra* to *Rhinocolura*, and thence to *Egypt*: and this trafic at length came into the hands of *David*, by his conquering the *Edomites*, and gaining the ports of the *Red Sea* called *Eloth* and *Ezion-Geber*, as may be understood by the 3000 talents of gold of *Ophir*, which *David* gave to the Temple, 1 *Chron.* xxix. 4. The *Egyptians* having the art of making linen-cloth, they began about this time to build long Ships with sails, in their port on those Seas near *Coptos*, and having learnt the skill of the *Edomites*, they began now to observe the positions of the Stars, and the length of the Solar Year, for enabling them to know the position of the Stars at any time, and to sail by them at all times, without sight of the shoar: and this gave a beginning to Astronomy and Navigation: for hitherto they had gone only by the shoar with oars, in round vessels of burden, first invented on that shallow sea by the posterity of *Abraham*, and in passing from island to island guided themselves by the sight of the islands in the day time, or by the sight of some of the Stars in the night. Their old year was the Lunisolar year, derived from *Noah* to all his posterity, 'till those days, and consisted of twelve months, each of thirty days, according to their calendar: and to the end of this calendar-year they now added five days, and thereby made up the Solar year of twelve months and five days, or 365 days.

The ancient *Egyptians* feigned[260] that *Rhea* lay secretly with *Saturn*, and *Sol* prayed that she might bring forth neither in any month, nor in the year; and that *Mercury* playing at dice with *Luna*, overcame, and took from the Lunar year the 72d part of every day, and thereof composed five days, and added them to the year of 360 days, that she might bring forth in them; and that the *Egyptians* celebrated those days as the birth-days of *Rhea*'s five children, *Osiris*, *Orus* senior, *Typhon*, *Isis*, and *Nephthe* the wife of *Typhon*: and therefore, according to the opinion of the ancient *Egyptians*, the five days were added to the Lunisolar calendar-year, in the Reign of *Saturn* and *Rhea*, the parents of *Osiris*, *Isis*, and *Typhon*; that is, in the Reign of *Ammon* and *Titæa*, the parents of the *Titans*; or in the latter half of the Reign of *David*, when those *Titans* were born, and by consequence soon after the flight of the *Edomites* from *David* into *Egypt*: but the Solstices not being yet settled, the beginning of this new year might not be fixed to the Vernal Equinox before the Reign of *Amenophis* the successor of *Orus* junior, the Son of *Osiris* and *Isis*.

When the *Edomites* fled from *David* with their young King *Hadad* into *Egypt*, it is probable that they carried thither also the use of letters: for letters were then in use among the posterity of *Abraham* in *Arabia Petræa*, and upon the borders of the *Red Sea*, the Law being written there by *Moses* in a book, and in tables of stone, long before: for *Moses* marrying the daughter of the prince of *Midian*, and dwelling with him forty years, learnt them among the *Midianites*: and *Job*, who lived[261] among their neighbours the *Edomites*, mentions the writing down or words, as there in use in his days, *Job.* xix. 23, 24. and there is no instance of letters for writing down sounds, being in use before the days of *David*, in any other nation besides the posterity of *Abraham*. The *Egyptians* ascribed this invention to *Thoth*, the secretary of *Osiris*; and therefore Letters began to be in use in *Egypt* in the days of *Thoth*, that is, a little after the flight of the *Edomites* from *David*, or about the time that *Cadmus* brought them into *Europe*.

Helladius[262] tells us, that a man called *Oes*, who appeared in the *Red Sea* with the tail of a fish, so they painted a sea-man, taught Astronomy and Letters: and *Hyginus*,[263] that *Euhadnes*, who came out of the Sea in *Chaldæa*, taught the *Chaldæans* Astrology the first of any man; he means Astronomy: and *Alexander Polyhistor*[264] tells us from *Berosus*, that *Oannes* taught the *Chaldæans* Letters, Mathematicks, Arts, Agriculture, Cohabitation in Cities, and the Construction of Temples; and that several such men came thither successively. *Oes*, *Euhadnes*, and *Oannes*, seem to be the same name a little varied by corruption; and this name seems to have been given in common to several sea-men, who came thither from time to time, and by consequence were merchants, and frequented those seas with their merchandise, or else fled from their enemies: so that Letters, Astronomy, Architecture and Agriculture, came into *Chaldæa* by sea, and were carried thither by sea-men, who frequented the *Persian Gulph*, and came thither from time to time, after all those things were practised in other countries whence they came, and by consequence in the days of *Ammon* and *Sesac*, *David* and *Solomon*, and their successors, or not long before. The *Chaldæans* indeed made *Oannes* older than the flood of *Xisuthrus*, but the *Egyptians* made *Osiris* as old, and I make them contemporary.

The *Red Sea* had its name not from its colour, but from *Edom* and *Erythra*, the names of *Esau*, which signify that colour: and some[265] tell us, that King *Erythra*, meaning *Esau*, invented the vessels, *rates*, in which they navigated that Sea, and was buried in an island thereof near the *Persian Gulph*: whence it follows, that the *Edomites* navigated that Sea from the days of *Esau*; and there is no need that the oldest *Oannes* should be older. There were boats upon rivers before, such as were the boats which carried the Patriarchs over *Euphrates* and *Jordan*, and the first nations over many other rivers, for peopling the earth, seeking new seats, and invading one another's territories: and after the example of such vessels, *Ishhmael* and *Midian* the sons of *Abraham*, and *Esau* his grandson, might build larger vessels to go to the islands upon the *Red Sea*, in searching for new seats, and by degrees learn to navigate that sea, as far as to the *Persian Gulph*: for ships were as old, even upon the *Mediterranean*, as the days of *Jacob*, *Gen.* xlix. 13. *Judg.* v. 17. but it is probable that the merchants of that sea were not forward to discover their Arts and Sciences, upon which their trade depended: it seems therefore that Letters and Astronomy, and the trade of Carpenters, were invented by the merchants of the *Red Sea*, for writing down their merchandise, and keeping their accounts, and guiding their ships in the night by the Stars, and building ships; and that they were propagated from *Arabia Petræa* into *Egypt*, *Chaldæa*, *Syria*, *Asia minor*, and *Europe*, much about one and the same time; the time in which *David* conquered and dispersed those merchants: for we hear nothing of Letters before the days of *David*, except among the posterity of *Abraham*; nothing of Astronomy, before the *Egyptians* under *Ammon* and *Sesac* applied themselves to that study, except the Constellations mentioned by *Job*, who lived in *Arabia Petræa* among the merchants; nothing of the trade of Carpenters, or good Architecture, before *Solomon* sent to *Hiram* King of *Tyre*, to supply him with such Artificers, saying that *there were none in* Israel *who could skill to hew timber like the* Zidonians.

Diodorus[266] tells us, *that the* Egyptians *sent many colonies out of* Egypt *into other countries; and that* Belus, *the son of* Neptune *and* Libya, *carried colonies thence into* Babylonia, *and seating himself on* Euphrates, *instituted priests free from taxes and publick expences, after the manner of* Egypt, *who were called* Chaldæans, *and who after the manner of* Egypt, *might observe the Stars:* and *Pausanias*[267] tells us, *that the* Belus *of the* Babylonians *had his name from* Belus *an* Egyptian, *the son of* Libya: and *Apollodorus;*[268] *that* Belus *the son of* Neptune *and* Libya, *and King of* Egypt, *was the father of* Ægyptus *and* Danaus, *that is,* Ammon: he tells us also, *that* Busiris *the son of* Neptune *and* Lisianassa [Libyanassa] *the daughter of* Epaphus, *was King of* Egypt; and *Eusebius* calls this King, Busiris *the son of* Neptune, *and of* Libya *the daughter of* Epaphus. By these things the later *Egyptians* seem to have made two *Belus's*, the one the father of *Osiris, Isis,* and *Neptune,* the other the son of *Neptune,* and father of *Ægyptus* and *Danaus:* and hence came the opinion of the people of *Naxus,* that there were two *Minos's* and two *Ariadnes,* the one two Generations older than the other; which we have confuted. The father of *Ægyptus* and *Danaus* was the father of *Osiris, Isis,* and *Typhon;* and *Typhon* was not the grandfather of *Neptune,* but *Neptune* himself.

Sesostris being brought up to hard labour by his father *Ammon,* warred first under his father, being the Hero or *Hercules* of the *Egyptians* during his father's Reign, and afterward their King: under his father, whilst he was very young, he invaded and conquered *Troglodytica,* and thereby secured the harbour of the *Red Sea,* near *Coptos* in *Egypt,* and then he invaded *Ethiopia,* and carried on his conquest southward, as far as to the region bearing cinnamon: and his father by the assistance of the *Edomites* having built a fleet on the *Red Sea,* he put to sea, and coasted *Arabia Fælix,* going to the *Persian Gulph* and beyond, and in those countries set up Columns with inscriptions denoting his conquests; and particularly he Set up a Pillar at *Dira,* a promontory in the straits of the *Red Sea,* next *Ethiopia,* and two Pillars in *India,* on the mountains near the mouth of the rivers *Ganges;* so[269] *Dionysius:*

[Greek: Entha te kai stêlai, Thêbaigeneos Dionysou]
[Greek: Hestasin pymatoio para rhoon Ôkeanoio,]
[Greek: Indôn hystatioisin en ouresin; entha te Gangês]
[Greek: Leukon hydor Nyssaion epi platamôna kylindei.]

Ubi etiamnum columnæ Thebis geniti Bacchi
Stant extremi juxta fluxum Oceani
Indorum ultimis in montibus: ubi & Ganges
Claram aquam Nyssæam ad planitiem devolvit.

After these things he invaded *Libya,* and fought the *Africans* with clubs, and thence is painted with a club in his hand: so[270] *Hyginus*; *Afri & Ægyptii primum fustibus dimicaverunt, postea Belus Neptuni filius gladio belligeratus est, unde bellum dictum est*: and after the conquest of *Libya*, by which *Egypt* was furnished with horses, and furnished *Solomon* and his friends; he prepared a fleet on the *Mediterranean*, and went on westward upon the coast of *Afric*, to search those countries, as far as to the Ocean and island *Erythra* or *Gades* in *Spain*; as *Macrobius*[271] informs us from *Panyasis* and *Pherecydes*: and there he conquered *Geryon*, and at the mouth of the *Straits* set up the famous Pillars.

[272]*Venit ad occasum mundique extrema Sesostris.*

Then he returned through *Spain* and the southern coasts of *France* and *Italy*, with the cattel of *Geryon*, his fleet attending him by sea, and left in *Sicily* the *Sicani*, a people which he had brought from *Spain*: and after his father's death he built Temples to him in his conquests; whence it came to pass, that *Jupiter Ammon* was worshipped in *Ammonia*, and *Ethiopia*, and *Arabia*, and as far as *India*, according to the[273] Poet:

Quamvis Æthiopum populis, Arabumque beatis
Gentibus, atque Indis unus sit Jupiter Ammon.

The *Arabians* worshipped only two Gods, *Coelus*, otherwise called *Ouranus*, or *Jupiter Uranius*, and *Bacchus*: and these were *Jupiter Ammon* and *Sesac*, as above: and so also the people of *Meroe* above *Egypt*[274] worshipped no other Gods but *Jupiter* and *Bacchus*, and had an Oracle of *Jupiter*, and these two Gods were *Jupiter Ammon* and *Osiris*, according to the language of *Egypt*.

At length *Sesostris*, in the fifth year of *Rehoboam*, came out of *Egypt* with a great army of *Libyans*, *Troglodytes* and *Ethiopians*, and spoiled the Temple, and reduced *Judæa* into servitude, and went on conquering, first eastward toward *India*, which he invaded, and then westward as far as *Thrace*: for *God had given him the kingdoms of the countries*, 2 *Chron.* xii. 2, 3, 8. In[275] this Expedition he spent nine years, setting up pillars with inscriptions in all his conquests, some of which remained in *Syria* 'till the days of *Herodotus*. He was accompanied with his son *Orus*, or *Apollo*, and with some singing women, called *the Muses*, one of which, called *Calliope*, was the mother of *Orpheus* an *Argonaut*: and the two tops of the mountain *Parnassus*, which were very high, were dedicated[276] the one to this *Bacchus*, and the other to his son *Apollo*: whence *Lucan*;[277]

Parnassus gemino petit æthera colle,
Mons Phoebo, Bromioque sacer.

In the fourteenth year of *Rehoboam* he returned back into *Egypt*; leaving *Æetes* in *Colchis*, and his nephew *Prometheus* at mount *Caucasus*, with part of his army, to defend his conquests from the *Scythians*. *Apollonius Rhodius*[278] and his scholiast tell us, that *Sesonchosis* King of all *Egypt*, that is *Sesac*, invading all *Asia*, and a great part of *Europe*, peopled many cities which he took; and that *Æa*, the Metropolis of *Colchis*, remained stable ever since his days with the posterity of those Egyptians *which he placed there, and that they preserved pillars or tables in which all the journies and the bounds of sea and land were described, for the use of them that were to go any whither:* these tables therefore gave a beginning to Geography.

Sesostris upon his returning home[279] divided *Egypt* by measure amongst the *Egyptians*; and this gave a beginning to Surveying and Geometry: and[280] *Jamblicus* derives this division of *Egypt*, and beginning of Geometry, from the Age of the Gods of *Egypt*. *Sesostris* also[281] divided *Egypt* into 36 *Nomes* or Counties, and dug a canal from the *Nile* to the head city of every *Nome*, and with the earth dug out of it, he caused the ground of the city to be raised higher, and built a Temple in every city for the worship of the *Nome*, and in the Temples set up Oracles, some of which remained 'till the days of *Herodotus*: and by this means the *Egyptians* of every *Nome* were induced to worship the great men of the Kingdom, to whom the *Nome*, the City, and the Temple or Sepulchre of the God, was dedicated: for every Temple had its proper God, and modes of worship, and annual festivals, at which the Council and People of the *Nome* met at certain times to sacrifice, and regulate the affairs of the *Nome*, and administer justice, and buy and sell; but *Sesac* and his Queen, by the names of *Osiris* and *Isis*, were worshipped in all *Egypt*: and because *Sesac*, to render the *Nile* more useful, dug channels from it to all the capital cities of *Egypt*; that river was consecrated to him, and he was called by its names, *Ægyptus, Siris, Nilus. Dionysius*[282] tells us, that the *Nile* was called *Siris* by the *Ethiopians*, and *Nilus* by the people of *Siene*. From the word *Nahal*, which signifies a torrent, that river was called *Nilus*; and *Dionysius*[283] tells us, that *Nilus* was that King who cut *Egypt* into canals, to make the river useful: in Scripture the river is called *Schichor*, or *Sihor*, and thence the *Greeks* formed the words *Siris, Sirius, Ser-Apis, O-Siris*; but *Plutarch*[284] tells us, that the syllable *O*, put before the word *Siris* by the *Greeks*, made it scarce intelligible to the *Egyptians*.

I have now told you the original of the *Nomes* of *Egypt* and of the Religions and Temples of the *Nomes*, and of the Cities built there by the Gods, and called by their names: whence *Diodorus*[285] tells us, that *of all the Provinces of the World, there were in* Egypt *only many cities built by the ancient Gods, as by* Jupiter, Sol, Hermes, Apollo, Pan, Eilithyia, *and, many others*: and *Lucian*[286] an *Assyrian*, who had travelled into *Phoenicia* and *Egypt*, tells us, that *the Temples of* Egypt *were very old, those in* Phoenicia *built by* Cinyras *as old, and those in* Assyria *almost as old as the former, but not altogether so old*: which shews that the Monarchy of *Assyria* rose up after the Monarchy of *Egypt*; as is represented in Scripture; and that the Temples of *Egypt* then standing, were those built by *Sesostris*, about the same time that the Temples of *Phoenicia* and *Cyprus* were built by *Cinyras, Benhadad*, and *Hiram*. This was not the first original of Idolatry, but only the erecting of much more sumptuous Temples than formerly to the founders of new Kingdoms: for Temples at first were very small;

> *Jupiter angusta vix totus stabat in æde.*
> *Ovid. Fast.* l. 1.

Altars were at first erected without Temples, and this custom continued in *Persia* 'till after the days of *Herodotus*: in *Phoenicia* they had Altars with little houses for eating the sacrifices much earlier, and these they called High Places: such was the High Place where *Samuel* entertained *Saul*; such was the House of *Dagon* at *Ashdod*, into which the *Philistims* brought the Ark; and the House of *Baal*, in which *Jehu* slew the Prophets of *Baal*; and such were the High Places of the *Canaanites* which *Moses* commanded *Israel* to destroy: he[287] commanded *Israel* to destroy the Altars, Images, High Places, and Groves of the *Canaanites*, but made no mention of their Temples, as he would have done had there been any in those days. I meet with no mention of sumptuous Temples before the days of *Solomon*: new Kingdoms begun then to build Sepulchres to their Founders in the form of Sumptuous Temples; and such Temples *Hiram* built in *Tyre*, *Sesac* in all *Egypt*, and *Benhadad* in *Damascus*.

For when *David*[288] smote *Hadad Ezer* King of *Zobah*, and slew the *Syrians* of *Damascus* who came to assist him, *Rezon the son of* Eliadah *fled from his lord* Hadad-Ezer, *and gathered men unto him and became Captain over a band, and Reigned in* Damascus, *over* Syria: he is called *Hezion*, 1 *King*. xv. 18. and his successors mentioned in history were *Tabrimon*, *Hadad* or *Ben-hadad*, *Benhadad* II. *Hazael*, *Benhadad* III. * * and *Rezin* the son of *Tabeah*. *Syria* became subject to *Egypt* in the days of *Tabrimon*, and recovered her liberty under *Benhadad* I; and in the days of *Benhadad* III, until the reign of the last *Rezin*, they became subject to *Israel*: and in the ninth year of *Hoshea* King of *Judah*, *Tiglath-pileser* King of *Assyria* captivated the *Syrians*, and put an end to their Kingdom: now *Josephus*[289] tells us, that *the* Syrians *'till his days worshipped both* Adar, *that is* Hadad *or* Benhadad, *and his successor* Hazael *as Gods, for their benefactions, and for building Temples by which they adorned the city of* Damascus: *for*, saith he, *they daily celebrate solemnities in honour of these Kings, and boast their antiquity, not knowing that they are novel, and lived not above eleven hundred years ago.* It seems these Kings built sumptuous Sepulchres for themselves, and were worshipped therein. *Justin*[290] calls the first of these two Kings *Damascus*, saying that *the city had its name from him, and that the* Syrians *in honour of him worshipped his wife* Arathes *as a Goddess, using her Sepulchre for a Temple.*

Another instance we have in the Kingdom of *Byblus*. In the[291] Reign of *Minos* King of *Crete*, when *Rhadamanthus* the brother of *Minos* carried colonies from *Crete* to the *Greek* islands, and gave the islands to his captains, he gave *Lemnos* to *Thoas*, or *Theias*, or *Thoantes*, the father of *Hypsipyle*, a *Cretan* worker in metals, and by consequence a disciple of the *Idæi Dactyli*, and perhaps a *Phoenician*: for the *Idæi Dactyli*, and *Telchines*, and *Corybantes* brought their Arts and Sciences from *Phoenicia*: and[292] *Suidas* saith, that he was descended from *Pharnaces* King of *Cyprus*; *Apollodorus*,[293] that he was the son of *Sandochus* a *Syrian*; and *Apollonius Rhodius*,[294] that Hypsipyle *gave* Jason *the purple cloak which the* Graces *made for* Bacchus, *who gave it to his son* Thoas, the father of *Hypsipyle*, and King of *Lemnos*: Thoas married[295] *Calycopis*, the mother of *Æneas*, and daughter of *Otreus* King of *Phrygia*, and for his skill on the harp was called *Cinyras*, and was said to be exceedingly beloved by *Apollo* or *Orus*: the great *Bacchus* loved his wife, and being caught in bed with her in *Phrygia* appeased him with wine, and composed the matter by making him King of *Byblus* and *Cyprus*; and then came over the *Hellespont* with his army, and conquered *Thrace*: and to these things the poets allude, in feigning that *Vulcan* fell from heaven into *Lemnos*, and that *Bacchus*[296] appeased him with wine, and reduced him back into heaven: he fell from the heaven of the *Cretan* Gods, when he went from *Crete* to *Lemnos* to work in metals, and was reduced back into heaven when *Bacchus* made him King of *Cyprus* and *Byblus*: he Reigned there 'till a very great age, living to the times of the *Trojan* war, and becoming exceeding rich: and after the death of his wife *Calycopis*,[297] he built Temples to her at *Paphos* and *Amathus*, in *Cyprus*; and at *Byblus* in *Syria*, and instituted Priests to her with Sacred Rites and lustful *Orgia*; whence she became the *Dea Cypria*, and the *Dea Syria*: and from Temples erected to her in these and other places, she was also called *Paphia, Amathusia, Byblia, Cytherea Salaminia, Cnidia, Erycina, Idalia. Fama tradit a Cinyra sacratum vetustissimum Paphiæ Veneris templum, Deamque ipsam conceptam mari huc appulsam: Tacit. Hist.* l. 2. c. 3. From her sailing from *Phrygia* to the island *Cythera*, and from thence to be Queen of *Cyprus*, she was said by the *Cyprians*, to be born of the froth of the sea, and was painted sailing upon a shell. *Cinyras* Deified also his son *Gingris*, by the name of *Adonis*; and for assisting the *Egyptians* with armour, it is probable that he himself was Deified by his friends the *Egyptians*, by the name of *Baal-Canaan*, or *Vulcan*: for *Vulcan* was celebrated principally by the *Egyptians*, and was a King according to *Homer*, and Reigned in *Lemnos*; and *Cinyras* was an inventor of arts,[298] and found out copper in *Cyprus*, and the smiths hammer, and anvil, and tongs, and laver; and imployed workmen in making armour, and other things of brass and iron, and was the only King celebrated in history for working in metals, and was King of *Lemnos*, and the husband of *Venus*; all which are the characters of *Vulcan*: and the *Egyptians* about the time of the death of *Cinyras, viz.* in the Reign of their King *Amenophis*, built a very sumptuous Temple at *Memphis* to *Vulcan*, and near it a smaller Temple to *Venus Hospita*; not an *Egyptian* woman but a foreigner, not *Helena* but *Vulcan's Venus*: for[299] *Herodotus* tells us, that the region round about this Temple was inhabited by *Tyrian Phoenicians*, and that[300] *Cambyses* going into this Temple at *Memphis*, very much derided the statue of *Vulcan* for its littleness; *For,* saith he, *this statue is most like those Gods which the* Phoenicians *call* Patæci, *and carry about in the fore part of their Ships in the form of* Pygmies: and[301] *Bochart* saith of this *Venus Hospita, Phoeniciam Venerem in Ægypto pro peregrina habitam.*

As the *Egyptians, Phoenicians* and *Syrians* in those days Deified their Kings and Princes, so upon their coming into *Asia minor* and *Greece*, they taught those nations to do the like, as hath been shewed above. In those days the writing of the *Thebans* and *Ethiopians* was in hieroglyphicks; and this way of writing seems to have spread into the lower *Egypt* before the days of *Moses*: for thence came the worship of their Gods in the various shapes of Birds, Beasts, and Fishes, forbidden in the second commandment. Now this emblematical way of writing gave occasion to the *Thebans* and *Ethiopians*, who in the days of *Samuel, David, Solomon,* and *Rehoboam* conquered *Egypt*, and the nations round about, and erected a great Empire, to represent and signify their conquering Kings and Princes, not by writing down their names, but by making various hieroglyphical figures; as by painting *Ammon* with Ram's horns, to signify the King who conquered *Libya*, a country abounding with sheep; his father *Amosis* with a Scithe, to signify that King who conquered the lower *Egypt*, a country abounding with corn; his Son *Osiris* by an Ox, because he taught the conquered nations to plow with oxen; *Bacchus* with Bulls horns for the same reason, and with Grapes because he taught the nations to plant vines, and upon a Tiger because he subdued *India*; *Orus* the son of *Osiris* with a Harp, to signify the Prince who was eminently skilled on that instrument; *Jupiter* upon an Eagle to signify the sublimity of his dominion, and with a Thunderbolt to represent him a warrior; *Venus* in a Chariot drawn with two Doves, to represent her amorous and lustful; *Neptune* with a Trident, to signify the commander of a fleet composed of three Squadrons; *Ægeon*, a Giant, with 50 heads, and an hundred hands, to signify *Neptune* with his men in a ship of fifty oars; *Thoth* with a Dog's head and wings at his cap and feet, and a *Caduceus* writhen about with two Serpents, to signify a man of craft, and an embassador who reconciled two contending nations; *Pan* with a Pipe and the legs of a Goat, to signify a man delighted in piping and dancing; and *Hercules* with Pillars and a Club, because *Sesostris* set up pillars in all his conquests, and fought against the *Libyans* with clubs: this is that *Hercules* who, according to[302] *Eudoxus*, was slain by *Typhon*; and according to *Ptolomæus Hephæstion*[303] was called *Nilus*, and who conquered *Geryon* with his three sons in *Spain*, and set up the famous pillars at the mouth of the *Straits*: for *Diodorus*[304] mentioning three *Hercules*'s, the *Egyptian*, the *Tyrian*, and the son of *Alcmena*, saith that *the oldest flourished among the* Egyptians, *and having conquered a great part of the world, set up the pillars in* Afric: and *Vasæus*,[305] that *Osiris*, called also *Dionysius, came into* Spain *and conquered* Geryon, *and was the first who brought Idolatry into* Spain. *Strabo*[306] tells us, that the *Ethiopians* called *Megabars* fought with clubs: and some of the *Greeks*[307] did so 'till the times of the *Trojan* war. Now from this hieroglyphical way of writing it came to pass, that upon the division of *Egypt* into *Nomes* by *Sesostris*, the great men of the Kingdom to whom the *Nomes* were dedicated, were represented in their Sepulchers or Temples of the *Nomes*, by various hieroglyphicks; as by an *Ox*, a *Cat*, a *Dog*, a *Cebus*, a *Goat*, a *Lyon*, a *Scarabæus*, an *Ichneumon*, a *Crocodile*, an *Hippopotamus*, an *Oxyrinchus*, an *Ibis*, a *Crow*, a *Hawk*, a *Leek*, and were worshipped by the *Nomes* in the shape of these creatures.

The[308] *Atlantides*, a people upon mount *Atlas* conquered by the *Egyptians* in the Reign of *Ammon*, related that *Uranus* was their first King, and reduced them from a savage course of life, and caused them to dwell in towns and cities, and lay up and use the fruits of the earth, and that he reigned over a great part of the world, and by his wife *Titæa* had eighteen children, among which were *Hyperion* and *Basilea* the parents of *Helius* and *Selene*; that the brothers of *Hyperion* slew him, and drowned his son *Helius*, the *Phaeton* of the ancients, in the *Nile*, and divided his Kingdom amongst themselves; and the country bordering upon the Ocean fell to the lot of *Atlas*, from whom the people were called *Atlantides*. By *Uranus* or *Jupiter Uranius*, *Hyperion*, *Basilea*, *Helius* and *Selene*, I understand *Jupiter Ammon*, *Osiris*, *Isis*, *Orus* and *Bubaste*; and by the sharing of the Kingdom of *Hyperion* amongst his brothers the *Titans*, I understand the division of the earth among the Gods mentioned in the Poem of *Solon*.

For *Solon* having travelled into *Egypt*, and conversed with the Priests of *Sais*; about their antiquities, wrote a Poem of what he had learnt, but did not finish it;[309] and this Poem fell into the hands of *Plato* who relates out of it, that at the mouth of the *Straits* near *Hercules*'s Pillars there was an Island called *Atlantis*, the people of which, nine thousand years before the days of *Solon*, reigned over *Libya* as far as *Egypt*; and over *Europe* as far as the *Tyrrhene* sea; and all this force collected into one body invaded *Egypt* and *Greece*, and whatever was contained within the Pillars of *Hercules*, but was resisted and stopt by the *Athenians* and other *Greeks*, and thereby the rest of the nations not yet conquered were preserved: he saith also that in those days the Gods, having finished their conquests, divided the whole earth amongst themselves, partly into larger, partly into smaller portions, and instituted Temples and Sacred Rites to themselves; and that the Island *Atlantis* fell to the lot of *Neptune*, who made his eldest Son *Atlas* King of the whole Island, a part of which was called *Gadir*; and that *in the history of the said wars mention was made of* Cecrops, Erechtheus, Erichthonius, *and others before* Theseus, *and also of the women who warred with the men, and of the habit and statue of* Minerva, *the study of war in those days being common to men and women.* By all these circumstances it is manifest that these Gods were the *Dii magni majorum gentium*, and lived between the age of *Cecrops* and *Theseus*; and that the wars which *Sesostris* with his brother *Neptune* made upon the nations by land and sea, and the resistance he met with in *Greece*, and the following invasion of *Egypt* by *Neptune*, are here described; and how the captains of *Sesostris* shared his conquests amongst themselves, as the captains of *Alexander* the great did his conquests long after, and instituting Temples and Priests and sacred Rites to themselves, caused the nations to worship them after death as Gods: and that the Island *Gadir* or *Gades*, with all *Libya*, fell to the lot of him who after death was Deified by the name of *Neptune*. The time therefore when these things were done is by *Solon* limited to the age of *Neptune*, the father of *Atlas*; for *Homer* tells us, that *Ulysses* presently after the *Trojan* war found *Calypso* the daughter of *Atlas* in the *Ogygian* Island, perhaps *Gadir*; and therefore it was but two Generations before the *Trojan* war. This is that *Neptune*, who with *Apollo* or *Orus* fortified *Troy* with a wall, in the Reign of *Laomedon* the father of *Priamus*, and left many natural children in *Greece*, some of which were *Argonauts*, and others were contemporary to the *Argonauts*; and therefore he flourished but one Generation before the *Argonautic* expedition, and by consequence about 400 years before *Solon* went into *Egypt*: but the Priests of *Egypt* in those 400 years had magnified the stories and antiquity of their Gods so exceedingly, as to make them nine thousand years older than *Solon*, and the Island *Atlantis* bigger than all *Afric* and *Asia* together, and full of people; and because in the days of *Solon* this great Island did not appear, they pretended that it was sunk into the sea with all its people: thus great was the vanity of the Priests of *Egypt* in magnifying their antiquities.

The *Cretans*[310] affirmed that *Neptune was the man who set out a fleet, having obtained this Præfecture of* his father *Saturn; whence posterity reckoned things done in the sea to be under his government, and mariners honoured him with sacrifices*: the invention of tall Ships with sails[311] is also ascribed to him. He was first worshipped in *Africa*, as *Herodotus*[312] affirms, and therefore Reigned over that province: for his eldest son *Atlas*, who succeeded him, was not only Lord of the Island *Atlantis*, but also Reigned over a great part of *Afric*, giving his name to the people called *Atlantii*, and to the mountain *Atlas*, and the *Atlantic Ocean*. The[313] outmost parts of the earth and promontories, and whatever bordered upon the sea and was washed by it, the *Egyptians* called *Neptys*; and on the coasts of *Marmorica* and *Cyrene*, *Bochart* and *Arius Montanus* place the *Naphthuhim*, a people sprung from *Mizraim*, *Gen.* x. 13; and thence *Neptune* and his wife *Neptys* might have their names, the words *Neptune*, *Neptys* and *Naphthuhim*, signifying the King, Queen, and people of the sea-coasts. The *Greeks* tell us that *Japetus* was the father of *Atlas*, and *Bochart* derives *Japetus* and *Neptune* from the same original: he and his son *Atlas* are celebrated in the ancient fables for making war upon the Gods of *Egypt*; as when *Lucian*[314] saith that *Corinth* being full of fables, tells the fight of *Sol* and *Neptune*, that is, of *Apollo* and *Python*, or *Orus* and *Typhon*; and where *Agatharcides*[315] relates how the Gods of *Egypt* fled from the Giants, 'till the *Titans* came in and saved them by putting *Neptune* to flight; and where *Hyginus*[316] tells the war between the Gods of *Ægypt*, and the *Titans* commanded by *Atlas*.

The *Titans* are the posterity of *Titæa*, some of whom under *Hercules* assisted the Gods, others under *Neptune* and *Atlas* warred against them: *for which reason*, saith *Plutarch*,[317] *the Priests of* Egypt *abominated the sea, and had* Neptune *in no honour*. By *Hercules*, I understand here the general of the forces of *Thebais* and *Ethiopia* whom the Gods or great men of *Egypt* called to their assistance, against the Giants or great men of *Libya*, who had slain *Osiris* and invaded *Egypt*: for *Diodorus*[318] saith that *when* Osiris *made his expedition over the world, he left his kinsman* Hercules *general of his forces over all his dominions, and* Antæus *governor of* Libya *and* Ethiopia. *Antæus* Reigned over all *Afric* to the *Atlantic Ocean*, and built *Tingis* or *Tangieres*: *Pindar*[319] tells us that he Reigned at *Irasa* a town of *Libya*, where *Cyrene* was afterwards built: he invaded *Egypt* and *Thebais*; for he was beaten by *Hercules* and the *Egyptians* near *Antæa* or *Antæopolis*, a town of *Thebais*; and *Diodorus*[320] tells us that *this town had its name from* Antæus, *whom* Hercules *slew in the days of* Osiris. *Hercules* overthrew him several times, and every time he grew stronger by recruits from *Libya*, his mother earth; but *Hercules* intercepted his recruits, and at length slew him. In these wars *Hercules* took the *Libyan* world from *Atlas*, and made *Atlas* pay tribute out of his golden orchard, the Kingdom of *Afric*. *Antæus* and *Atlas* were both of them sons of *Neptune* both of them Reigned over all *Libya* and *Afric*, between *Mount Atlas* and the *Mediterranean* to the very Ocean; both of them invaded *Egypt*, and contended with *Hercules* in the wars of the Gods, and therefore they are but two names of one and the same man; and even the name *Atlas* in the oblique cases seems to have been compounded of the name *Antæus* and some other word, perhaps the word *Atal*, cursed, put before it: the invasion of *Egypt* by *Antæus*, *Ovid* hath relation unto, where he makes *Hercules* say,

> *Sævoque alimenta parentis*
> *Antæo eripui.*

This war was at length composed by the intervention of *Mercury*, who in memory thereof was said to reconcile two contending serpents, by casting his Ambassador's rod between them: and thus much concerning the ancient state of *Egypt*, *Libya*, and *Greece*, described by *Solon*.

The mythology of the *Cretans* differed in some things from that of *Egypt* and *Libya*: for in the *Cretan* mythology, *Coelus* and *Terra*, or *Uranus* and *Titæa* were the parents of *Saturn* and *Rhea*, and *Saturn* and *Rhea* were the parents of *Jupiter* and *Juno*; and *Hyperion*, *Japetus* and the *Titans* were one Generation older than *Jupiter*; and *Saturn* was expelled his Kingdom and castrated by his son *Jupiter*: which fable hath no place in the mythology of *Egypt*.

During the Reign of *Sesac*, *Jeroboam* being in subjection to *Egypt*; set up the Gods of *Egypt* in *Dan* and *Bethel*; and *Israel was without the true God, and without a teaching Priest and without law: and in those times there was no peace to him that went out, nor to him that came in, but great vexations were upon all the inhabitants of the countries; and nation was destroyed of nation, and city of city: for God did vex them with all adversity.* 2 *Chron.* xv. 3, 5, 6. But in the fifth year of *Asa* the land of *Judah* became quiet from war, and from thence had quiet ten years; and *Asa* took away the altars of strange Gods, and brake down the Images, and built the fenced cities of *Judah* with walls and towers and gates and bars, having rest on every side, and got up an army of 580000 men, with which in the fifteenth year of his Reign he met *Zerah* the *Ethiopian*, who came out against him with an army of a thousand thousand *Ethiopians* and *Libyans*: the way of the *Libyans* was through *Egypt*, and therefore *Zerah* was now Lord of *Egypt*: they fought at *Mareshah* near *Gerar*, between *Egypt* and *Judæa*, and *Zerah* was beaten, so that he could not recover himself: and from all this I seem to gather that *Osiris* was slain in the fifth year of *Asa*, and thereupon *Egypt* fell into civil wars, being invaded by the *Libyans*, and defended by the *Ethiopians* for a time; and after ten years more being invaded by the *Ethiopians*, who slew *Orus* the son and successor of *Osiris*, drowning him in the *Nile*, and seized his Kingdom. By these civil wars of *Egypt*, the land of *Judah* had rest ten years. *Osiris* or *Sesostris* reigned long, *Manetho* saith 48 years; and by this reckoning he began to Reign about the 17th year of *Solomon*; and *Orus* his son was drowned in the 15th year of *Asa*: for *Pliny*[321] tells us, *Ægyptiorum bellis attrita est Æthiopia, vicissim imperitando serviendoque, clara & potens etiam usque ad Trojana bella Memnone regnante.* Ethiopia, served *Egypt* 'till the death of *Sesostris*, and no longer; for *Herodotus*[322] tells us that *he alone enjoyed the Empire of* Ethiopia: then the *Ethiopians* became free, and after ten years became Lords of *Egypt* and *Libya*, under *Zerah* and *Amenophis*.

When *Asa* by his victory over *Zerah* became safe from *Egypt*, he assembled all the people, and they offered sacrifices out of the spoils, and entered into a covenant upon oath to seek the Lord; and in lieu of the vessels taken away by *Sesac, he brought into the house of God the things that his father had dedicated, and that he himself had dedicated, Silver and Gold, and Vessels. 2 Chron.* xv.

When *Zerah* was beaten, so that he could not recover himself, the people[323] of the lower *Egypt* revolted from the *Ethiopians*, and called in to their assistance two hundred thousand *Jews* and *Canaanites*; and under the conduct of one *Osarsiphus*, a Priest of *Egypt*, called *Usorthon, Osorchon, Osorchor*, and *Hercules Ægyptius* by *Manetho*, caused the *Ethiopians* now under *Memnon* to retire to *Memphis*: and there *Memnon* turned the river *Nile* into a new channel, built a bridge over it and fortified that pass, and then went back into *Ethiopia*: but after thirteen years, he and his young son *Ramesses* came down with an army from *Ethiopia*, conquered the lower *Egypt*, and drove out the *Jews* and *Phoenicians*; and this action the *Egyptian* writers and their followers call the second expulsion of the Shepherds, taking *Osarsiphus* for *Moses*.

Tithonus a beautiful youth, the elder brother of *Priamus*, went into *Ethiopia*, being carried thither among many captives by *Sesostris*: and the *Greeks*, before the days of *Hesiod*, feigned that *Memnon* was his son: *Memnon* therefore, in the opinion of those ancient *Greeks*, was one Generation younger than *Tithonus*, and was born after the return of *Sesostris* into *Egypt*: suppose about 16 or 20 years after the death of *Solomon*. He is said to have lived very long, and so might die about 95 years after *Solomon*, as we reckoned above: his mother, called *Cissia* by *Æschylus*, in a statue erected to her in *Egypt*,[324] was represented as the daughter, the wife, and the mother of a King, and therefore he was the son of a King; which makes it probable that *Zerah*, whom he succeeded in the Kingdom of *Ethiopia*, was his father.

Historians[325] agree that *Menes* Reigned in *Egypt* next after the Gods, and turned the river into a new channel, and built a bridge over it, and built *Memphis* and the magnificent Temple of *Vulcan*: he built *Memphis* over-against the place where *Grand Cairo* now stands, called by the *Arabian* historians *Mesir*: he built only the body of the Temple of *Vulcan*, and his successors *Ramesses* or *Rhampsinitus, Moeris, Asychis*, and *Psammiticus* built the western, northern eastern, and southern portico's thereof: *Psammiticus*, who built the last portico of this Temple, Reigned three hundred years after the victory of *Asa* over *Zerah*, and it is not likely that this Temple could be above three hundred years in building, or that any *Menes* could be King of all *Egypt* before the expulsion of the Shepherds. The last of the Gods of *Egypt* was *Orus*, with his mother *Isis*, and sister *Bubaste*, and secretary *Thoth*, and unkle *Typhon*; and the King who reigned next after all their deaths, and turned the river and built a bridge over it, and built *Memphis* and the Temple of *Vulcan*, was *Memnon* or *Amenophis*, called by the *Egyptians Amenoph*; and therefore he is *Menes*: for the names *Amenoph*, or *Menoph*, and *Menes* do not much differ; and from *Amenoph* the city *Memphis* built by *Menes* had its *Egyptian* names *Moph, Noph, Menoph* or *Menuf*, as it is still called by the *Arabian* historians: the necessity of fortifying this place against *Osarsiphus* gave occasion to the building of it.

In the time of the revolt of the lower *Egypt* under *Osarsiphus*, and the retirement of *Amenophis* into *Ethiopia, Egypt* being then in the greatest distraction, the *Greeks* built the ship *Argo*, and sent in it the flower of *Greece* to *Æetes* in *Colchis*, and to many other Princes on the coasts of the *Euxine* and *Mediterranean* seas; and this ship was built after the pattern of an *Egyptian* ship with fifty oars, in which *Danaus* with his fifty daughters a few years before fled from *Egypt* into *Greece*, and was the first long ship with sails built by the *Greeks*: and such an improvement of navigation, with a design to send the flower of *Greece* to many Princes upon the sea-coasts of the *Euxine* and *Mediterranean* seas, was too great an undertaking to be set on foot, without the concurrence of the Princes and States of *Greece*, and perhaps the approbation of the *Amphictyonic* Council; for it was done by the dictate of the Oracle. This Council met every half year upon state-affairs for the welfare of *Greece*, and therefore knew of this expedition, and might send the *Argonauts* upon an embassy to the said Princes; and for concealing their design might make the fable of the golden fleece, in relation to the ship of *Phrixus* whose ensign was a golden ram: and probably their design was to notify the distraction of *Egypt*, and the invasion thereof by the *Ethiopians* and *Israelites*, to the said Princes, and to persuade them to take that opportunity to revolt from *Egypt*, and set up for themselves, and make a league with the *Greeks*: for the *Argonauts* went through[326] the Kingdom of *Colchis* by land to the *Armenians*, and through *Armenia* to the *Medes*; which could not have been done if they had not made friendship with the nations through which they passed: they visited also *Laomedon* King of the *Trojans*, *Phineus* King of the *Thracians*, *Cyzicus* King of the *Doliones*, *Lycus* King of the *Mariandyni*, the coasts of *Mysia* and *Taurica Chersonesus*, the nations upon the *Tanais*, the people about *Byzantium*, and the coasts of *Epirus*, *Corsica*, *Melita*, *Italy*, *Sicily*, *Sardinia*, and *Gallia* upon the *Mediterranean*; and from thence they[327] crossed the sea to *Afric*, and there conferred with *Euripylus* King of *Cyrene*: and[328] *Strabo* tells us that *in* Armenia *and* Media, *and the neighbouring places, there were frequent monuments of the expedition of* Jason; *as also about* Sinope, *and its sea-coasts, the* Propontis *and the* Hellespont, *and in the* Mediterranean: and a message by the flower of *Greece* to so many nations could be on no other account than state-policy; these nations had been invaded by the *Egyptians*, but after this expedition we hear no more of their continuing in subjection to *Egypt*.

The[329] *Egyptians* originally lived on the fruits of the earth, and fared hardly, and abstained from animals, and therefore abominated Shepherds: *Menes* taught them to adorn their beds and tables with rich furniture and carpets, and brought in amongst them a sumptuous, delicious and voluptuous way of life: and about a hundred years after his death, *Gnephacthus* one of his successors cursed him for it, and to reduce the luxury of *Egypt*, caused the curse to be entered in the Temple of *Jupiter* at *Thebes*; and by this curse the honour of *Menes* was diminished among the *Egyptians*.

The Kings of *Egypt* who expelled the Shepherds and Succeeded them, Reigned I think first at *Coptos*, and then at *Thebes*, and then at *Memphis*. At *Coptos* I place *Misphragmuthosis* and *Amosis* or *Thomosis* who expelled the Shepherds, and abolished their custom of sacrificing men, and extended the *Coptic* language, and the name of [Greek: Aia Koptou], *Aegyptus*, to the conquest. Then *Thebes* became the Royal City of *Ammon*, and from him was called *No-Ammon*, and his conquest on the west of *Egypt* was called *Ammonia*. After him, in the same city of *Thebes*, Reigned *Osiris*, *Orus*, *Menes* or *Amenophis*, and *Ramesses*: but *Memphis* and her miracles were not yet celebrated in *Greece*; for *Homer* celebrates *Thebes* as in its glory in his days, and makes no mention of *Memphis*. After *Menes* had built *Memphis*, *Moeris* the successor of *Ramesses* adorned it, and made it the seat of the Kingdom, and this was almost two Generations after the *Trojan* war. *Cinyras*, the *Vulcan* who married *Venus*, and under the Kings of *Egypt* Reigned over *Cyprus* and part of *Phoenicia*, and made armour for those Kings, lived 'till the times of the *Trojan* war: and upon his death *Menes* or *Memnon* might Deify him, and found the famous Temple of *Vulcan* in that city for his worship, but not live to finish it. In a plain[330] not far from *Memphis* are many small Pyramids, said to be built by *Venephes* or *Enephes*; and I suspect that *Venephes* and *Enephes* have been corruptly written for *Menephes* or *Amenophis*, the letters *AM* being almost worn out in some old manuscript: for after the example of these Pyramids, the following Kings, *Moeris* and his successors, built others much larger. The plain in which they were built was the burying-place of that city, as appears by the Mummies there found; and therefore the Pyramids were the sepulchral monuments of the Kings and Princes of that city: and by these and such like works the city grew famous soon after the days of *Homer*, who therefore flourished in the Reign of *Ramesses*.

Herodotus[331] is the oldest historian now extant who wrote of the antiquities of *Egypt*, and had what he wrote from the Priests of that country: and *Diodorus*, who wrote almost 400 years after him, and had his relations also from the Priests of *Egypt*, placed many nameless Kings between those whom *Herodotus* placed in continual succession. The Priests of *Egypt* had therefore, between the days of *Herodotus* and *Diodorus*, out of vanity, very much increased the number of their Kings: and what they did after the days of *Herodotus*, they began to do before his days; for he tells us that they recited to him out of their books, the names of 330 Kings who Reigned after *Menes*, but did nothing memorable, except *Nitocris* and *Moeris* the last of them: all these Reigned at *Thebes*, 'till *Moeris* translated the seat of the Empire from *Thebes* to *Memphis*. After *Moeris* he reckons *Sesostris*, *Pheron*, *Proteus*, *Rhampsinitus*, *Cheops*, *Cephren*, *Mycerinus*, *Asychis*, *Anysis*, *Sabacon*, *Anysis* again, *Sethon*, twelve contemporary Kings, *Psammitichus*, *Nechus*, *Psammis*, *Apries*, *Amasis*, and *Psammenitus*. The *Egyptians* had before the days of *Solon* made their monarchy 9000 years old, and now they reckon'd to *Herodotus* a succession of 330 Kings Reigning so many Generations, that is about 11000 years, before *Sesostris*: but the Kings who Reigned long before *Sesostris* might Reign over several little Kingdoms in several parts of *Egypt*, before the rise of their Monarchy; and by consequence before the days of *Eli* and *Samuel*, and so are not under our consideration: and these names may have been multiplied by corruption; and some of them, as *Athothes* or *Thoth*, the secretary of *Osiris*; *Tosorthrus* or *Æsculapius* a Physician who invented building with square stones; and *Thuor* or *Polybus* the husband of *Alcandra*, were only Princes of *Egypt*. If with *Herodotus* we omit the names of those Kings who did nothing memorable, and consider only those whose actions are recorded, and who left splendid monuments of their having Reigned over *Egypt*, such as were Temples, Statues, Pyramids, Obelisks, and Palaces dedicated or ascribed to them, these Kings reduced into good order will give us all or almost all the Kings of *Egypt*, from the days of the expulsion of the Shepherds and founding of the Monarchy, downwards to the conquest of *Egypt* by *Cambyses*: for *Sesostris* Reigned in the Age of the Gods of *Egypt*: being Deified by the names of *Osiris*, *Hercules* and *Bacchus*, as above; and therefore *Menes*, *Nitocris*, and *Moeris* are to be placed after him; *Menes* and his son *Ramesses* Reigned next after the Gods, and therefore *Nitocris* and *Moeris* Reigned after *Ramesses*. *Moeris* is set down immediately before *Cheops*, three times in the Dynastys of the Kings of *Egypt* composed by *Eratosthenes*, and once in the Dynasties of *Manetho*; and in the same Dynasties *Nitocris* is set after the builders of the three great Pyramids, and according to *Herodotus* her brother Reigned before her, and was slain, and she revenged his death; and according to *Syncellus* she built the third great Pyramid; and the builders of the Pyramids Reigned at *Memphis*, and by consequence after *Moeris*. Now from these things I gather that the Kings of *Egypt* mentioned by *Herodotus* ought to be placed in this order; *Sesostris*, *Pheron*, *Proteus*, *Menes*, *Rhampsinitus*, *Moeris*, *Cheops*, *Cephren*, *Mycerinus*, *Nitocris*, *Asychis*, *Anysis*, *Sabacon*, *Anysis* again, *Sethon*, twelve contemporary Kings, *Psammitichus*, *Nechus*, *Psammis*, *Apries*, *Amasis*, *Psammenitus*.

Pheron is by *Herodotus* said to be the son and successor of *Sesostris*. He was Deified by the name of *Orus*.

Proteus Reigned in the lower *Egypt* when *Paris* sailed thither; that is at the end of the *Trojan* war, according to[332] *Herodotus*: and at that time *Amenophis* was King of *Egypt* and *Ethiopia*: but in his absence *Proteus* might be governor of some part of the lower *Egypt* under him; for *Homer* places *Proteus* upon the sea-coasts, and makes him a sea God, and calls him the servant of *Neptune*; and *Herodotus* saith that he rose up from among the common people, and that *Proteus* was his name translated into *Greek*, and this name in *Greek* signifies only a Prince or President. He succeeded *Pheron*, and was succeeded by *Rhampsinitus* according to *Herodotus*; and so was contemporary to *Amenophis*.

Amenophis Reigned next after *Orus* and *Isis* the last of the Gods; he Reigned at first over all *Egypt*, and then over *Memphis* and the upper parts of *Egypt*; and by conquering *Osarsiphus*, who had revolted from him, became King of all *Egypt* again, about 51 years after the death of *Solomon*. He built *Memphis* and ordered the worship of the Gods of *Egypt*, and built a Palace at *Abydus*, and the *Memnonia* at *This* and *Susa*, and the magnificent Temple of *Vulcan* in *Memphis*; the building with square stones being found out before by *Tosorthrus*, the *Æsculapius* of *Egypt*: he is by corruption of his name called *Menes*, *Mines*, *Minæus*, *Mineus*, *Minies*, *Mnevis*, *Enephes*, *Venephes*, *Phamenophis*, *Osymanthyas*, *Osimandes*, *Ismandes*, *Imandes*, *Memnon*, *Arminon*.

Amenophis was succeeded by his son, called by *Herodotus*, *Rhampsinitus*, and by others *Ramses*, *Ramises*, *Rameses*, *Ramesses*,[333] *Ramestes*, *Rhampses*, *Remphis*. Upon an Obelisk erected by this King in *Heliopolis*, and sent to *Rome* by the Emperor *Constantius*, was an inscription, interpreted by *Hermapion* an *Egyptian* Priest, expressing that the King was long lived, and Reigned over a great part of the earth: and *Strabo*,[334] an eye-witness, tells us, that in the monuments of the Kings of *Egypt*, above the *Memnonium* were inscriptions upon Obelisks, expressing the riches of the Kings, and their Reigning as far as *Scythia*, *Bactria*, *India* and *Ionia:* and *Tacitus*[335] tells us from an inscription seen at *Thebes* by *Cæsar Germanicus*, and interpreted to him by the *Egyptian* Priests, that this King *Ramesses* had an army of 700000 men, and Reigned over *Libya*, *Ethiopia*, *Media*, *Persia*, *Bactria*, *Scythia*, *Armenia*, *Cappadocia*, *Bithynia*, and *Lycia*; whence the Monarchy of *Assyria* was not yet risen. This King was very covetous, and a great collector of taxes, and one of the richest of all the Kings of *Egypt*, and built the western portico of the Temple of *Vulcan*.

Moeris inheriting the riches of *Ramesses*, built the northern portico of that Temple more sumptuously, and made the Lake of *Moeris*, with two great Pyramids of brick in the midst of it: and for preserving the division of *Egypt* into equal shares amongst the soldiers, this King wrote a book of surveying, which gave a beginning to Geometry. He is called also *Maris*, *Myris*, *Meres*, *Marres*, *Smarres*; and more corruptly, by changing [Greek: M] into [Greek: A, T, B, S, YCH, L], &c. *Ayres*, *Tyris*, *Byires*, *Soris*, *Uchoreus*, *Lachares*, *Labaris*, &c.

Diodorus[336] places *Uchoreus* between *Osymanduas* and *Myris*, that is between *Amenophis* and *Moeris*, and saith that he built *Memphis*, and fortified it to admiration with a mighty rampart of earth, and a broad and deep trench, which was filled with the water of the *Nile*, and made there a vast and deep Lake for receiving the water of the *Nile* in the time of its overflowing, and built palaces in the city; and that this place was so commodiously seated that most of the Kings who Reigned after him preferred it before *Thebes*, and removed the Court from thence to this place, so that the magnificence of *Thebes* from that time began to decrease, and that of *Memphis* to increase, 'till *Alexander* King of *Macedon* built *Alexandria*. These great works of *Uchoreus* and those of *Moeris* savour of one and the same genius, and were certainly done by one and the same King, distinguished into two by a corruption of the name as above; for this Lake of *Uchoreus* was certainly the same with that of *Moeris*.

After the example of the two brick Pyramids made by *Moeris*, the three next Kings, *Cheops*, *Cephren* and *Mycerinus* built the three great Pyramids at *Memphis*; and therefore Reigned in that city. *Cheops* shut up the Temples of the *Nomes*, and prohibited the worship of the Gods of *Egypt*, designing no doubt to have been worshipped himself after death: he is called also *Chembis*, *Chemmis*, *Chemnis*, *Phiops*, *Apathus*, *Apappus*, *Suphis*, *Saophis*, *Syphoas*, *Syphaosis*, *Soiphis*, *Syphuris*, *Anoiphis*, *Anoisis:* he built the biggest of the three great Pyramids which stand together; and his brother *Cephren* or *Cerpheres* built the second, and his son *Mycerinus* founded the third: this last King was celebrated for clemency and justice; he shut up the dead body of his daughter in a hollow ox, and caused her to be worshipped daily with odours: he is called also *Cheres*, *Cherinus*, *Bicheres*, *Moscheres*, *Mencheres*. He died before the third Pyramid was finished, and his sister and successor *Nitocris* finished it.

Then Reigned *Asychis*, who built the eastern portico of the Temple of *Vulcan* very splendidly, and among the small Pyramids a large Pyramid of brick, made of mud dug out of the Lake of *Moeris*: and these are the Kings who Reigned at *Memphis*, and spent their time in adorning that city, until the *Ethiopians* and the *Assyrians* and others revolted, and *Egypt* lost all her dominion abroad, and became again divided into several small Kingdoms.

One of those Kingdoms was I think at *Memphis*, under *Gnephactus*, and his son and successor *Bocchoris*. *Africanus* calls *Bocchoris* a *Saite*; but *Sais* at this time had other Kings: *Gnephactus*, otherwise called *Neochabis* and *Technatis*, cursed *Menes* for his luxury, and caused the curse to be entered in the Temple of *Jupiter* at *Thebes*; and therefore Reigned over *Thebais*: and *Bocchoris* sent in a wild bull upon the God *Mnevis* which was worshipped at *Heliopolis*. Another of those Kingdoms was at *Anysis*, or *Hanes*, *Isa.* xxx. 4. under its King *Anysis* or *Amosis*; a third was at *Sais*, under *Stephanathis*, *Nechepsos*, and *Nechus*; and a fourth was at *Tanis* or *Zoan*, under *Petubastes*, *Osorchon* and *Psammis*: and *Egypt* being weakened by this division, was invaded and conquered by the *Ethiopians* under *Sabacon*, who slew *Bocchoris* and *Nechus*, and made *Anysis* fly. The Olympiads began in the Reign of *Petubastes*, and the Æra of *Nabonassar* in the 22d year of the Reign of *Bocchoris*, according to *Africanus*; and therefore the division, of *Egypt* into many Kingdoms began before the Olympiads, but not above the length of two Kings Reigns before them.

After the study of Astronomy was set on foot for the use of navigation, and the *Egyptians* by the Heliacal Risings and Settings of the Stars had determined the length of the Solar year of 365 days, and by other observations had fixed the Solstices, and formed the fixt Stars into Asterisms, all which was done in the Reign of *Ammon*, *Sesac*, *Orus*, and *Memnon*; it may be presumed that they continued to observe the motions of the Planets; for they called them after the names of their Gods; and *Nechepsos* or *Nicepsos* King of *Sais*, by the assistance of *Petosiris* a Priest of *Egypt*, invented Astrology, grounding it upon the aspects of the Planets, and the qualities of the men and women to whom they were dedicated: and in the beginning of the Reign of *Nabonassar* King of *Babylon*, about which time the *Ethiopians* under *Sabacon* invaded *Egypt*, those *Egyptians* who fled from him to *Babylon*, carried thither the *Egyptian* year of 365 days, and the study of Astronomy and Astrology, and founded the Æra of *Nabonassar*, dating it from the first year of that King's Reign, which was the 22d year *of Bocchoris* as above, and beginning the year on the same day with the *Egyptians* for the sake of their calculations. So *Diodorus*[337]: *they say that the* Chaldæans *in* Babylon, *being Colonies of the* Egyptians, *became famous for Astrology, having learnt it from the Priests of* Egypt: and *Hestiæus*, who wrote an history of *Egypt*, speaking of a disaster of the invaded *Egyptians*, saith[338] that *the Priests who survived this disaster, taking with them the* Sacra *of* Jupiter Enyalius, *came to* Sennaar *in* Babylonia. From the 15th year of *Asa*, in which *Zerah* was beaten, and *Menes* or *Amenophis* began his Reign, to the beginning of the Æra of *Nabonassar*, were 200 years; and this interval of time allows room for about nine or ten Reigns of Kings, at about twenty years to a Reign one with another; and so many Reigns there were, according to the account set down above out of *Herodotus*; and therefore that account, as it is the oldest, and was received by *Herodotus* from the Priests of

Thebes, Memphis, and *Heliopolis,* three principal cities of *Egypt,* agrees also with the course of nature, and leaves no room for the Reigns of the many nameless Kings which we have omitted. These omitted Kings Reigned before *Moeris,* and by consequence at *Thebes;* for *Moeris* translated the seat of the Empire from *Thebes* to *Memphis:* they Reigned after *Ramesses;* for *Ramesses* was the son and successor of *Menes,* who Reigned next after the Gods. Now *Menes* built the body of the Temple of *Vulcan, Ramesses* the first portico, and *Moeris* the second portico thereof; but the *Egyptians,* for making their Gods and Kingdom look ancient, have inserted between the builders of the first and second portico of this Temple, three hundred and thirty Kings of *Thebes,* and supposed that these Kings Reigned eleven thousand years; as if any Temple could stand so long. This being a manifest fiction, we have corrected it, by omitting those interposed Kings, who did nothing, and placing *Moeris* the builder of the second portico, next after *Ramesses* the builder of the first.

In the Dynasties of *Manetho; Sevechus* is made the successor of *Sabacon,* being his son; and perhaps he is the *Sethon* of *Herodotus,* who became Priest of *Vulcan,* and neglected military discipline: for *Sabacon* is that *So* or *Sua* with whom *Hoshea* King of *Israel* conspired against the *Assyrians,* in the fourth year of *Hezekiah, Anno Nabonass.* 24. *Herodotus* tells us twice or thrice, that *Sabacon* after a long Reign of fifty years relinquished *Egypt* voluntarily, and that *Anysis* who fled from him, returned and Reigned again in the lower *Egypt* after him, or rather with him: and that *Sethon* Reigned after *Sabacon,* and went to *Pelusium* against the army of *Sennacherib,* and was relieved with a great multitude of mice, which eat the bow-strings of the *Assyrians;* in memory of which the statue of *Sethon,* seen by *Herodotus,*[339] was made with a Mouse in its hand. A Mouse was the *Egyptian* symbol of destruction, and the Mouse in the hand of *Sethon* signifies only that he overcame the *Assyrians* with a great destruction. The Scriptures inform us, that when *Sennacherib* invaded *Judæa* and besieged *Lachish* and *Libnah,* which was in the 14th year of *Hezekiah, Anno Nabonass.* 34. the King of *Judah* trusted upon *Pharaoh* King of *Egypt,* that is upon *Sethon,* and that *Tirhakah* King of *Ethiopia* came out also to fight against *Sennacherib,* 2 *King.* xviii. 21. & xix. 9. which makes it probable, that when *Sennacherib* heard of the Kings of *Egypt* and *Ethiopia* coming against him, he went from *Libnah* towards *Pelusium* to oppose them, and was there surprized and set upon in the night by them both, and routed with as great a slaughter as if the bow-strings of the *Assyrians* had been eaten by mice. Some think that the *Assyrians* were smitten by lightning, or by a fiery wind which sometimes comes from the southern parts of *Chaldæa.* After this victory *Tirhakah* succeeding *Sethon,* carried his arms westward through *Libya* and *Afric* to the mouth of the *Straits:* but *Herodotus* tells us, that the Priests of *Egypt* reckoned *Sethon* the last King of *Egypt,* who Reigned before the division of *Egypt* into twelve contemporary Kingdoms, and by consequence before the invasion of *Egypt* by the *Assyrians.*

For *Asserhadon* King of *Assyria,* in the 68th year of *Nabonassar,* after he had Reigned about thirty years over *Assyria,* invaded the Kingdom of *Babylon,* and then carried into captivity many people from *Babylon,* and *Cuthah,* and *Ava,* and

Hamath, and *Sepharvaim*, placing them in the Regions of *Samaria* and *Damascus*: and from thence they carried into *Babylonia* and *Assyria* the remainder of the people of *Israel* and *Syria*, which had been left there by *Tiglath-pileser*. This captivity was 65 years after the first year of *Ahaz*, Isa. vii. 1, 8. & 2. King. xv. 37. & xvi. 5. and by consequence in the twentieth year of *Manasseh*, Anno Nabonass. 69. and then *Tartan* was sent by *Asserhadon* with an army against *Ashdod* or *Azoth*, a town at that time subject to *Judæa*, 2 *Chron*. xxvi. 6. and took it, *Isa*. xx. 1: and this post being secured, the *Assyrians* beat the *Jews*, and captivated *Manasseh*, and subdued *Judæa*: and in these wars, *Isaiah* was saw'd asunder by the command of *Manasseh*, for prophesying against him. Then the *Assyrians* invaded and subdued *Egypt* and *Ethiopia*, and carried the *Egyptians* and *Ethiopians* into captivity, and thereby put an end to the Reign of the *Ethiopians* over *Egypt*, Isa. vii. 18. & viii. 7. & x. 11, 12, & xix. 23. & xx. 4. In this war the city *No-Ammon* or *Thebes*, which had hitherto continued in a flourishing condition, was miserably wasted and led into captivity, as is described by *Nahum*, chap. iii. ver. 8, 9, 10; for *Nahum* wrote after the last invasion of *Judæa* by the *Assyrians*, chap. i. ver. 15; and therefore describes this captivity as fresh in memory: and this and other following invasions of *Egypt* under *Nebuchadnezzar* and *Cambyses*, put an end to the glory of that city. *Asserhadon* Reigned over the *Egyptians* and *Ethiopians* three years, *Isa*. xx. 3, 4. that is until his death, which was in the year of *Nabonassar* 81, and therefore invaded *Egypt*, and put an end to the Reign of the *Ethiopians* over the *Egyptians*, in the year of *Nabonassar* 78; so that the *Ethiopians* under *Sabacon*, and his successors *Sethon* and *Tirhakah*, Reigned over *Egypt* about 80 years: *Herodotus* allots 50 years to *Sabacon*, and *Africanus* fourteen years to *Sethon*, and eighteen to *Tirhakah*.

The division of *Egypt* into more Kingdoms than one, both before and after the Reign of the *Ethiopians*, and the conquest of the *Egyptians* by *Asserhadon*, the prophet *Isaiah*[340] seems allude unto in these words: *I will set*, saith he, *the* Egyptians *against the* Egyptians, *and they shall fight every one against his brother, and every one against his neighbour, city against city, and Kingdom against Kingdom, and the Spirit of* Egypt *shall fail.—And the* Egyptians *will I give over into the hand of a cruel Lord* [viz. *Asserhadon*] *and a fierce King shall Reign over them.—Surely the Princes of* Zoan [Tanis] *are fools, the counsel of the wise Councellors of* Pharaoh *is become brutish: how long say ye unto* Pharaoh, *I am the son of the ancient Kings.—The Princes of* Zoan *are become fools: the Princes of* Noph [Memphis] *are deceived,—even they that were the stay of the tribes thereof.—In that day there shall be a high-way out of* Egypt *into* Assyria, *and the* Egyptians *shall serve the* Assyrians.

After the death of *Asserhadon*, *Egypt* remained subject to twelve contemporary Kings, who revolted from the *Assyrians*, and Reigned together fifteen years; including I think the three years of *Asserhadon*, because the *Egyptians* do not reckon him among their Kings. They[341] built the Labyrinth adjoining to the Lake of *Moeris* which was a very magnificent structure, with twelve Halls in it, for their Palaces: and then *Psammitichus*, who was one of the twelve, conquered all the rest. He built the last Portico of the Temple of *Vulcan*, founded by *Menes* about 260 years before, and Reigned 54 years, including the fifteen years of his Reign with the twelve Kings. Then Reigned *Nechaoh* or *Nechus*, 17 years; *Psammis* six years; *Vaphres, Apries, Eraphius,* or *Hophra,* 25 years; *Amasis* 44 years; and *Psammenitus* six months, according to *Herodotus. Egypt* was subdued by *Nebuchadnezzar* in the last year but one of *Hophra, Anno Nabonass.* 178, and remained in subjection to *Babylon* forty years, *Jer.* xliv. 30. & *Ezek.* xxix. 12, 13, 14, 17, 19. that is, almost all the Reign of *Amasis,* a plebeian set over *Egypt* by the conqueror: the forty years ended with the death of *Cyrus;* for he Reigned over *Egypt* and *Ethiopia,* according to *Xenophon.* At that time therefore those nations recovered their liberty; but after four or five years more they were invaded and conquered by *Cambyses, Anno Nabonass.* 223 or 224, and have almost ever since remained in servitude, as was predicted by the Prophets.

The Reigns of *Psammitichus, Nechus, Psammis, Apries, Amasis,* and *Psammenitus,* set down by *Herodotus,* amount unto 146½ years: and so many years there were from the 78th year of *Nabonassar,* in which the dominion of the *Ethiopians* over *Egypt* came to an end, unto the 224th year of *Nabonassar,* in which *Cambyses* invaded *Egypt,* and put an end to that Kingdom: which is an argument that *Herodotus* was circumspect and faithful in his narrations, and has given us a good account of the antiquities of *Egypt,* so far as the Priests of *Egypt* at *Thebes, Memphis,* and *Heliopolis,* and the *Carians* and *Ionians* inhabiting *Egypt,* were then able to inform him: for he consulted them all; and the *Cares* and *Ionians* had been in *Egypt* from the time of the Reign of the twelve contemporary Kings.

Pliny[342] tells us, that the *Egyptian* Obelisks were of a sort of stone dug near *Syene* in *Thebais,* and that the first Obelisk was made by *Mitres,* who Reigned in *Heliopolis;* that is, by *Mephres* the predecessor of *Misphragmuthosis;* and that afterwards other Kings made others: *Sochis,* that is *Sesochis,* or *Sesac,* four, each of 48 cubits in length; *Ramises,* that is *Ramesses,* two; *Smarres,* that is *Moeris,* one of 48 cubits in length; *Eraphius,* or *Hophra,* one of 48; and *Nectabis,* or *Nectenabis,* one of 80. *Mephres* therefore extended his dominion over all the upper *Egypt,* from *Syene* to *Heliopolis,* and after him, *Misphragmuthosis* and *Amosis,* Reigned *Ammon* and *Sesac,* who erected the first great Empire in the world: and these four, *Amosis, Ammon, Sesac,* and *Orus,* Reigned in the four ages of the great Gods of *Egypt;* and *Amenophis* was the *Menes* who Reigned next after them: he was Succeeded by *Ramesses,* and *Moeris,* and some time after by *Hophra.*

Diodorus[343] recites the same Kings of *Egypt* with *Herodotus,* but in a more confused order, and repeats some of them twice, or oftener, under various names, and omits others: his Kings are these; *Jupiter Ammon* and *Juno, Osiris* and *Isis, Horus, Menes, Busiris* I, *Busiris* II, *Osymanduas, Uchoreus, Myris, Sesoosis* I, *Sesoosis* II, *Amasis, Actisanes, Mendes* or *Marrus, Proteus, Remphis, Chembis, Cephren, Mycerinus* or *Cherinus, Gnephacthus, Bocchoris, Sabacon,* twelve contemporary Kings, *Psammitichus,* * * *Apries, Amasis.* Here I take *Sesoosis* I, and *Sesoosis* II, *Busiris* I, and *Busiris* II, to be the same Kings with *Osiris* and *Orus:* also *Osymanduas* to be the same with *Amenophis* or *Menes:* also *Amasis,* and *Actisanes,* an *Ethiopian* who conquered him, to be the same with *Anysis* and *Sabacon* in *Herodotus:* and *Uchoreus, Mendes, Marrus,* and *Myris,* to be only several names of one and the same King. Whence the catalogue of *Diodorus* will be reduced to this: *Jupiter*

Ammon and *Juno*; *Osiris, Busiris* or *Sesoosis*, and *Isis*; *Horus, Busiris* II, or *Sesoosis* II; *Menes*, or *Osymanduas*; *Proteus*; *Remphis* or *Ramesses*; *Uchoreus, Mendes, Marrus*, or *Myris*; *Chembis* or *Cheops*; *Cephren*; *Mycerinus*; * * *Gnephacthus*; *Bocchoris*; *Amasis*, or *Anysis*; *Actisanes*, or *Sabacon*; * twelve contemporary Kings; *Psammitichus*; * * *Apries*, *Amasis*: to which, if in their proper places you add *Nitocris, Asychis, Sethon, Nechus*, and *Psammis*, you will have the catalogue of *Herodotus*.

The Dynasties of *Manetho* and *Eratosthenes* seem to be filled with many such names of Kings as *Herodotus* omitted: when it shall be made appear that any of them Reigned in *Egypt* after the expulsion of the Shepherds, and were different from the Kings described above, they may be inserted in their proper places.

Egypt was conquered by the *Ethiopians* under *Sabacon*, about the beginning of the *Æra* of *Nabonassar*, or perhaps three or four years before, that is, about three hundred years before *Herodotus* wrote his history; and about eighty years after that conquest, it was conquered again by the *Assyrians* under *Asserhadon*: and the history of *Egypt* set down by *Herodotus* from the time of this last conquest, is right both as to the number, and order, and names of the Kings, and as to the length of their Reigns: and therein he is now followed by historians, being the only author who hath given us so good a history of *Egypt*, for that interval of time. If his history of the earlier times be less accurate, it was because the archives of *Egypt* had suffered much during the Reign of the *Ethiopians* and *Assyrians*: and it is not likely that the Priests of *Egypt*, who lived two or three hundred years after the days of *Herodotus*, could mend the matter: on the contrary, after *Cambyses* had carried away the records of *Egypt*, the Priests were daily feigning new Kings, to make their Gods and nation look ancient; as is manifest by comparing *Herodotus* with *Diodorus Siculus*, and both of them with what *Plato* relates out of the Poem of *Solon*: which Poem makes the wars of the great Gods of *Egypt* against the *Greeks*, to have been in the days of *Cecrops, Erechtheus* and *Erichthonius*, and a little before those of *Theseus*; these Gods at that time instituting Temples and Sacred Rites to themselves. I have therefore chosen to rely upon the stories related to *Herodotus* by the Priests of *Egypt* in those days, and corrected by the Poem of *Solon*, so as to make these Gods of *Egypt* no older than *Cecrops* and *Erechtheus*, and their successor *Menes* no older than *Theseus* and *Memnon*, and the Temple of *Vulcan* not above 280 years in building: rather than to correct *Herodotus* by *Manetho, Eratosthenes, Diodorus*, and others, who lived after the Priests of *Egypt* had corrupted their Antiquities much more than they had done in the days of *Herodotus*.

CHAP. III

Of the ASSYRIAN *Empire.*

AS the Gods or ancient Deified Kings and Princes of *Greece, Egypt,* and *Syria* of *Damascus,* have been made much ancienter than the truth, so have those of *Chaldæa* and *Assyria:* for *Diodorus*[344] tells us, that when *Alexander* the great was in *Asia,* the *Chaldæans* reckoned 473000 years since they first began to observe the Stars; and *Ctesias,* and the ancient *Greek* and *Latin* writers who copy from him, have made the *Assyrian* Empire as old as *Noah's* flood within 60 or 70 years, and tell us the names of all the Kings of *Assyria* downwards, from *Belus* and his feigned son *Ninus,* to *Sardanapalus* the last King of that Monarchy: but the names of his Kings, except two or three, have no affinity with the names of the *Assyrians* mentioned in Scripture; for the *Assyrians* were usually named after their Gods, *Bel* or *Pul; Chaddon, Hadon, Adon,* or *Adonis; Melech* or *Moloch; Atsur* or *Assur; Nebo; Nergal; Merodach:* as in these names, *Pul, Tiglath-Pul-Assur, Salman-Assur, Adra-Melech, Shar-Assur, Assur-Hadon, Sardanapalus* or *Assur-Hadon-Pul, Nabonassar* or *Nebo-Adon-Assur, Bel Adon, Chiniladon* or *Chen-El-Adon, Nebo-Pul-Assur, Nebo-Chaddon-Assur, Nebuzaradon* or *Nebo-Assur-Adon, Nergal-Assur, Nergal-Shar-Assur, Labo-Assur-dach, Sheseb-Assur, Beltes-Assur, Evil-Merodach, Shamgar-Nebo, Rabsaris* or *Rab-Assur, Nebo-Shashban, Mardocempad* or *Merodach-Empad.* Such were the *Assyrian* names; but those in *Ctesias* are of another sort, except *Sardanapalus,* whose name he had met with in *Herodotus.* He makes *Semiramis* as old as the first *Belus;* but *Herodotus* tells us, that she was but five Generations older than the mother of *Labynetus:* he represents that the city *Ninus* was founded by a man of the same name, and *Babylon* by *Semiramis;* whereas either *Nimrod* or *Assur* founded those and other cities, without giving his own name to any of them: he makes the *Assyrian* Empire continue about 1360 years, whereas *Herodotus* tells us that it lasted only 500 years, and the numbers of *Herodotus* concerning those ancient times are all of them too long: he makes *Nineveh* destroyed by the *Medes* and *Babylonians,* three hundred years before the Reign of *Astibares* and *Nebuchadnezzar* who destroyed it, and sets down the names of seven or eight feigned Kings of *Media,* between the destruction of *Nineveh* and the Reigns of *Astibares* and *Nebuchadnezzar,* as if the Empire of the *Medes,* erected upon the ruins of the *Assyrian* Empire, had lasted 300 years, whereas it lasted but 72: and the true Empire of the *Assyrians* described in Scripture, whose Kings were *Pul, Tiglath-pilesar, Shalmaneser, Sennacherib, Asserhadon,* &c. he mentions not, tho' much nearer to his own times; which shews that he was ignorant of the antiquities of the *Assyrians.* Yet something of truth there is in the bottom of some of his stories, as there uses to be in Romances; as, that *Nineveh* was destroyed by the *Medes* and *Babylonians;* that *Sardanapalus* was the last King of the *Assyrian* Empire; and that *Astibares* and *Astyages* were Kings of the *Medes:* but he has made all things too ancient, and out of vainglory taken too great a liberty in feigning names and stories to please his reader.

When the *Jews* were newly returned from the *Babylonian* captivity, they confessed their Sins in this manner, *Now therefore our God,* —— *let not all the trouble seem little before thee that hath come upon us, on our Kings, on our Princes, and on our Priests, and on our Prophets, and on our fathers, and on all thy people, since the time of the Kings of* Assyria, *unto this day;* Nehem. ix. 32. that is, since the time of the Kingdom of *Assyria*, or since the rise of that Empire; and therefore the *Assyrian* Empire arose when the Kings of *Assyria* began to afflict the inhabitants of *Palestine*; which was in the days of *Pul*: he and his successors afflicted *Israel*, and conquered the nations round about them; and upon the ruin of many small and ancient Kingdoms erected their Empire, conquering the *Medes* as well as other nations: but of these conquests *Ctesias* knew not a word, no not so much as the names of the conquerors, or that there was an *Assyrian* Empire then standing; for he supposes that the *Medes* Reigned at that time, and that the *Assyrian* Empire was at an end above 250 years before it began.

However we must allow that *Nimrod* founded a Kingdom at *Babylon*, and perhaps extended it into *Assyria*: but this Kingdom was but of small extent, if compared with the Empires which rose up afterwards; being only within the fertile plains of *Chaldæa*, *Chalonitis* and *Assyria*, watered by the *Tigris* and *Euphrates*: and if it had been greater, yet it was but of short continuance, it being the custom in those early ages for every father to divide his territories amongst his sons. So *Noah* was King of all the world, and *Cham* was King of all *Afric*, and *Japhet* of all *Europe* and *Asia minor*; but they left no standing Kingdoms. After the days of *Nimrod*, we hear no more of an *Assyrian* Empire 'till the days of *Pul*. The four Kings who in the days of *Abraham* invaded the southern coast of *Canaan* came from the countries where *Nimrod* had Reigned, and perhaps were some of his posterity who had shared his conquests. In the time of the Judges of *Israel*, *Mesopotamia* was under its own King, *Judg*. iii. 8. and the King of *Zobah* Reigned on both sides of the River *Euphrates* 'till *David* conquered him, 2 *Sam*. viii, and x. The Kingdoms of *Israel*, *Moab*, *Ammon*, *Edom*, *Philistia*, *Zidon*, *Damascus*, and *Hamath* the great, continued subject to other Lords than the *Assyrians* 'till the days of *Pul* and his successors; and so did the house of *Eden*, *Amos* i. 5. 2 *Kings* xix. 12. and *Haran* or *Carrhæ*, *Gen*. xii. 2 *Kings* xix. 12. and *Sepharvaim* in *Mesopotamia*, and *Calneh* near *Bagdad*, *Gen*. x. 10, *Isa*. x. 9, 2 *Kings* xvii. 31. *Sesac* and *Memnon* were great conquerors, and Reigned over *Chaldæa*, *Assyria*, and *Persia*, but in their histories there is not a word of any opposition made to them by an *Assyrian* Empire then standing: on the contrary, *Susiana*, *Media*, *Persia*, *Bactria*, *Armenia*, *Cappadocia*, &c. were conquered by them, and continued subject to the Kings of *Egypt* 'till after the long Reign of *Ramesses* the son of *Memnon*, as above.

Homer mentions *Bacchus* and *Memnon* Kings of *Egypt* and *Persia*, but knew nothing of an *Assyrian* Empire. *Jonah* prophesied when *Israel* was in affliction under the King of *Syria*, and this was in the latter part of the Reign of *Jehoahaz*, and first part of the Reign of *Joash*, Kings of *Israel*, and I think in the Reign of *Moeris* the successor of *Ramesses* King of *Egypt*, and about sixty years before the Reign of *Pul*; and *Nineveh* was then a city of large extent, but full of pastures for cattle, so that it contained but about 120000 persons. It was not yet grown so great and potent as not to be terrified at the preaching of *Jonah*, and to fear being invaded by its neighbours and ruined within forty days: it had some time before got free from the dominion of *Egypt*, and had got a King of its own; but its King was not yet called King of *Assyria*, but only King of *Nineveh, Jonah* iii. 6, 7. and his proclamation for a fast was not published in several nations, nor in all *Assyria*, but only in *Nineveh*, and perhaps in the villages thereof; but soon after, when the dominion of *Nineveh* was established at home, and exalted over all *Assyria* properly so called, and this Kingdom began to make war upon the neighbouring nations, its Kings were no longer called Kings of *Nineveh* but began to be called Kings of *Assyria*.

 Amos prophesied in the Reign of *Jeroboam* the Son of *Joash* King of *Israel*, soon after *Jeroboam* had subdued the Kingdoms of *Damascus* and *Hamath*, that is, about ten or twenty years before the Reign of *Pul*: and he[345] thus reproves *Israel* for being lifted up by those conquests; *Ye which rejoyce in a thing of nought, which say, have we not taken to us horns by our strength? But behold I will raise up against you a nation, O house of* Israel, *saith the Lord the God of Hosts, and they shall afflict you from the entring in of* Hamath *unto the river of the wilderness.* God here threatens to raise up a nation against *Israel*; but what nation he names not; that he conceals 'till the *Assyrians* should appear and discover it. In the prophesies of *Isaiah, Jeremiah, Ezekiel, Hosea, Micah, Nahum, Zephaniah* and *Zechariah*, which were written after the Monarchy grew up, it is openly named upon all occasions; but in this of *Amos* not once, tho' the captivity of *Israel* and *Syria* be the subject of the prophesy, and that of *Israel* be often threatned: he only saith in general that *Syria* should go into captivity unto *Kir*, and that *Israel*, notwithstanding her present greatness, should go into captivity beyond *Damascus*; and that God would raise up a nation to afflict them: meaning that he would raise up above them from a lower condition, a nation whom they yet feared not: for so the *Hebrew* word [Hebrew: mqm] signifies when applied to men, as in *Amos* v. 2. 1 *Sam.* xii. 11. *Psal.* cxiii. 7. *Jer.* x. 20. l. 32. *Hab.* i. 6. *Zech.* xi. 16. As *Amos* names not the *Assyrians*, at the writing of this prophecy they made no great figure in the world, but were to be raised up against *Israel*, and by consequence rose up in the days of *Pul* and his successors: for after *Jeroboam* had conquered *Damascus* and *Hamath*, his successor *Menahem* destroyed *Tiphsah* with its territories upon *Euphrates*, because they opened not to him: and therefore *Israel* continued in its greatness 'till *Pul*, probably grown formidable by some victories, caused *Menahem* to buy his peace. *Pul* therefore Reigning presently after the prophesy of *Amos*, and being the first upon record who began to fulfill it, may be justly reckoned the first conqueror and founder of this Empire. For *God stirred up the spirit of* Pul, *and the spirit of* Tiglath-pileser *King of* Assyria, 1 *Chron.* v. 20.

 The same Prophet *Amos*, in prophesying against *Israel*, threatned them in this manner, with what had lately befallen other Kingdoms: *Pass ye*,[346] saith he, *unto* Calneh *and see, and from thence go ye to* Hamath *the great, then go down to* Gath *of the* Philistims. *Be they better than these Kingdoms?* These Kingdoms were not yet conquered by the *Assyrians*, except that of *Calneh* or *Chalonitis* upon *Tigris*, between *Babylon* and *Nineveh*. *Gath* was newly vanquished[347] by *Uzziah* King of

Judah, and *Hamath*[348] by *Jeroboam* King of *Israel:* and while the Prophet, in threatning *Israel* with the *Assyrians,* instances in desolations made by other nations, and mentions no other conquest of the *Assyrians* than that of *Chalonitis* near *Nineveh;* it argues that the King of *Nineveh* was now beginning his conquests, and had not yet made any great progress in that vast career of victories, which we read of a few years after.

For about seven years after the captivity of the ten Tribes, when *Sennacherib* warred in *Syria,* which was in the 16th Olympiad, he[349] sent this message to the King of *Judah: Behold, thou hast heard that the Kings of* Assyria *have done to all Lands by destroying them utterly, and shalt thou be delivered? Have the Gods of the nations delivered them which the Gods of my fathers have destroyed, as* Gozan *and* Haran *and* Reseph, *and the children of* Eden *which were in* [the Kingdom of] Thelasar? *Where is the King of* Hamath, *and the King of* Arpad, *and the King of the city of* Sepharvaim, *and of* Hena *and* Ivah? And *Isaiah*[350] thus introduceth the King of *Assyria* boasting: *Are not my Princes altogether as Kings? Is not* Calno [or *Calneh*] *as* Carchemish? *Is not* Hamath *as* Arpad? *Is not* Samaria *as* Damascus? *As my hand hath found the Kingdoms of the Idols, and whose graven Images did excel them of* Jerusalem *and of* Samaria; *shall I not as I have done unto* Samaria *and her Idols, so do to* Jerusalem *and her Idols?* All this desolation is recited as fresh in memory to terrify the *Jews,* and these Kingdoms reach to the borders of *Assyria,* and to shew the largeness of the conquests they are called *all lands,* that is, all round about *Assyria.* It was the custom of the Kings of *Assyria,* for preventing the rebellion of people newly conquered, to captivate and transplant those of several countries into one another's lands, and intermix them variously: and thence it appears[351] that *Halah,* and *Habor,* and *Hara,* and *Gozan,* and the cities of the *Medes* into which *Galilee* and *Samaria* were transplanted; and *Kir* into which *Damascus* was transplanted; and *Babylon* and *Cuth* or the *Susanchites,* and *Hamath,* and *Ava,* and *Sepharvaim,* and the *Dinaites,* and the *Apharsachites,* and the *Tarpelites,* and the *Archevites,* and the *Dehavites,* and the *Elamites,* or *Persians,* part of all which nations were led captive by *Asserhadon* and his predecessors into *Samaria;* were all of them conquered by the *Assyrians* not long before.

In these conquests are involved on the west and south side of *Assyria,* the Kingdoms of *Mesopotamia,* whose royal seats were *Haran* or *Carrhæ,* and *Carchemish* or *Circutium,* and *Sepharvaim,* a city upon *Euphrates,* between *Babylon* and *Nineveh,* called *Sipparæ* by *Berosus, Abydenus,* and *Polyhistor,* and *Sipphara* by *Ptolomy;* and the Kingdoms of *Syria* seated at *Samaria, Damascus, Gath, Hamath, Arpad,* and *Reseph,* a city placed by *Ptolomy* near *Thapsacus:* on the south side and south east side were *Babylon* and *Calneh,* or *Calno,* a city which was founded by *Nimrod,* where *Bagdad* now stands, and gave the name of *Chalonitis* to a large region under its government; and *Thelasar* or *Talatha,* a city of the children of *Eden,* placed by *Ptolomy* in *Babylonia,* upon the common stream of *Tigris* and *Euphrates,* which was therefore the river of Paradise; and the *Archevites* at *Areca* or *Erech,* a city built by *Nimrod* on the east side of *Pasitigris,* between *Apamia* and the *Persian Gulph;* and the *Susanchites* at *Cuth,* or *Susa,* the metropolis of *Susiana:* on the east were *Elymais,* and some cities of the *Medes,* and *Kir,*[352] a city and large region of *Media,* between *Elymais,* and *Assyria,* called *Kirene* by the *Chaldee*

Paraphrast and *Latin* Interpreter, and *Carine* by *Ptolomy*: on the north-east were *Habor* or *Chaboras*, a mountainous region between *Assyria* and *Media*; and the *Apharsachites*, or men of *Arrapachitis*, a region originally peopled by *Arphaxad*, and placed by *Ptolomy* at the bottom of the mountains next *Assyria*: and on the north between *Assyria* and the *Gordiæan* mountains was *Halah* or *Chalach*, the metropolis of *Calachene*: and beyond these upon the *Caspian* sea was *Gozan*, called *Gauzania* by *Ptolomy*. Thus did these new conquests extend every way from the province of *Assyria* to considerable distances, and make up the great body of that Monarchy: so that well might the King of *Assyria* boast how his armies had destroyed all lands. All these nations[353] had 'till now their several Gods, and each accounted his God the God of his own land, and the defender thereof, against the Gods of the neighbouring countries, and particularly against the Gods of *Assyria*; and therefore they were never 'till now united under the *Assyrian* Monarchy, especially since the King of *Assyria* doth not boast of their being conquered by the *Assyrians* oftner than once: but these being small Kingdoms the King of *Assyria* easily overflowed them: *Know ye not*, saith[354] *Sennacherib* to the *Jews, what I and my fathers have done unto all the People of other lands?—for no God of any nation or kingdom was able to deliver his people out of mine hand, and out of the hand of my fathers: how much less shall your God deliver you out of mine hand?* He and his fathers therefore, *Pul, Tiglath-pileser*, and *Shalmaneser*, were great conquerors, and with a current of victories had newly overflowed all nations round about *Assyria*, and thereby set up this Monarchy.

Between the Reigns of *Jeroboam* II, and his son *Zachariah*, there was an interregnum of about ten or twelve years in the Kingdom of *Israel*: and the prophet *Hosea*[355] in the time of that interregnum, or soon after, mentions the King of *Assyria* by the name of *Jareb*, and another conqueror by the name of *Shalman*; and perhaps *Shalman* might be the first part of the name of *Shalmaneser*, and *Iareb*, or *Irib*, for it may be read both ways, the last part of the name of his successor *Sennacherib*: but whoever these Princes were, it appears not that they Reigned before *Shalmaneser*. *Pul*, or *Belus*, seems to be the first who carried on his conquests beyond the province of *Assyria*: he conquered *Calneh* with its territories in the Reign of *Jerboam*, *Amos* i. 1. vi. 2. & *Isa*. x. 8, 9. and invaded *Israel* in the Reign of *Menahem*, 2 *King*. xv. 19. but stayed not in the land, being bought off by *Menahem* for a thousand talents of silver: in his Reign therefore the Kingdom of *Assyria* was advanced on this side *Tigris*: for he was a great warrior, and seems to have conquered *Haran*, and *Carchemish*, and *Reseph*, and *Calneh*, and *Thelasar*, and might found or enlarge the city of *Babylon*, and build the old palace.

Herodotus tells us, that one of the gates of *Babylon* was[356] called the gate of *Semiramis*, and than she adorned the walls of the city, and the Temple of *Belus*, and that she[357] was five Generations older than *Nitocris* the mother of *Labynitus*, or *Nabonnedus*, the last King of *Babylon*; and therefore she flourished four Generations, or about 134 years, before *Nebuchadnezzar*, and by consequence in the Reign of *Tiglath-pileser* the successor of *Pul*: and the followers of *Ctesias* tell us, that she built *Babylon*, and was the widow of the son and successor of *Belus*, the founder of the *Assyrian* Empire; that is, the widow of one of the sons of *Pul*:

but[358] *Berosus* a *Chaldæan* blames the *Greeks* for ascribing the building of *Babylon* to *Semiramis*; and other authors ascribe the building of this city to *Belus* himself, that is to *Pul*; so *Curtius*[359] tells us; *Semiramis Babylonem condiderat, vel ut plerique credidere Belus, cujus regia ostenditur.* and *Abydenus*, who had his history from the ancient monuments of the *Chaldæans*, writes,[360] [Greek: Legetai Bêlon Babylôna teichei peribalein; tôi chronôi de tôi ikneumenôi aphanisthênai. teichisai de authis Nabouchodonosoron, to mechri tês Makedoniôn archês diameinan eon chalkopylon.] *'Tis reported that* Belus *compassed* Babylon *with a wall, which in time was abolished: and that* Nebuchadnezzar *afterwards built a new wall with brazen gates, which stood 'till the time of the* Macedonian *Empire:* and so *Dorotheas*[361] an ancient Poet of *Sidon*;

[Greek: Archaiê Babylôn, Tyriou Bêloio polisma.]
The ancient city Babylon *built by the* Tyrian Belus;

That is, by the *Syrian* or *Assyrian Belus*; the words *Tyrian*, *Syrian*, and *Assyrian*, being anciently used promiscuously for one another: *Herennius*[362] tells us, that it was built by the son of *Belus*; and this son might be *Nabonassar*. After the conquest of *Calneh*, *Thelasar*, and *Sippare*, *Belus* might seize *Chaldæa*, and begin to build *Babylon*, and leave it to his younger son: for all the Kings of *Babylon* in the Canon of *Ptolemy* are called *Assyrians*, and *Nabonassar* is the first of them: and *Nebuchadnezzar*[363] reckoned himself descended from *Belus*, that is, from the *Assyrian Pul*: and the building of *Babylon* is ascribed to the *Assyrians* by[364] *Isaiah*: *Behold*, saith he, *the land of the* Chaldeans: *This people was not 'till the* Assyrian *founded it for them that dwell in the wilderness,* [that is, for the *Arabians*.] *They set up the towers thereof, they raised up the palaces thereof.* From all this it seems therefore that *Pul* founded the walls and the palaces of *Babylon*, and left the city with the province of *Chaldæa* to his younger son *Nabonassar*; and that *Nabonassar* finished what his father began, and erected the Temple of *Jupiter Belus* to his father: and that *Semiramis* lived in those days, and was the Queen of *Nabonassar*, because one of the gates of *Babylon* was called the gate of *Semiramis*, as *Herodotus* affirms: but whether she continued to Reign there after her husband's death may be doubted.

Pul therefore was succeeded at *Nineveh* by his elder son *Tiglath-pileser*, at the same time that he left *Babylon* to his younger son *Nabonassar*. *Tiglath-pileser*, the second King of *Assyria*, warred in *Phoenicia*, and captivated *Galilee* with the two Tribes and an half, in the days of *Pekah* King of *Israel*, and placed them in *Halah*, and *Habor*, and *Hara*, and at the river *Gozan*, places lying on the western borders of *Media*, between *Assyria* and the *Caspian* sea, 2 *King.* xv. 29, &c: 1 *Chron.* v. 26. and about the fifth or sixth year of *Nabonassar*, he came to the assistance of the King of *Judah* against the Kings of *Israel* and *Syria*, and overthrew the Kingdom of *Syria*, which had been seated at *Damascus* ever since the days of King *David*, and carried away the *Syrians* to *Kir* in *Media*, as *Amos* had prophesied, and placed other nations in the regions of *Damascus*, 2 *King.* xv. 37, & xvi. 5, 9. *Amos* i. 5. *Joseph. Antiq.* l. 9. c. 13. whence it seems that the *Medes* were conquered before, and that the Empire of the *Assyrians* was now grown great: for *the God of* Israel *stirred up the spirit of* Pul *King of* Assyria, *and the spirit of* Tiglath-pileser *King of* Assyria to make war, 1 *Chron.* v. 26.

Shalmaneser or *Salmanasser,* called *Enemessar* by *Tobit,* invaded[365] all *Phoenicia,* took the city of *Samaria,* and captivated *Israel,* and placed them in *Chalach* and *Chabor,* by the river *Gozan,* and in the cities of the *Medes;* and *Hosea*[366] seems to say that he took *Arbela*: and his successor *Sennacherib* said that his fathers had conquered also *Gozan,* and *Haran* or *Carrhæ,* and *Reseph* or *Resen,* and the children of *Eden,* and *Arpad* or the *Aradii,* 2 *King.* xix. 12.

Sennacherib the son of *Shalmaneser* in the 14th year of *Hezekiah* invaded *Phoenicia,* and took several cities of *Judah,* and attempted *Egypt*; and *Sethon* or *Sevechus* King of *Egypt* and *Tirhakah* King of *Ethiopia* coming against him, he lost in one night 185000 men, as some say by a plague, or perhaps by lightning, or a fiery wind which blows sometimes in the neighbouring deserts, or rather by being surprised by *Sethon* and *Tirhakah*: for the *Egyptians* in memory of this action erected a statue to *Sethon,* holding in his hand a mouse, the *Egyptian* symbol of destruction. Upon this defeat *Sennacherib* returned in haste to *Nineveh,* and[367] his Kingdom became troubled, so that *Tobit* could not go into *Media,* the *Medes* I think at this time revolting: and he was soon after slain by two of his sons who fled into *Armenia,* and his son *Asserhadon* succeeded him. At that time did *Merodach Baladan* or *Mardocempad* King of *Babylon* send an embassy to *Hezekiah* King of *Judah.*

Asserhadon,[368] called *Sarchedon* by *Tobit, Asordan* by the LXX, and *Assaradin* in *Ptolomy*'s Canon, began his Reign at *Nineveh,* in the year of *Nabonassar* 42; and in the year 68 extended it over *Babylon*: then he carried the remainder of the *Samaritans* into captivity, and peopled *Samaria* with captives brought from several parts of his Kingdom, the *Dinaites,* the *Apharsachites,* the *Tarpelites,* the *Apharsites,* the *Archevites,* the *Babylonians,* the *Susanchites,* the *Dehavites,* the *Elamites, Ezra* iv. 2, 9. and therefore he Reigned over all these nations. *Pekah* and *Rezin* Kings of *Samaria* and *Damascus,* invaded *Judæa* in the first year of *Ahaz,* and within 65 years after, that is in the 21st year of *Manasseh, Anno Nabonass.* 69, *Samaria* by this captivity ceased to be a people, *Isa.* vii. 8. Then *Asserhadon* invaded *Judæa,* took *Azoth,* carried *Manasseh* captive to *Babylon,* and[369] captivated also *Egypt, Thebais,* and *Ethiopia* above *Thebais*: and by this war he seems to have put an end to the Reign of the *Ethiopians* over *Egypt,* in the year of *Nabonassar* 77 or 78.

In the Reign of *Sennacherib* and *Asserhadon,* the *Assyrian* Empire seems arrived at its greatness, being united under one Monarch, and containing *Assyria, Media, Apolloniatis, Susiana, Chaldæa, Mesopotamia, Cilicia, Syria, Phoenicia, Egypt, Ethiopia,* and part of *Arabia,* and reaching eastward into *Elymais,* and *Parætacene,* a province of the *Medes*: and if *Chalach* and *Chabor* be *Colchis* and *Iberia,* as some think, and as may seem probable from the circumcision used by those nations 'till the days of *Herodotus,* we are also to add these two Provinces, with the two *Armenia's, Pontus* and *Cappadocia,* as far as to the river *Halys*: for[370] *Herodotus* tells us, that the people of *Cappadocia* as far as to that river were called *Syrians* by the *Greeks,* both before and after the days or *Cyrus,* and that the *Assyrians* were also called *Syrians* by the *Greeks.*

Yet the *Medes* revolted from the *Assyrians* in the latter end of the Reign of *Sennacherib*, I think upon the slaughter of his army near *Egypt* and his flight to *Nineveh*: for at that time the estate of *Sennacherib* was troubled, so that *Tobit* could not go into *Media* as he had done before, *Tobit* i. 15. and some time after, *Tobit* advised his son to go into *Media* where he might expect peace, while *Nineveh*, according to the prophesy of *Jonah*, should be destroyed. *Ctesias* wrote that *Arbaces* a *Mede* being admitted to see *Sardanapalus* in his palace, and observing his voluptuous life amongst women, revolted with the *Medes*, and in conjunction with *Belesis* a *Babylonian* overcame him, and caused him to set fire to his palace and burn himself: but he is contradicted by other authors of better credit; for *Duris* and[371] many others wrote that *Arbaces* upon being admitted into the palace of *Sardanapalus*, and seeing his effeminate life, slew himself; and *Cleitarchus*, that *Sardanapalus* died of old age, after he had lost his dominion over *Syria*: he lost it by the revolt of the western nations; and *Herodotus*[372] tells us, that the *Medes* revolted first, and defended their liberty by force of arms against the *Assyrians*, without conquering them; and at their first revolting had no King, but after some time set up *Dejoces* over them, and built *Ecbatane* for his residence; and that *Dejoces* Reigned only over *Media*, and had a peaceable Reign of 54 years, but his son and successor *Phraortes* made war upon his neighbours, and conquered *Persia*; and that the *Syrians* also, and other western nations, at length revolted from the *Assyrians*, being encouraged thereunto by the example of the *Medes*; and that after the revolt of the western nations, *Phraortes* invaded the *Assyrians*, but was slain by them in that war, after he had Reigned twenty and two years. He was succeeded by *Astyages*.

Now *Asserhadon* seems to be the *Sardanapalus* who died of old age after the revolt of *Syria*, the name *Sardanapalus* being derived from *Asserhadon-Pul*. *Sardanapalus* was the[373] son of *Anacyndaraxis*, *Cyndaraxis*, or *Anabaxaris*, King of *Assyria*; and this name seems to have been corruptly written for *Sennacherib* the father of *Asserhadon*. *Sardanapalus* built *Tarsus* and *Anchiale* in one day, and therefore Reigned over *Cilicia*, before the revolt of the western nations: and if he be the same King with *Asserhadon*, he was succeeded by *Saosduchinus* in the year of *Nabonassar* 81; and by this revolution *Manasseh* was set at liberty to return home and fortify *Jerusalem*: and the *Egyptians* also, after the *Assyrians* had harrassed *Egypt* and *Ethiopia* three years, *Isa.* xx. 3, 4. were set at liberty, and continued under twelve contemporary Kings of their own nation, as above. The *Assyrians* invaded and conquered the *Egyptians* the first of the three years, and Reigned over them two years more: and these two years are the interregnum which *Africanus*, from *Manetho*, places next before the twelve Kings. The *Scythians* of *Touran* or *Turquestan* beyond the river *Oxus* began in those days to infest *Persia*, and by one of their inroads might give occasion to the revolt of the western nations.

In the year of *Nabonassar* 101, *Saosduchinus*, after a Reign of twenty years, was succeeded at *Babylon* by *Chyniladon*, and I think at *Nineveh* also, for I take *Chyniladon* to be that *Nabuchodonosor* who is mentioned in the book of *Judith*; for the history of that King suits best with these times: for there it is said that

Nabuchodonosor *King of the* Assyrians *who Reigned at* Nineveh, *that great city, in the twelfth year of his Reign made war upon* Arphaxad *King of the* Medes, and was then left alone by a defection of the auxiliary nations of *Cilicia, Damascus, Syria, Phoenicia, Moab, Ammon,* and *Egypt*; and without their help routed the army of the *Medes,* and slew *Arphaxad:* and *Arphaxad* is there said to have built *Ecbatane* and therefore was either *Dejoces,* or his son *Phraortes,* who might finish the city founded by his father: and *Herodotus*[374] tells the same story of a King of *Assyria,* who routed the *Medes,* and slew their King *Phraortes*; and saith that in the time of this war the *Assyrians* were left alone by the defection of the auxiliary nations, being otherwise in good condition: *Arphaxad* was therefore the *Phraortes* of *Herodotus,* and by consequence was slain near the beginning of the Reign of *Josiah:* for this war was made after *Phoenicia, Moab, Ammon,* and *Egypt* had been conquered and revolted, *Judith* i. 7, 8, 9. and by consequence after the Reign of *Asserhadon* who conquered them: it was made when the *Jews* were newly returned from captivity, *and the Vessels and Altar and Temple were sanctified after the profanation, Judith* iv. 3. that is soon after *Manasseh* their King had been carried captive to *Babylon* by *Asserhadon*; and upon the death of that King, or some other change in the *Assyrian* Empire, had been released with the *Jews* from that captivity, and had repaired the Altar, and restored the sacrifices and worship of the Temple, 2 *Chron.* xxxiii. 11, 16. In the *Greek* version of the book of *Judith,* chap. v. 18. it is said, that *the Temple of God was cast to the ground*; but this is not said in *Jerom's* version; and in the *Greek* version, chap. iv. 3, and chap. xvi. 20, it is said, that *the vessels, and the altar, and the house were sanctified after the prophanation,* and in both versions, chap. iv. 11, the Temple is represented standing.

After this war *Nabuchodonosor* King of *Assyria,* in the 13th year of his Reign, according to the version of *Jerom,* sent his captain *Holofernes* with a great army to avenge himself on all the west country; because they had disobeyed his commandment: and *Holofernes* went forth with an army of 12000 horse, and 120000 foot of *Assyrians, Medes* and *Persians,* and reduced *Cilicia, Mesopotamia,* and *Syria,* and *Damascus,* and part of *Arabia,* and *Ammon,* and *Edom,* and *Madian,* and then came against *Judæa:* and this was done when the government was in the hands of the High-Priest and Antients of *Israel, Judith* iv. 8. and vii. 23. and by consequence not in the Reign of *Manasseh* or *Amon,* but when *Josiah* was a child. In times of prosperity the children of *Israel* were apt to go after false Gods, and in times of affliction to repent and turn to the Lord. So *Manasseh* a very wicked King, being captivated by the *Assyrians,* repented; and being released from captivity restored the worship of the true God: So when we are told that *Josiah in the eighth year of his Reign, while he was yet young, began to seek after the God of* David *his father, and in the twelfth year of his Reign began to purge* Judah *and* Jerusalem *from Idolatry, and to destroy the High Places, and Groves, and Altars and Images of Baalim,* 2 *Chron.* xxxiv. 3. we may understand that these acts of religion were occasioned by impending dangers, and escapes from danger. When *Holofernes* came against the western nations, and spoiled them, then were the *Jews* terrified, and they fortified *Judæa,* and *cryed unto God with great fervency, and humbled themselves in sackcloth, and put ashes on their heads, and cried unto the God of* Israel *that he would not give their wives and their children and cities for a prey, and the Temple for a profanation: and the High-priest, and all the Priests put on sackcloth and ashes, and offered daily burnt offerings with vows and free gifts of the people, Judith* iv. and then began *Josiah* to seek after the God of his father *David*: and after *Judith* had slain *Holofernes*, and the *Assyrians* were fled, and the *Jews* who pursued them were returned to *Jerusalem, they worshipped the Lord, and offered burnt offerings and gifts, and continued feasting before the sanctuary for the space of three months, Judith* xvi. 18, and then did *Josiah* purge *Judah* and *Jerusalem* from Idolatry. Whence it seems to me that the eighth year of *Josiah* fell in with the fourteenth or fifteenth of *Nabuchodonosor*, and that the twelfth year of *Nabuchodonosor*, in which *Phraortes* was slain, was the fifth or sixth of *Josiah*. *Phraortes* Reigned 22 years according to *Herodotus*, and therefore succeeded his father *Dejoces* about the 40th year of *Manasseh, Anno Nabonass.* 89, and was slain by the *Assyrians*, and succeeded by *Astyages, Anno Nabonass.* 111. *Dejoces* Reigned 53 years according to *Herodotus*, and these years began in the 16th year of *Hezekiah*; which makes it probable that the *Medes* dated them from the time of their revolt: and according to all this reckoning, the Reign of *Nabuchodonosor* fell in with that of *Chyniladon*; which makes it probable that they were but two names of one and the same King.

Soon after the death of *Phraortes*[375] the *Scythians* under *Madyes* or *Medus* invaded *Media*, and beat the *Medes* in battle, *Anno Nabonass.* 113, and went thence towards *Egypt*, but were met in *Phoenicia* by *Psammitichus* and bought off, and returning Reigned over a great part of *Asia*: but in the end of about 28 years were expelled; many of their Princes and commanders being slain in a feast by the *Medes* under the conduct of *Cyaxeres*, the successor of *Astyages*, just before the destruction of *Nineveh*, and the rest being soon after forced to retire.

In the year of *Nabonassar* 123,[376] *Nabopolassar* the commander of the forces of *Chyniladon* the King of *Assyria* in *Chaldæa* revolted from him, and became King of *Babylon*; and *Chyniladon* was either then, or soon after, succeeded at *Nineveh* by the last King of *Assyria*, called *Sarac* by *Polyhistor*: and at length *Nebuchadnezzar*, the son of *Nabopolassar*, married *Amyite* the daughter of *Astyages* and sister of *Cyaxeres*; and by this marriage the two families having contracted affinity, they conspired against the *Assyrians*; and *Nabopolasser* being now grown old, and *Astyages* being dead, their sons *Nebuchadnezzar* and *Cyaxeres* led the armies of the two nations against *Nineveh*, slew *Sarac*, destroyed the city, and shared the Kingdom of the *Assyrians*. This victory the *Jews* refer to the *Chaldæans*; the *Greeks* to the *Medes*; *Tobit, Polyhistor, Josephus*, and *Ctesias* to both. It gave a beginning to the great successes of *Nebuchadnezzar* and *Cyaxeres*, and laid the foundation of the two collateral Empires of the *Babylonians* and *Medes*; these being branches of the *Assyrian* Empire: and thence the time of the fall of the *Assyrian* Empire is determined, the conquerors being then in their youth. In the Reign of *Josiah*, when *Zephaniah* prophesied, *Nineveh* and the Kingdom of *Assyria* were standing, and their fall was predicted by that Prophet, *Zeph.* i. 1, and ii. 13. and in the end of his Reign *Pharaoh Nechoh* King of *Egypt*, the successor of *Psammitichus*, went up against the King of *Assyria* to the river *Euphrates*, to fight against *Carchemish* or *Circutium*, and in his way thither slew *Josiah*, 2 *Kings* xxiii. 29.

2 *Chron.* xxxv. 20. and therefore the last King of *Assyria* was not yet slain. But in the third and fourth year of *Jehoiakim* the successor of *Josiah*, the two conquerors having taken *Nineveh* and finished their war in *Assyria*, prosecuted their conquests westward, and leading their forces against the King of *Egypt*, as an invader of their right of conquest, they beat him at *Carchemish*, and[377] took from him whatever he had newly taken from the *Assyrians*: and therefore we cannot err above a year or two, if we refer the destruction of *Nineveh*, and fall of the *Assyrian* Empire, to the second year of *Jehoiakim*, *Anno Nabonass.* 140. The name of the last King *Sarac* might perhaps be contracted from *Sarchedon*, as this name was from *Asserhadon*, *Asserhadon-Pul*, or *Sardanapalus*.

While the *Assyrians* Reigned at *Nineveh*, *Persia* was divided into several Kingdoms; and amongst others there was a Kingdom of *Elam*, which flourished in the days of *Hezekiah*, *Manasseh*, *Josiah*, and *Jehoiakim* Kings of *Judah*, and fell in the days of *Zedekiah*, *Jer.* xxv. 25, and xlix. 34, and *Ezek.* xxxii. 24. This Kingdom seems to have been potent, and to have had wars with the King of *Touran* or *Scythia* beyond the river *Oxus* with various success, and at length to have been subdued by the *Medes* and *Babylonians*, or one of them. For while *Nebuchadnezzar* warred in the west, *Cyaxeres* recovered the *Assyrian* provinces of *Armenia*, *Pontus*, and *Cappadocia*, and then they went eastward against the provinces of *Persia* and *Parthia*. Whether the *Pischdadians*, whom the *Persians* reckon to have been their oldest Kings, were Kings of the Kingdom of *Elam*, or of that of the *Assyrians*, and whether *Elam* was conquered by the *Assyrians* at the same time with *Babylonia* and *Susiana* in the Reign of *Asserhadon*, and soon after revolted, I leave to be examined.

CHAP. IV

Of the two Contemporary Empires of the Babylonians *and* Medes.

BY the fall of the *Assyrian* Empire the Kingdoms of the *Babylonians* and *Medes* grew great and potent. The Reigns of the Kings of *Babylon* are stated in *Ptolemy's* Canon: for understanding of which you are to note that every King's Reign in that Canon began with the last *Thoth* of his predecessor's Reign, as I gather by comparing the Reigns of the *Roman* Emperors in that Canon with their Reigns recorded in years, months, and days, by other Authors: whence it appears from that Canon that *Asserhadon* died in the year of *Nabonassar* 81, *Saosduchinus* his successor in the year 101, *Chyniladon* in the year 123, *Nabopolassar* in the year 144, and *Nebuchadnezzar* in the year 187. All these Kings, and some others mentioned in the Canon, Reigned successively over *Babylon*, and this last King died in the 37th year of *Jechoniah*'s captivity, 2 *Kings* xxv. 27. and therefore *Jechoniah* was captivated in the 150th year of *Nabonassar*.

This captivity was in the eighth year of *Nebuchadnezzar*'s Reign, 2 *Kings* xxiv. 12. and eleventh of *Jehoiakim*'s: for the first year of *Nebuchadnezzar*'s Reign was the fourth of *Jehoiakim*'s, *Jer.* xxv. i. and *Jehoiakim* Reigned eleven years before this captivity, 2 *Kings* xxiii. 36. 2 *Chron.* xxxvi. 5, and *Jechoniah* three months, ending with the captivity; and the tenth year of *Jechoniah*'s captivity, was the eighteenth year of *Nebuchadnezzar*'s Reign, *Jer.* xxxii. 1. and the eleventh year of *Zedekiah*, in which *Jerusalem* was taken, was the nineteenth of *Nebuchadnezzar*, *Jer.* lii. 5, 12. and therefore *Nebuchadnezzar* began his Reign in the year of *Nabonassar* 142, that is, two years before the death of his father *Nabopolassar*, he being then made King by his father; and *Jehoiakim* succeeded his father *Josiah* in the year of *Nabonassar* 139; and *Jerusalem* was taken and the Temple burnt in the year of *Nabonassar* 160, about twenty years after the destruction of *Nineveh*.

The Reign of *Darius Hystaspis* over *Persia*, by the Canon and the consent of all Chronologers, and by several Eclipses of the Moon, began in spring in the year of *Nabonassar* 227: and *in the fourth year of King* Darius, *in the 4th day of the ninth month, which is the month* Chisleu, *when the* Jews *had sent unto the house of God, saying, should I weep in the fifth month as I have done these so many years? the word of the Lord came unto* Zechariah, *saying, speak to all the people of the Land, and to the Priests, saying; when ye fasted and mourned in the fifth and seventh month even those seventy years, did ye at all fast unto me?* Zech. vii. Count backwards those seventy years in which they fasted in the fifth month for the burning of the Temple, and in the seventh for the death of *Gedaliah*; and the burning of the Temple and death of *Gedaliah*, will fall upon the fifth and seventh *Jewish* months, in the year of *Nabonassar* 160, as above.

As the *Chaldæan* Astronomers counted the Reigns of their Kings by the years of *Nabonassar*, beginning with the month *Thoth*, so the *Jews*, as their Authors tell us, counted the Reigns of theirs by the years of *Moses*, beginning every year with the month *Nisan*: for if any King began his Reign a few days before this month began, it was reckoned to him for a whole year, and the beginning of this month was accounted the beginning of the second year of his

Reign; and according to this reckoning the first year of *Jehojakim* began with the month *Nisan*, *Anno Nabonass.* 139, tho' his Reign might not really begin 'till five or six months after; and the fourth year of *Jehoiakim*, and first of *Nebuchadnezzar*, according to the reckoning of the *Jews*, began with the month *Nisan*, *Anno Nabonass.* 142; and the first year of *Zedekiah* and of *Jeconiah*'s captivity, and ninth year of *Nebuchadnezzar*, began with the month *Nisan*, in the year of *Nabonassar* 150; and the tenth year of *Zedekiah*, and 18th of *Nebuchadnezzar*, began with the month *Nisan* in the year of *Nabonassar* 159. Now in the ninth year of *Zedekiah*, *Nebuchadnezzar* invaded *Judæa* and the cities thereof and in the tenth month of that year, and tenth day of the month, he and his host besieged *Jerusalem*, 2 *Kings* xxv. 1. *Jer.* xxxiv. 1, xxxix. 1, and lii. 4. From this time to the tenth month in the second year of *Darius* are just seventy years, and accordingly, *upon the 24th day of the eleventh month of the second year of* Darius, *the word of the Lord came unto* Zechariah,—*and the Angel of the Lord said, Oh Lord of Hosts, how long wilt thou not have mercy on* Jerusalem, *and on the cities of* Judah, *against which thou hast had indignation, these threescore and ten years,* Zech. i. 7, 12. So then the ninth year of *Zedekiah*, in which this indignation against *Jerusalem* and the cities of *Judah* began, commenced with the month *Nisan* in the year of *Nabonassar* 158; and the eleventh year of *Zedekiah*, and nineteenth of *Nebuchadnezzar*, in which the city was taken and the Temple burnt, commenced with the month *Nisan* in the year of *Nabonassar* 160, as above.

By all these characters the years of *Jehoiakim*, *Zedekiah*, and *Nebuchadnezzar*, seem to be sufficiently determined, and thereby the Chronology of the *Jews* in the Old Testament is connected with that of later times: for between the death of *Solomon* and the ninth year of *Zedekiah* wherein *Nebuchadnezzar* invaded *Judæa*, and began the Siege of *Jerusalem*, there were 390 years, as is manifest both by the prophesy of *Ezekiel*, chap. iv, and by summing up the years of the Kings of *Judah*; and from the ninth year of *Zedekiah* inclusively to the vulgar *Æra* of *Christ*, there were 590 years: and both these numbers, with half the Reign of *Solomon*, make up a thousand years.

In the[378] end of the Reign of *Josiah*, *Anno Nabonass.* 139, *Pharaoh Nechoh*, the successor of *Psammitichus*, came with a great army out of *Egypt* against the King of *Assyria*, and being denied passage through *Judæa*, beat the *Jews* at *Megiddo* or *Magdolus* before *Egypt*, slew *Josiah* their King, marched to *Carchemish* or *Circutium*, a town of *Mesopotamia* upon *Euphrates*, and took it, possest himself of the cities of *Syria*, sent for *Jehoahaz* the new King of *Judah* to *Riblah* or *Antioch*, deposed him there, made *Jehojakim* King in the room of *Josiah*, and put the Kingdom of *Judah* to tribute: but the King of *Assyria* being in the mean time besieged and subdued, and *Nineveh* destroyed by *Assuerus* King of the *Medes*, and *Nebuchadnezzar* King of *Babylon*, and the conquerors being thereby entitled to the countries belonging to the King of *Assyria*, they led their victorious armies against the King of *Egypt* who had seized part of them. For *Nebuchadnezzar*, assisted[379] by *Astibares*, that is, by *Astivares*, *Assuerus*, *Acksweres*, *Axeres*, or *Cy-Axeres*, King of the *Medes*, in the[380] third year of *Jehoiakim*, came with an army of *Babylonians*, *Medes*, *Syrians*, *Moabites* and *Ammonites*, to the number of 10000 chariots, and 180000 foot, and 120000 horse, and laid waste *Samaria, Galilee, Scythopolis*, and the *Jews* in *Galaaditis*, and besieged *Jerusalem*, and took King *Jehoiakim* alive, and[381] bound him in chains for a time, and carried to *Babylon Daniel* and others of the people, and part of what Gold and Silver and Brass they found in the Temple: and in[382] the fourth year of *Jehoiakim*, which was the twentieth of *Nabopolassar*, they routed the army of *Pharaoh Nechoh* at *Carchemish*, and by pursuing the war took from the King of *Egypt* whatever pertained to him from the river of *Egypt* to the river of *Euphrates*. This King of *Egypt* is called by *Berosus*,[383] the *Satrapa* of *Egypt, Coele-Syria*, and *Phoenicia*; and this victory over him put an end to his Reign in *Coele-Syria* and *Phoenicia*, which he had newly invaded, and gave a beginning to the Reign of *Nebuchadnezzar* there: and by the conquests over *Assyria* and *Syria* the small Kingdom of *Babylon* was erected into a potent Empire.

Whilst *Nebuchadnezzar* was acting in *Syria*,[384] his father *Nabopolassar* died, having Reigned 21 years; and *Nebuchadnezzar* upon the news thereof, having ordered his affairs in *Syria* returned to *Babylon*, leaving the captives and his army with his servants to follow him: and from henceforward he applied himself sometimes to war, conquering *Sittacene, Susiana, Arabia, Edom, Egypt*, and some other countries; and sometimes to peace, adorning the Temple of *Belus* with the spoils that he had taken; and the city of *Babylon* with magnificent walls and gates, and stately palaces and pensile gardens, as *Berosus* relates; and amongst other things he cut the new rivers *Naarmalcha* and *Pallacopas* above *Babylon* and built the city of *Teredon*.

Judæa was now in servitude under the King of *Babylon*, being invaded and subdued in the third and fourth years of *Jehoiakim, and* Jehoiakim *served him three years, and then turned and rebelled,* 2 *King.* xxiv. 1. While *Nebuchadnezzar* and the army of the *Chaldæans* continued in *Syria, Jehojakim* was under compulsion; after they returned to *Babylon, Jehojakim* continued in fidelity three years, that is, during the 7th, 8th and 9th years of his Reign, and rebelled in the tenth: whereupon in the return or end of the year, that is in spring, he sent[385] and besieged *Jerusalem*, captivated *Jeconiah* the son and successor of *Jehoiakim*, spoiled the Temple, and carried away to *Babylon* the Princes, craftsmen, smiths, and all that were fit for war: and, when none remained but the poorest of the people, made[386] *Zedekiah* their King, and bound him upon oath to serve the King of *Babylon*: this was in spring in the end of the eleventh year of *Jehoiakim*, and beginning of the year of *Nabonassar* 150.

Zedekiah notwithstanding his oath[387] revolted, and made a covenant with the King of *Egypt*, and therefore *Nebuchadnezzar* in the ninth year of *Zedekiah*[388] invaded *Judæa* and the cities thereof, and in the tenth *Jewish* month of that year besieged *Jerusalem* again, and in the eleventh year of *Zedekiah*, in the 4th and 5th months, after a siege of one year and an half, took and burnt the City and Temple.

Nebuchadnezzar after he was made King by his father Reigned over *Phoenicia* and *Coele-Syria* 45 years, and[389] after the death of his father 43 years, and[390] after the captivity of *Jeconiah* 37; and then was succeeded by his son *Evilmerodach*, called *Iluarodamus* in *Ptolemy*'s Canon. *Jerome*[391] tells us, that *Evilmerodach* Reigned seven years in his father's life-time, while his father did eat grass with oxen, and after his father's restoration was put in prison with *Jeconiah* King of *Judah* 'till the death of his father, and then succeeded in the Throne. In the fifth year of *Jeconiah*'s captivity, *Belshazzar* was next in dignity to his father *Nebuchadnezzar*, and was designed to be his successor, *Baruch* i. 2, 10, 11, 12, 14, and therefore *Evilmerodach* was even then in disgrace. Upon his coming to the Throne[392] he brought his friend and companion *Jeconiah* out of prison on the 27th day of the twelfth month; so that *Nebuchadnezzar* died in the end of winter, *Anno Nabonass.* 187.

Evilmerodach Reigned two years after his father's death, and for his lust and evil manners was slain by his sister's husband *Neriglissar*, or *Nergalassar*, *Nabonass.* 189, according to the Canon.

Neriglissar, in the name of his young son *Labosordachus*, or *Laboasserdach*, the grand-child of *Nebuchadnezzar* by his daughter, Reigned four years, according to the Canon and *Berosus*, including the short Reign of *Laboasserdach* alone: for *Laboasserdach*, according to *Berosus* and *Josephus*, Reigned nine months after the death of his father, and then for his evil manners was slain in a feast, by the conspiracy of his friends with *Nabonnedus* a *Babylonian*, to whom by consent they gave the Kingdom: but these nine months are not reckoned apart in the Canon.

Nabonnedus or *Nabonadius*, according to the Canon, began his Reign in the year of *Nabonassar* 193, Reigned seventeen years, and ended his Reign in the year of *Nabonassar* 210, being then vanquished and *Babylon* taken by *Cyrus*.

Herodotus calls this last King of *Babylon*, *Labynitus*, and says that he was the son of a former *Labynitus*, and of *Nitocris* an eminent Queen of *Babylon*: by the father he seems to understand that *Labynitus*, who, as he tells us, was King of *Babylon* when the great Eclipse of the Sun predicted by *Thales* put an end to the five years war between the *Medes* and *Lydians*; and this was the great *Nebuchadnezzar*. *Daniel*[393] calls the last King of *Babylon*, *Belshazzar*, and saith that *Nebuchadnezzar* was his father: and *Josephus* tells us,[394] that the last King of *Babylon* was called *Naboandel* by the *Babylonians*, and Reigned seventeen years; and therefore he is the same King of *Babylon* with *Nabonnedus* or *Labynitus*; and this is more agreeable to sacred writ than to make *Nabonnedus* a stranger to the royal line: for all *nations were to serve* Nebuchadnezzar *and his posterity, till the very time of his land should come, and many nations should serve themselves of him*, Jer. xxvii. 7. *Belshazzar* was born and lived in honour before the fifth year of *Jeconiah*'s captivity, which was the eleventh year of *Nebuchadnezzar*'s Reign; and therefore he was above 34 years old at the death of *Evilmerodach*, and so could be no other King than *Nabonnedus*: for *Laboasserdach* the grandson of *Nebuchadnezzar* was a child when he Reigned.

Herodotus[395] tells us, that there were two famous Queens of *Babylon*, *Semiramis* and *Nitocris*; and that the latter was more skilful: she observing that the Kingdom of the *Medes*, having subdued many cities, and among others *Nineveh*, was become great and potent, intercepted and fortified the passages out of *Media* into *Babylonia*; and the river which before was straight, she made crooked with great windings, that it might be more sedate and less apt to overflow: and on the side of the river above *Babylon*, in imitation of the Lake of *Moeris* in *Egypt*, she dug a Lake every way forty miles broad, to receive the water of the river, and keep it for watering the land. She built also a bridge over the river in the middle of *Babylon*, turning the stream into the Lake 'till the bridge was built. *Philostratus* saith,[396] that she made a bridge under the river two fathoms broad, meaning an arched vault over which the river flowed, and under which they might walk cross the river: he calls her [Greek: Mêdeia], a *Mede*.

Berosus tells us, that *Nebuchadnezzar* built a pensile garden upon arches, because his wife was a *Mede* and delighted in mountainous prospects, such as abounded in *Media*, but were wanting in *Babylonia*: she was *Amyite* the daughter of *Astyages*, and sister of *Cyaxeres*, Kings of the *Medes. Nebuchadnezzar* married her upon a league between the two families against the King of *Assyria*: but *Nitocris* might be another woman who in the Reign of her son *Labynitus*, a voluptuous and vicious King, took care of his affairs, and for securing his Kingdom against the *Medes*, did the works above mentioned. This is that Queen mentioned in *Daniel*, chap. v. ver. 10.

Josephus[397] relates out of the *Tyrian* records, that in the Reign of *Ithobalus* King of *Tyre*, that city was besieged by *Nebuchadnezzar* thirteen years together: in the end of that siege *Ithobalus* their King was slain, *Ezek.* xxviii. 8, 9, 10. and after him, according to the *Tyrian* records, Reigned *Baal* ten years, *Ecnibalus* and *Chelbes* one year, *Abbarus* three months, *Mytgonus* and *Gerastratus* six years, *Balatorus* one year, *Merbalus* four years, and *Iromus* twenty years: and in the fourteenth year of *Iromus*, say the *Tyrian* records, the Reign of *Cyrus* began in *Babylonia*; therefore the siege of *Tyre* began 48 years and some months before the Reign of *Cyrus* in *Babylonia*: it began when *Jerusalem* had been newly taken and burnt, with the Temple, *Ezek.* xxvi and by consequence after the eleventh year of *Jeconiah*'s captivity, or 160th year of *Nabonassar*, and therefore the Reign of *Cyrus* in *Babylonia* began after the year of *Nabonassar* 208: it ended before the eight and twentieth year of *Jeconiah*'s captivity, or 176th year of *Nabonassar*, *Ezek.* xxix. 17. and therefore the Reign of *Cyrus* in *Babylonia* began before the year of *Nabonassar* 211. By this argument the first year of *Cyrus* in *Babylonia* was one of the two intermediate years 209, 210. *Cyrus* invaded *Babylonia* in the year of *Nabonassar* 209;[398] *Babylon* held out, and the next year was taken, *Jer.* li. 39, 57. by diverting the river *Euphrates*, and entring the city through the emptied channel, and by consequence after midsummer: for the river, by the melting of the snow in *Armenia*, overflows yearly in the beginning of summer, but in the heat of dimmer grows low.[399] *And that night was the King of* Babylon *slain, and* Darius *the* Mede, *or King of the* Medes, *took the Kingdom being about threescore and two years old*: so then *Babylon* was taken a month or two after the summer solstice, in the year of *Nabonassar* 210; as the Canon also represents.

The Kings of the *Medes* before *Cyrus* were *Dejoces*, *Phraortes*, *Astyages*, *Cyaxeres*, or *Cyaxares*, and *Darius*: the three first Reigned before the Kingdom grew great, the two last were great conquerors, and erected the Empire; for *Æschylus*, who flourished in the Reigns of *Darius Hystaspis*, and *Xerxes*, and died in the 76th

Olympiad, introduces *Darius* thus complaining of those who persuaded his son *Xerxes* to invade *Greece*;[400]

[Greek: Toigar sphin ergon estin exeirgasmenon]
[Greek: Megiston, aieimnêston hoion oudepô,]
[Greek: To d' asty Sousôn exekeinôsen peson;]
[Greek: Ex houte timên Zeus anax tênd' ôpasen]
[Greek: En andra pasês Asiados mêlotrophou]
[Greek: Tagein, echonta skêptron euthyntêrion]
[Greek: Mêdos gar ên ho prôtos hêgemôn stratou;]
[Greek: Allos d' ekeinou pais tod' ergon ênyse;]
[Greek: Phrenes gar autou thymon oiakostrophoun.]
[Greek: Tritos d' ap' autou Kyros, eudaimôn anêr,] &c.

They have done a work
The greatest, and most memorable, such as never happen'd,
For it has emptied the falling Sufa:
From the time that King Jupiter *granted this honour,*
That one man should Reign over all fruitful Asia,
Having the imperial Scepter.
For he that first led the Army was a Mede;
The next, who was his son, finisht the work,
For prudence directed his soul;
The third was Cyrus, *a happy man,* &c.

The Poet here attributes the founding of the *Medo-Persian* Empire to the two immediate predecessors of *Cyrus*, the first of which was a *Mede*, and the second was his son: the second was *Darius* the *Mede*, the immediate predecessor of *Cyrus*, according to *Daniel*; and therefore the first was the father of *Darius*, that is, *Achsuerus, Assuerus, Oxyares, Axeres*, Prince *Axeres*, or *Cy-Axeres*, the word *Cy* signifying a Prince: for *Daniel* tells us, that *Darius* was the son of *Achsuerus*, or *Ahasuerus*, as the *Masoretes* erroneously call him, of the seed of the *Medes*, that is, of the seed royal: this is that *Assuerus* who together with *Nebuchadnezzar* took and destroyed *Nineveh*, according to *Tobit*: which action is by the *Greeks* ascribed to *Cyaxeres*, and by *Eupolemus* to *Astibares*, a name perhaps corruptly written for *Assuerus*. By this victory over the *Assyrians*, and subversion of their Empire seated at *Nineveh*, and the ensuing conquests of *Armenia, Cappadocia* and *Persia*, he began to extend the Reign of one man over all *Asia*; and his son *Darius* the *Mede*, by conquering the Kingdoms of *Lydia* and *Babylon*, finished the work: and the third King was *Cyrus*, a happy man for his great successes under and against *Darius*, and large and peaceable dominion in his own Reign.

Cyrus lived seventy years, according to *Cicero*, and Reigned nine years over *Babylon*, according to *Ptolemy*'s Canon, and therefore was 61 years old at the taking of *Babylon*; at which time *Darius* the *Mede* was 62 years old, according to *Daniel*: and therefore *Darius* was two Generations younger than *Astyages*, the grandfather of *Cyrus*: for *Astyages*, according to both[401] *Herodotus* and *Xenophon*, gave his daughter *Mandane* to *Cambyses* a Prince of *Persia*, and by them became the grandfather of *Cyrus*; and *Cyaxeres* was the son of *Astyages*, according[402] to *Xenophon*, and gave his Daughter to *Cyrus*. This daughter,[403] saith *Xenophon*, was reported to be very handsome, and used to play with *Cyrus* when they were both children, and to say that she would marry him: and therefore they were much of the same age. *Xenophon* saith that *Cyrus* married her after the taking of *Babylon*; but she was then an old woman: it's more probable that he married her while she was young and handsome, and he a young man; and that because he was the brother-in-law of *Darius* the King, he led the armies of the Kingdom until he revolted: so then *Astyages*, *Cyaxeres* and *Darius* Reigned successively over the *Medes*; and *Cyrus* was the grandson of *Astyages*, and married the sister of *Darius*, and succeeded him in the Throne.

Herodotus therefore[404] hath inverted the order of the Kings *Astyages* and *Cyaxeres*, making *Cyaxeres* to be the son and successor of *Phraortes*, and the father and predecessor of *Astyages* the father of *Mandane*, and grandfather of *Cyrus*, and telling us, that this *Astyages* married *Ariene* the daughter of *Alyattes* King of *Lydia*, and was at length taken prisoner and deprived of his dominion by *Cyrus*: and *Pausanias* hath copied after *Herodotus*, in telling us that *Astyages* the son of *Cyaxeres* Reigned in *Media* in the days of *Alyattes* King of *Lydia*. *Cyaxeres* had a son who married *Ariene* the daughter of *Alyattes*; but this son was not the father of *Mandane*, and grandfather of *Cyrus*, but of the same age with *Cyrus*: and his true name is preserved in the name of the *Darics*, which upon the conquest of *Croesus* by the conduct of his General *Cyrus*, he coyned out of the gold and silver of the conquered *Lydians*: his name was therefore *Darius*, as he is called by *Daniel*; for *Daniel* tells us, that this *Darius* was a *Mede*, and that his father's name was *Assuerus*, that is *Axeres* or *Cyaxeres*, as above: considering therefore that *Cyaxeres* Reigned long, and that no author mentions more Kings of *Media* than one called *Astyages*, and that *Æschylus* who lived in those days knew but of two great Monarchs of *Media* and *Persia*, the father and the son, older than *Cyrus*; it seems to me that *Astyages*, the father of *Mandane* and grandfather of *Cyrus*, was the father and predecessor of *Cyaxeres*; and that the son and successor of *Cyaxeres* was called *Darius*. *Cyaxeres*,[405] according to *Herodotus*, Reigned 40 years, and his successor 35, and *Cyrus*, according to *Xenophon*, seven: *Cyrus* died *Anno Nabonass*. 219, according to the Canon, and therefore *Cyaxeres* died *Anno Nabonass*. 177, and began his Reign *Anno Nabonass*. 137, and his father *Astyages* Reigned 26 years, beginning his Reign at the death of *Phraortes*, who was slain by the *Assyrians*, *Anno Nabonass*. 111, as above.

Of all the Kings of the *Medes*, *Cyaxeres* was greatest warrior. *Herodotus*[406] saith that he was much more valiant than his ancestors, and that he was the first who divided the Kingdom into provinces, and reduced the irregular and undisciplined forces of the *Medes* into discipline and order: and therefore by the testimony of *Herodotus* he was that King of the *Medes* whom *Æschylus* makes the first conqueror and founder of the Empire; for *Herodotus* represents him and his son to have been the two immediate predecessors of *Cyrus*, erring only in the name of the son. *Astyages* did nothing glorious: in the beginning of his Reign a great body of *Scythians* commanded by *Madyes*,[407] invaded *Media* and *Parthia*, as above, and Reigned there about 28 years; but at length his son *Cyaxeres* circumvented and slew them in a feast, and made the rest fly to their brethren in *Parthia*; and immediately after, in conjunction with *Nebuchadnezzar*, invaded and subverted the Kingdom of *Assyria*, and destroyed *Nineveh*.

In the fourth year of *Jehoiakim*, which the *Jews* reckon to be the first of *Nebuchadnezzar*, dating his Reign from his being made King by his father, or from the month *Nisan* preceding, when the victors had newly shared the Empire of the *Assyrians*, and in prosecuting their victory were invading *Syria* and *Phoenicia*, and were ready to invade the nations round about; God[408] threatned that *he would take all the families of the North*, that is, the armies of the *Medes, and* Nebuchadnezzar *the King of* Babylon, *and bring them against* Judæa *and against the nations round about, and utterly destroy those nations, and make them an astonishment and lasting desolations, and cause them all to drink the wine-cup of his fury*; and in particular, he names *the Kings of* Judah *and* Egypt, *and those of* Edom, *and* Moab, *and* Ammon, *and* Tyre, *and* Zidon, *and the Isles of the Sea, and* Arabia, *and* Zimri, *and all the Kings of* Elam, *and all the Kings of the* Medes, *and all the Kings of the North, and the King of* Sesac; *and that after seventy years, he would also punish the King of* Babylon. Here, in numbering the nations which should suffer, he omits the *Assyrians* as fallen already, and names the Kings of *Elam* or *Persia*, and *Sesac* or *Susa*, as distinct from those of the *Medes* and *Babylonians*; and therefore the *Persians* were not yet subdued by the *Medes*, nor the King of *Susa* by the *Chaldæans*; and as by the punishment of the King of *Babylon* he means the conquest of *Babylon* by the *Medes*; so by the punishment of the *Medes* he seems to mean the conquest of the *Medes* by *Cyrus*.

After this, in the beginning of the Reign of *Zedekiah*, that is, in the ninth year of *Nebuchadnezzar*, God threatned that *he would give the Kingdoms of* Edom, Moab, *and* Ammon, *and* Tyre *and* Zidon, *into the hand of* Nebuchadnezzar *King of* Babylon, *and that all the nations should serve him, and his son, and his son's son until the very time of his land should come, and many nations and great Kings should serve themselves of him*, Jer. xxvii. And at the same time God thus predicted the approaching conquest of the *Persians* by the *Medes* and their confederates: *Behold*, saith he, *I will break the bow of* Elam, *the chief of their might: and upon* Elam *will I bring the four winds from the four quarters of heaven, and will scatter them towards all those winds, and there shall be no nation whither the outcasts of* Elam *shall not come: for I will cause* Elam *to be dismayed before their enemies, and before them that seek their life; and I will bring evil upon them, even my fierce anger, saith the Lord; and I will send the sword after them 'till I have consumed them; and I will set my throne in* Elam, *and will destroy from thence the King and the Princes, saith the Lord: but it shall come to pass in the latter days*, viz. in the Reign of *Cyrus, that I will bring again the captivity of* Elam, *saith the Lord*. Jer. xlix. 35, *&c.* The *Persians* were therefore hitherto a free nation under their own King, but soon after this were invaded, subdued, captivated, and dispersed into the nations round about, and continued in servitude until the Reign of *Cyrus*: and since the *Medes* and *Chaldæans* did not conquer the *Persians* 'till after the ninth year of

Nebuchadnezzar, it gives us occasion to enquire what that active warrior *Cyaxeres* was doing next after the taking of *Nineveh*.

When *Cyaxeres* expelled the *Scythians*,[409] some of them made their peace with him, and staid in *Media*, and presented to him daily some of the venison which they took in hunting: but happening one day to catch nothing, *Cyaxeres* in a passion treated them with opprobrious language: this they resented, and soon after killed one of the children of the *Medes*, dressed it like venison, and presented it to *Cyaxeres*, and then fled to *Alyattes* King of *Lydia*; whence followed a war of five years between the two Kings *Cyaxeres* and *Alyattes*: and thence I gather that the Kingdoms of the *Medes* and *Lydians* were now contiguous, and by consequence that *Cyaxeres*, soon after the conquest of *Nineveh*, seized the regions belonging to the *Assyrians*, as far as to the river *Halys*. In the sixth year of this war, in the midst of a battel between the two Kings, there was a total Eclipse of the Sun, predicted by *Thales*;[410] and this Eclipse fell upon the 28th of *May*, *Anno Nabonass.* 163, forty and seven years before the taking of *Babylon*, and put an end to the battel: and thereupon the two Kings made peace by the mediation of *Nebuchadnezzar* King of *Babylon*, and *Syennesis* King of *Cilicia*; and the peace was ratified by a marriage, between *Darius* the son of *Cyaxeres* and *Ariene* the daughter of *Alyattes*. *Darius* was therefore fifteen or sixteen years old at the time of this marriage; for he was 62 years old at the taking of *Babylon*.

In the eleventh year of *Zedekiah's* Reign, the year in which *Nebuchadnezzar* took *Jerusalem* and destroyed the Temple, *Ezekiel* comparing the Kingdoms of the East to trees in the garden of *Eden*, thus mentions their being conquered by the Kings of the *Medes* and *Chaldæans*: *Behold*, saith he, *the* Assyrian *was a Cedar in* Lebanon *with fair branches,—his height was exalted above all the trees of the field,—and under his shadow dwelt all great nations,—not any tree in the garden of God was like unto him in his beauty:—but I have delivered him into the hand of the mighty one of the heathen,— I made the nations to shake at the sound of his fall, when I cast him down to the grave with them that descend into the pit: and all the trees of* Eden, *the choice and best of* Lebanon, *all that drink water, shall be comforted in the nether parts of the earth: they also went down into the grave with him, unto them that be slain with the sword, and they that were his arm, that dwelt under his shadow in the midst of the heathen,* Ezek. xxxi.

The next year *Ezekiel*, in another prophesy, thus enumerates the principal nations who had been subdued and slaughtered by the conquering sword of *Cyaxeres* and *Nebuchadnezzar*. Asthur *is there and all her company*, viz. in *Hades* or the lower parts of the earth, where the dead bodies lay buried, *his graves are about him; all of them slain, fallen by the sword, which caused their terrour in the land of the living. There is* Elam, *and all her multitude round about her grave, all of them slain, fallen by the sword, which are gone down uncircumcised into the nether parts of the earth, which caused their terrour in the land of the living: yet have they born their shame with them that go down into the pit.— There is* Meshech, Tubal, *and all her multitude*[411]*; her graves are round about him: all of them uncircumcised, slain by the sword, though they caused their terrour in the land of the living.—There is* Edom, *her Kings, and all her Princes, which with their might are laid by them that were slain by the sword.—There be the Princes of the North all of them, and all the* Zidonians, *which with their terrour are gone down with the slain,* Ezek. xxxii. Here by

the Princes of the North I understand those on the north of *Judæa*, and chiefly
the Princes of *Armenia* and *Cappadocia*, who fell in the wars which *Cyaxeres* made
in reducing those countries after the taking of *Nineveh*. *Elam* or *Persia* was
conquered by the *Medes*, and *Susiana* by the *Babylonians*, after the ninth, and
before the nineteenth year of *Nebuchadnezzar*: and therefore we cannot err much
if we place these conquests in the twelfth or fourteenth year of *Nebuchadnezzar*.
in the nineteenth, twentieth, and one and twentieth year of this King, he invaded
and[412] conquered *Judæa, Moab, Ammon, Edom*, the *Philistims* and *Zidon*; and[413] the
next year he besieged *Tyre*, and after a siege of thirteen years he took it, in the
35th year of his Reign; and then he[414] invaded and conquered *Egypt, Ethiopia* and
Libya; and about eighteen or twenty years after the death of this King, *Darius* the
Mede conquered the Kingdom of *Sardes*; and after five or six years more he
invaded and conquered the Empire of *Babylon*: and thereby finished the work of
propagating the *Medo-Persian* Monarchy over all *Asia*, as *Æschylus* represents.

Now this is that *Darius* who coined a great number of pieces of pure gold
called *Darics*, or *Stateres Darici*: for *Suidas, Harpocration*, and the Scholiast of
Aristophanes][415] tell us, that these were coined not by the father of *Xerxes*, but by
an earlier *Darius*, by *Darius* the first, by the first King of the *Medes* and *Persians*
who coined gold money. They were stamped on one side with the effigies of an
Archer, who was crowned with a spiked crown, had a bow in his left hand, and
an arrow in his right, and was cloathed with a long robe; I have seen one of
them in gold, and another in silver: they were of the same weight and value with
the *Attic Stater* or piece of gold money weighing two *Attic* drachms. *Darius* seems
to have learnt the art and use of money from the conquered Kingdom of the
Lydians, and to have recoined their gold: for the *Medes*, before they conquered
the *Lydians*, had no money. *Herodotus*[416] tells us, that *when* Croesus *was preparing to
invade* Cyrus, *a certain* Lydian *called* Sandanis *advised him, that he was preparing an
expedition against a nation who were cloathed with leathern breeches, who eat not such victuals
as they would, but such as their barren country afforded; who drank no wine, but water only,
who eat no figs nor other good meat, who had nothing to lose, but might get much from the*
Lydians: *for the* Persians, saith *Herodotus, before they conquered the* Lydians, *had nothing
rich or valuable*: and[417] *Isaiah* tells us, that *the* Medes *regarded not silver, nor delighted in
gold*; but the *Lydians* and *Phrygians* were exceeding rich, even to a proverb: *Midas
& Croesus*, saith[418] *Pliny, infinitum possederant. Jam Cyrus devicta Asia [auri] pondo
xxxiv millia invenerat, præter vasa aurea aurumque factum, & in eo folia ac platanum
vitemque. Qua victoria argenti quingenta millia talentorum reportavit, & craterem
Semiramidis cujus pondus quindecim talentorum colligebat. Talentum autem Ægyptium pondo
octoginta capere Varro tradit.* What the conqueror did with all this gold and silver
appears by the *Darics*. The *Lydians*, according to[419] *Herodotus*, were the first who
coined gold and silver, and *Croesus* coined gold monies in plenty, called *Croesei*;
and it was not reasonable that the monies of the Kings of *Lydia* should continue
current after the overthrow of their Kingdom, and therefore *Darius* recoined it
with his own effigies, but without altering the current weight and value: he
Reigned then from before the conquest of *Sardes* 'till after the conquest of
Babylon.

And since the cup of *Semiramis* was preserved 'till the conquest of *Croesus* by *Darius*, it is not probable that she could be older than is represented by *Herodotus*.

This conquest of the Kingdom of *Lydia* put the *Greeks* into fear of the *Medes*: for *Theognis*, who lived at *Megara* in the very times of these wars, writes thus,[420]

[Greek: Pinômen, charienta met' allêloisi legontes,]
[Greek: Mêden ton Mêdôn deidiotes polemon.]

Let us drink, talking pleasant things with one another,
Not fearing the war of the Medes.

And again,[421]

[Greek: Autos de straton hybristên Mêdôn aperyke]
[Greek: Têsde poleus, hina soi laoi en euphrosynêi]
[Greek: Êros eperchomenou kleitas pempôs' hekatombas,]
[Greek: Terpomenoi kitharê kai eratêi thaliêi,]
[Greek: Paianônte chorois, iachôsi te, son peri bômon.]
[Greek: Ê gar egôge dedoik', aphradiên esorôn]
[Greek: Kai stasin Hellênôn laophthoron; alla sy Phoibe,]
[Greek: Hilaos hêmeterên tênde phylasse polin.]

Thou Apollo *drive away the injurious army of the* Medes
From this city, that the people may with joy
Send thee choice hecatombs in the spring,
Delighted with the harp and chearful feasting,
And chorus's of Poeans *and acclamations about thy altar.*
For truly I am afraid, beholding the folly
And sedition of the Greeks, *which corrupts the people: but thou*
Apollo,
Being propitious, keep this our city.

The Poet tells us further that discord had destroyed *Magnesia, Colophon,* and *Smyrna,* cities of *Ionia* and *Phrygia,* and would destroy the *Greeks*; which is as much as to say that the *Medes* had then conquered those cities.

The *Medes* therefore Reigned 'till the taking of *Sardes*: and further, according to *Xenophon* and the Scriptures, they Reigned 'till the taking of *Babylon*: for *Xenophon*[422] tells us, that after the taking of *Babylon, Cyrus* went to the King of the *Medes* at *Ecbatane* and succeeded him in the Kingdom: and *Jerom*,[423] that Babylon *was taken by* Darius *King of the* Medes *and his kinsman* Cyrus: and the Scriptures tell us, that *Babylon* was destroyed by *a nation out of the north, Jerem.* l. 3, 9, 41. *by the Kingdoms of* Ararat Minni, *or* Armenia, *and* Ashchenez, *or* Phrygia minor—, Jer. *li.* 27. *by the* Medes, Isa. *xiii. 17, 19.* by the Kings of the *Medes* and the captains and rulers thereof, and all the land of his dominion, Jer. *li. 11, 28. The Kingdom of* Babylon *was* numbered and finished and broken and given to the *Medes* and

Persians, Dan. v. 26. 28. first to the Medes *under* Darius, *and then to the* Persians *under* Cyrus: *for* Darius *Reigned over* Babylon *like a conqueror, not observing the laws of the* Babylonians, *but introducing the immutable laws of the conquering nations, the* Medes *and* Persians, Dan. *vi. 8, 12, 15; and the* Medes *in his Reign are set before the* Persians, Dan. *ib. & v. 28, & viii. 20. as the* Persians *were afterwards in the Reign of* Cyrus *and his successors set before the* Medes, Esther *i. 3, 14, 18, 19.* Dan. *x. 1, 20. and xi. 2. which shews that in the Reign of* Darius *the* Medes *were uppermost.*

You may know also by the great number of provinces in the Kingdom of *Darius,* that he was King of the *Medes* and *Persians:* for upon the conquest of *Babylon,* he set over the whole Kingdom an hundred and twenty Princes, *Dan.* vi. 1. and afterwards when *Cambyses* and *Darius Hystaspis* had added some new territories, the whole contained but 127 provinces.

The extent of the *Babylonian* Empire was much the same with that of *Nineveh* after the revolt of the *Medes.* Berosus saith that *Nebuchadnezzar* held *Egypt, Syria, Phoenicia* and *Arabia:* and *Strabo* adds *Arbela* to the territories of *Babylon;* and saying that *Babylon* was anciently the metropolis of Assyria, he thus describes the limits of this *Assyrian* Empire. *Contiguous,*[424] saith he, to *Persia* and *Susiana* are the *Assyrians:* for so they call *Babylonia,* and the greatest part of the region about it: part of which is *Arturia,* wherein is *Ninus [or Nineveh;]* and *Apolloniatis,* and the *Elymæans,* and the *Parætacæ,* and *Chalonitis* by the mountain *Zagrus,* and the fields near *Ninus,* and *Dolomene,* and *Chalachene,* and *Chazene,* and *Adiabene,* and the nations of *Mesopotamia* near the *Gordyæans,* and the *Mygdones* about *Nisibis,* unto *Zeugma* upon *Euphrates;* and a large region on this side *Euphrates* inhabited by the *Arabians* and *Syrians* properly so called, as far as *Cilicia* and *Phoenicia* and *Libya* and the sea of *Egypt* and the *Sinus Issicus: and a little after describing the extent of the* Babylonian *region, he bounds it on the north, with the* Armenians *and* Medes *unto the mountain* Zagrus; *on the east side, with* Susa *and* Elymais *and* Parætacene, *inclusively; on the south, with the* Persian Gulph *and* Chaldæa; *and on the west, with the* Arabes Scenitæ *as far as* Adiabene *and* Gordyæa: *afterwards speaking of* Susiana *and* Sitacene, *a region between* Babylon *and* Susa, *and of* Parætacene *and* Cossæa *and* Elymais, *and of the* Sagapeni *and* Siloceni, *two little adjoining Provinces, he concludes,*[425] and these are the nations which inhabit *Babylonia* eastward: to the north are *Media* and *Armenia, exclusively,* and westward are *Adiabene* and *Mesopotamia, inclusively;* the greatest part of *Adiabene* is plain, the same being part of *Babylonia:* in same places it borders on *Armenia:* for the *Medes, Armenians* and *Babylonians* warred frequently on one another. Thus far *Strabo.*

When *Cyrus* took *Babylon,* he changed the Kingdom into a Satrapy or Province: whereby the bounds were long after known: and by this means *Herodotus*[426] gives us an estimate of the bigness of this Monarchy in proportion to that of the *Persians,* telling us that whilst every region over which the King of *Persia* Reigned in his days, was distributed for the nourishment of his army, besides the tributes, the *Babylonian* region nourished him four months of the twelve in the year, and all the rest of *Asia* eight: so the power of the region, *saith he,* is equivalent to the third part of *Asia,* and its Principality, which the *Persians* call a *Satrapy,* is far the best of all the Provinces.

Babylon[427] was a square city of 120 furlongs, or 15 miles on every side, compassed first with a broad and deep ditch, and then with a wall fifty cubits thick, and two hundred high. *Euphrates* flowed through the middle of it southward, a few leagues on this side *Tigris:* and in the middle of one half westward stood the King's new Palace, built by *Nebuchadnezzar;* and in the middle of the other half stood the Temple of Belus, with the old Palace between that Temple and the river: this old Palace was built by the Assyrians, according to[428] *Isaiah,* and by consequence, by *Pul* and his son *Nabonassar,* as above: they founded the city for the *Arabians,* and set up the towers thereof, and raised the Palaces thereof: and at that time *Sabacon* the *Ethiopian* invaded *Egypt,* and made great multitudes of *Egyptians* fly from him into Chaldæa, and carry thither their Astronomy, and Astrology, and Architecture, and the form of their year, which they preserved there in the *Æra* of *Nabonassar:* for the practice of observing the Stars began in Egypt in the days of *Ammon,* as above, and was propagated from thence in the Reign of his son Sesac into Afric, Europe, and *Asia* by conquest; and then *Atlas* formed the Sphere of the *Libyans,* and *Chiron* that of the *Greeks,* and the *Chaldæans* also made a Sphere of their own. But Astrology was invented in *Egypt* by Nichepsos, or *Necepsos,* one of the Kings of the lower *Egypt,* and *Petosiris* his Priest, a little before the days of *Sabacon,* and propagated thence into *Chaldæa,* where *Zoroaster* the Legislator of the *Magi* met with it: so *Paulinus,*

Quique magos docuit mysteria vana Necepsos:

And *Diodorus,*[429] they say that the *Chaldæans* in *Babylonia* are colonies of the *Egyptians,* and being taught by the Priests of *Egypt* became famous for Astrology. By the influence of the same colonies, the Temple of *Jupiter Belus* in *Babylon* seems to have been erected in the form of the *Egyptian* Pyramids: for[430] this Temple was a solid Tower or Pyramid a furlong square, and a furlong high, with seven retractions, which made it appear like eight towers standing upon one another, and growing less and less to the top: and in the eighth tower was a Temple with a bed and a golden table, kept by a woman, after the manner of the *Egyptians* in the Temple of *Jupiter Ammon* at Thebes; and above the Temple was a place for observing the Stars: they went up to the top of it by steps on the outside, and the bottom was compassed with a court, and the court with a building two furlongs in length on every side.

The *Babylonians* were extreamly addicted to Sorcery, Inchantments, Astrology and Divinations, Isa. xlvii. 9, 12, 13. Dan. ii. 2, & v. 11. and to the worship of Idols, Jer. l. 2, 40. and to feasting, wine and women. *Nihil urbis ejus corruptius moribus, nec ad irritandas illiciendasque immodicas voluptates instructius. Liberos conjugesque cum hospitibus stupro coire, modo pretium flagitii detur, parentes maritique patiuntur. Convivales ludi tota Perside regibus purpuratisque cordi sunt: Babylonii maxime in vinum & quæ ebrietatem sequuntur effusi sunt. Fœminarum convivia ineuntium in principio modestus est habitus; dein summa quæque amicula exuunt, paulatimque pudorem profanant: ad ultimum, honos auribus sit, ima corporum velamenta projiciunt. Nec meretricum hoc dedecus est, sed matronarum virginumque, apud quas comitas habetur vulgati corporis vilitas.*

Q. Curtius, lib. v. cap. 1. And this lewdness of their women, coloured over with the name of civility, was encouraged even by their religion: for it was the custom for their women once in their life to sit in the Temple of *Venus* for the use of strangers; which Temple they called *Succoth Benoth*, the Temple of Women: and when any woman was once sat there, she was not to depart 'till some stranger threw money into her bosom, took her away and lay with her; and the money being for sacred uses, she was obliged to accept of it how little soever, and follow the stranger.

The *Persians* being conquered by the *Medes* about the middle of the Reign of *Zedekiah*, continued in subjection under them 'till the end of the Reign of *Darius* the *Mede:* and *Cyrus*, who was of the Royal Family of the *Persians*, might be *Satrapa* of *Persia*, and command a body of their forces under *Darius;* but was not yet an absolute and independant King: but after the taking of Babylon, when he had a victorious army at his devotion, and *Darius* was returned from *Babylon* into Media, he revolted from *Darius*, in conjunction with the *Persians* under him;[431] they being incited thereunto by *Harpagus* a *Mede*, whom *Xenophon* calls *Artagerses* and *Atabazus*, and who had assisted *Cyrus* in conquering *Croesus* and *Asia minor*, and had been injured by *Darius*. *Harpagus* was sent by *Darius* with an army against *Cyrus*, and in the midst of a battel revolted with part of the army to *Cyrus:* *Darius* got up a fresh army, and the next year the two armies fought again: this last battel was fought at *Pasargadæ* in *Persia*, according to[432] *Strabo;* and there *Darius* was beaten and taken Prisoner by *Cyrus*, and the Monarchy was by this victory translated to the *Persians*. The last King of the *Medes* is by *Xenophon* called *Cyaxares*, and by *Herodotus*, *Astyages* the father of *Mandane:* but these Kings were dead before, and *Daniel* lets us know that *Darius* was the true name of the last King, and *Herodotus*,[433] that the last King was conquered by *Cyrus* in the manner above described; and the *Darics* coined by the last King testify that his name was *Darius*.

This victory over Darius was about two years after the taking of *Babylon:* for the Reign or *Nabonnedus* the last King of the *Chaldees*, whom *Josephus* calls *Naboandel* and *Belshazzar*, ended in the year of *Nabonassar* 210, nine years before the death of *Cyrus*, according to the Canon: but after the translation of the Kingdom of the *Medes* to the *Persians*, *Cyrus* Reigned only seven years, according to[434] *Xenophon;* and spending the seven winter months yearly at *Babylon*, the three spring months yearly at *Susa*, and the two Summer months at *Ecbatane*, he came the seventh time into *Persia*, and died there in the spring, and was buried at *Pasargadae*. By the Canon and the common consent of all Chronologers, he died in the year of *Nabonassar* 219, and therefore conquered *Darius* in the year of *Nabonassar* 212, seventy and two years after the destruction of *Nineveh*, and beat him the first time in the year of *Nabonassar* 211, and revolted from him, and became King of the *Persians*, either the same year, or in the end of the year before. At his death he was seventy years old according to *Herodotus*, and therefore he was born in the year of *Nabonassar* 149, his mother Mandane being the sister of *Cyaxeres*, at that time a young man, and also the sister of *Amyite* the wife of *Nebuchadnezzar*, and his father *Cambyses* being of the old Royal Family of the *Persians*.

CHAP. V

A Description of the TEMPLE of Solomon.

[435]THE Temple of *Solomon* being destroyed by the *Babylonians,* it may not be amiss here to give a description of that edifice.

This[436] Temple looked eastward, and stood in a square area, called the *Separate Place:* and[437] before it stood the *Altar,* in the center of another square area, called the *Inner Court,* or *Court of the Priests:* and these two square areas, being parted only by a marble rail, made an area 200 cubits long from west to east, and 100 cubits broad: this area was compassed on the west with a wall, and[438] on the other three sides with a pavement fifty cubits broad, upon which stood the buildings for the Priests, with cloysters under them: and the pavement was faced on the inside with a marble rail before the cloysters: the whole made an area 250 cubits long from west to east, and 200 broad, and was compassed with an outward Court, called also the *Great Court, or Court of the People,*[439] which was an hundred cubits on every side; for there were but two Courts built by *Solomon:* and the outward Court was about four cubits lower than the inward, and was compassed on the west with a wall, and on the other three sides[440] with a pavement fifty cubits broad, upon which stood the buildings for the People. All this was the[441] *Sanctuary,* and made a square area 500 cubits long, and 500 broad, and was compassed with a walk, called the *Mountain of the House:* and this walk being 50 cubits broad, was compassed with a wall six cubits broad, and six high, and six hundred long on every side: and the cubit was about 21½, or almost 22 inches of the *English* foot, being the sacred cubit of the Jews, which was an hand-breadth, or the sixth part of its length bigger than the common cubit.

The *Altar* stood in the center of the whole; and in the buildings of[442] both Courts over against the middle of the *Altar,* eastward, southward, and northward, were gates[443] 25 cubits broad between the buildings, and 40 long; with porches of ten cubits more, looking towards the *Altar Court,* which made the whole length of the gates fifty cubits cross the pavements. Every gate had two doors, one at either[444] end, ten cubits wide, and twenty high, with posts and thresholds six cubits broad: within the gates was an area 28 cubits long between the thresholds, and 13 cubits wide: and on either side of this area were three posts, each six cubits square, and twenty high, with arches five cubits wide between them: all which posts and arches filled the 28 cubits in length between the thresholds; and their breadth being added to the thirteen cubits, made the whole breadth of the gates 25 cubits. These posts were hollow, and had rooms in them with narrow windows for the porters, and a step before them a cubit broad: and the walls of the porches being six cubits thick, were also hollow for several uses.[445] At the east gate of the *Peoples Court,* called the *King's gate,*[446] were six porters, at the south gate were four, and at the north gate were four: the people[447] went in and out at the south and north gates: the[448] east gate was opened only for the King, and in this gate he ate the Sacrifices. There were also four gates or doors in the western wall of the *Mountain of the House:* of these[449] the most northern, called *Shallecheth*, or the *gate of the causey*, led to the King's palace, the valley between being filled up with a causey: the next gate, called *Parbar*, led to the suburbs *Millo*: the third and fourth gates, called *Asuppim*, led the one to *Millo*, the other to the city of *Jerusalem*, there being steps down into the valley and up again into the city. At the gate *Shallecheth* were four porters; at the other three gates were six porters, two at each gate: the house of the porters who had the charge of the north gate of the *People's Court*, had also the charge of the gates *Shallecheth* and *Parbar*: and the house of the porters who had the charge of the south gate of the *People s Court*, had also the charge of the other two gates called *Asuppim*.

They came through the four western gates into the *Mountain of the House*, and[450] went up from the *Mountain of the House*, to the gates of the *People's Court* by seven steps, and from the *People's Court* to the gates of the *Priest's Court* by eight steps:[451] and the arches in the sides of the gates of both courts led into cloysters[452] under a double building, supported by three rows of marble pillars, which butted directly upon the middles of the square posts, ran along from thence upon the pavements towards the corners of the Courts: the axes of the pillars in the middle row being eleven cubits distant from the axes of the pillars in the other two rows on either hand; and the building joining to the sides of the gates: the pillars were three cubits in diameter below, and their bases four cubits and an half square. The gates and buildings of both Courts were alike, and[453] faced their Courts: the cloysters of all the buildings, and the porches of all the gates looking towards the *Altar*. The row of pillars on the backsides of the cloysters adhered to marble walls, which bounded the cloysters and supported the buildings:[454] these buildings were three stories high above the cloysters, and[455] were supported in each of those stories by a row of cedar beams, or pillars of cedar, standing above the middle row of the marble pillars: the buildings on either side of every gate of the *People's Court*, being 187½ cubits long, were distinguished into five chambers on a floor, running in length from the gates to the corners or the Courts: there[456] being in all thirty chambers in a story, where the People ate the Sacrifices, or thirty exhedras, each of which contained three chambers, a lower, a middle, and an upper: every exhedra was 37½ cubits long, being supported by four pillars in each row,[457] whose bases were 4½ cubits square, and the distances between their bases 6½ cubits, and the distances between the axes of the pillars eleven cubits: and where two[458] exhedras joyned, there the bases of their pillars joyned; the axes of those two pillars being only 4½ cubits distant from one another: and perhaps for strengthning the building, the space between the axes of these two pillars in the front was filled up with a marble column 4½ cubits square, the two pillars standing half out on either side of the square column. At the ends of these buildings[459] in the four corners of the *Peoples Court*, were little Courts fifty cubits square on the outside of their walls, and forty on the inside thereof, for stair-cases to the buildings, and kitchins to bake and boil the Sacrifices for the People, the kitchin being thirty cubits broad, and the stair-case ten. The buildings on either side of the gates of the *Priests Court* were also 37½ cubits long, and contained each of them one great chamber in a story, subdivided into smaller rooms, for the Great Officers of the Temple, and Princes of the Priests: and in the south-east and north-east corners of this court, at the ends of the buildings, were kitchins and stair-cases for the Great Officers; and perhaps rooms for laying up wood for the *Altar.*

In the eastern gate of the *Peoples Court,* sat a Court of Judicature, composed of 23 Elders. The eastern gate of the *Priests Court,* with the buildings on either side, was for the High-Priest, and his deputy the *Sagan,* and for the *Sanhedrim* or Supreme Court of Judicature, composed of seventy Elders.[460] The building or exhedra on the eastern side of the southern gate, was for the Priests who had the oversight of the charge of the *Sanctuary* with its treasuries: and these were, first, two *Catholikim,* who were High-Treasurers and Secretaries to the High-Priest, and examined, stated, and prepared all acts and accounts to be signed and sealed by him; then seven *Amarcholim,* who kept the keys of the seven locks of every gate of the *Sanctuary,* and those also of the treasuries, and had the oversight, direction, and appointment of all things in the *Sanctuary;* then three or more *Gisbarim,* or Under-Treasurers, or Receivers, who kept the Holy Vessels, and the Publick Money, and received or disposed of such sums as were brought in for the service of the Temple, and accounted for the same. All these, with the High-Priest, composed the Supreme Council for managing the affairs of the Temple.

The Sacrifices[461] were killed on the northern side of the *Altar,* and flea'd, cut in pieces and salted in the northern gate of the Temple; and therefore the building or exhedra on the eastern side of this gate, was for the Priests who had the oversight of the charge of the *Altar,* and Daily Service: and these Officers were, He that received money of the People for purchasing things for the Sacrifices, and gave out tickets for the same; He that upon sight of the tickets delivered the wine, flower and oyl purchased; He that was over the lots, whereby every Priest attending on the *Altar* had his duty assigned; He that upon sight of the tickets delivered out the doves and pigeons purchased; He that administred physic to the Priests attending; He that was over the waters; He that was over the times, and did the duty of a cryer, calling the Priests or Levites to attend in their ministeries; He that opened the gates in the morning to begin the service, and shut them in the evening when the service was done, and for that end received the keys of the *Amarcholim,* and returned them when he had done his duty; He that visited the night-watches; He that by a Cymbal called the Levites to their stations for singing; He that appointed the Hymns and set the Tune; and He that took care of the Shew-Bread: there were also Officers who took care of the Perfume, the Veil, and the Wardrobe of the Priests.

The exhedra on the western side of the south gate, and that on the western side of the north gate, were for the Princes of the four and twenty courses of the Priests, one exhedra for twelve of the Princes,[462] and the other exhedra for the other twelve: and upon the pavement on either side of the *Separate Place*[463] were other buildings without cloysters, for the four and twenty courses of the Priests to eat the Sacrifices, and lay up their garments and the most holy things: each pavement being 100 cubits long, and 50 broad, had buildings on either side of it twenty cubits broad, with a walk or alley ten cubits broad between them: the building which bordered upon the *Separate Place* was an hundred cubits long, and that next the *Peoples Court* but fifty, the other fifty cubits westward[464] being for a stair-case and kitchin: these buildings[465] were three stories high, and the middle story was narrower in the front than the lower story, and the upper story still narrower, to make room for galleries; for they had galleries before them, and under the galleries were closets for laying up the holy things, and the garments of the Priests, and these galleries were towards the walk or alley, which ran between the buildings.

They went up from the *Priests Court* to the Porch of the Temple by ten steps: and the[466] House of the Temple was twenty cubits broad, and sixty long within; or thirty broad, and seventy long, including the walls; or seventy cubits broad, and 90 long, including a building of treasure-chambers which was twenty cubits broad on three sides of the House; and if the Porch be also included, the Temple was[467] an hundred cubits long. The treasure-chambers were built of cedar, between the wall of the Temple, and another wall without: they were[468] built in two rows three stories high, and opened door against door into a walk or gallery which ran along between them, and was five cubits broad in every story; So that the breadth of the chambers on either side of the gallery, including the breadth of the wall to which they adjoined, was ten cubits; and the whole breadth of the gallery and chambers, and both walls, was five and twenty cubits: the chambers[469] were five cubits broad in the lower story, six broad in the middle story, and seven broad in the upper story; for the wall of the Temple was built with retractions of a cubit, to rest the timber upon. *Ezekiel* represents the chambers a cubit narrower, and the walls a cubit thicker than they were in *Solomon's* Temple: there were[470] thirty chambers in a story, in all ninety chambers, and they were five cubits high in every story. The[471] Porch of the Temple was 120 cubits high, and its length from south to north equalled the breadth of the House: the House was three stories high, which made the height of the *Holy Place* three times thirty cubits, and that of the *Most Holy* three times twenty: the upper rooms were treasure-chambers; they[472] went up to the middle chamber by winding stairs in the southern shoulder of the House, and from the middle into the upper.

Some time after this Temple was built, the *Jews*[473] added a New Court, on the eastern side of the *Priests Court,* before the *King's gate,* and therein built[474] a covert for the Sabbath: this Court was not measured by *Ezekiel,* but the dimensions thereof may be gathered from those of the *Womens Court,* in the second Temple, built after the example thereof: for when *Nebuchadnezzar* had destroyed the first Temple, *Zerubbabel,* by the commissions of *Cyrus* and *Darius,* built another upon the same area, excepting the *Outward Court,* which was left open to the *Gentiles:* and this Temple[475] was sixty cubits long, and sixty broad, being only two stories in height, and having only one row of treasure-chambers about it: and on either side of the *Priests Court* were double buildings for the Priests, built upon three rows of marble pillars in the lower story, with a row of cedar beams or pillars in the stories above: and the cloyster in the lower story looked towards the *Priests Court:* and the *Separate Place,* and *Priests Court,* with their buildings on the north and south sides, and the *Womens Court,* at the east end, took up an area three hundred cubits long, and two hundred broad, the Altar standing in the center of the whole. *The Womens Court* was so named, because the women came into it as well as the men: there were galleries for the women, and the men worshipped upon the ground below: and in this state the second Temple continued all the Reign of the *Persians;* but afterwards suffered some alterations, especially in the days of *Herod.*

This description of the Temple being taken principally from *Ezekiel's* Vision thereof; and the ancient *Hebrew* copy followed by the Seventy, differing in some readings from the copy followed by the editors of the present *Hebrew,* I will here subjoin that part of the Vision which relates to the *Outward Court,* as I have deduced it from the present *Hebrew,* and the version of the Seventy compared together.

Ezekiel chap. xl. ver. 5, &c.

[476]*And behold a wall on the outside of the House round about,* at the distance of fifty cubits from it, aabb: *and in the man's hand a measuring reed six cubits long by the cubit, and an hand-breadth: so he measured the breadth of the building,* or wall, *one reed, and the height one reed.*[477] *Then came he unto the gate* of the House, *which looketh towards the east, and went up the seven steps thereof,* AB, *and measured the threshold of the gate,* CD, *which was one reed broad, and the* Porters *little chamber,* EFG, *one reed long, and one reed broad; and the arched passage between the little chambers,* FH, *five cubits: and the second little chamber,* HIK, *a reed broad and a reed long; and the arched passage,* IL, *five cubits: and the third little chamber* LMN, *a reed long and a reed broad: and the threshold of the gate next the porch of the gate within,* OP, *one reed: and he measured the porch of the gate,* QR, *eight cubits; and the posts thereof* ST, st, *two cubits; and the porch of the gate,* QR, *was inward,* or toward the inward court; *and the little chambers,* EF, HI, LM, ef, hi, lm, *were outward,* or *to the east; three on this side, and three on that side* of the gate. *There was one measure of the three, and one measure of the posts on this side, and on that side; and he measured the breadth of the door of the gate,* Cc, or Dd, *ten cubits; and the breadth of the gate* within between the little chambers, Ee or Ff, *thirteen cubits; and the limit,* or *margin,* or *step before the little chambers,* EM, *one cubit on this side, and the step,* em, *one cubit on the other side; and the little chambers,* EFG, HIK, LMN, efg, hik, lmn, *were six cubits* broad *on this side, and six cubits* broad *on that side: and he measured* the whole breadth of *the gate, from the* further *wall of one little chamber to the* further *wall of another little chamber: the breadth,* Gg, or Kk, or Nn, *was twenty and five cubits* through; *door,* FH, *against door,* fh: *and he measured the posts,* EF, HI, *and* LM, ef, hi, *and* lm, *twenty cubits* high; *and at the posts there were gates,* or arched passages, FH, IL, fh, il, *round about; and from the* eastern *face of the gate at the entrance,* Cc, *to the* western *face of the porch of the gate within,* Tt, *were fifty cubits: and there were narrow windows to the little chambers, and to the porch within the gate, round about, and likewise to the posts; even windows were round about within: and upon each post were palm trees.*

Then he brought me into the Outward Court, and lo there were chambers, and a pavement with pillars upon it in the court round about,[478] *thirty chambers* in length *upon the pavement, supported by the pillars,* ten chambers on every side, except the western: *and the pavement butted upon the shoulders or sides of the gates below,* every gate having five chambers or exhedræ on either side. *And he measured the breadth* of the Outward Court, *from the fore-front of the lower-gate, to the fore-front of the inward court, an hundred cubits eastward.*

Then he brought me northward, and there was a gate that looked towards the north; he measured the length thereof, and the breadth thereof, and the little chambers thereof, three on this side, and three on that side, and the posts thereof, and the porch thereof, and it was according to the measures of the first gate; its length was fifty cubits, and its breadth was five and twenty: and the windows thereof, and the porch and the palm-trees thereof were according to the measures of the gate which looked to the east, and they went up to it by seven steps: and its porch was before them, that is inward. *And there was a gate of the inward court over against this gate of the north, as* in the gates *to the eastward: and he measured from gate to gate an hundred cubits.*

A Description of THE TEMPLE OF SOLOMON

ABCD. *The Separate Place in which stood the Temple.*
ABEF. *The Court of* $y^\wedge\{e\}$ *Priests.*
G. The Altar.
DHLKICEFD. *A Pavement compassing three sides of the foremention'd Courts, and upon which stood the Buildings for the Priests, with Cloysters under them.*
MNOP. *The Court of the People.*
MQTSRN. *A Pavement compassing three sides of the Peoples Court, upon which stood the Buildings for the People, with Cloysters under them.*
UXYZ. *The Mountain of the House.*
aabb. *A Wall enclosing the whole.*
c. *The Gate Shallecheth.*
d. *The Gate Parbar.*
ef. *The two Gates Assupim.*
g. *The East Gate of the Peoples Court, call'd the Kings Gate.*
hh. *The North and South Gates of the same Court.*
iiii. *The chambers over the Cloysters of the Peoples Court where the People ate the Sacrifices, 30 Chambers in each Story.*
kkkk. *Four little Courts serving for Stair Cases and Kitchins for the People.*
l. *The Eastern Gate of the Priests Court, over which sate the Sanhedrin.*
m. *The Southern Gate of the Priests Court.*
n. *The Northern Gate of the same Court, where the Sacrifices were flea'd &c.*
opqrst. *The Buildings over the Cloysters for the Priests, viz six large Chambers (subdivided) in each Story, whereof* o *and* p *were for the High Priest and Sagan,* q *for the Overseers of the Sanctuary and Treasury,* r *for the Overseers of the Altar and Sacrifice and* s *and* t *for the Princes of the twenty four Courses of Priests.*
uu. *Two Courts in which were Stair Cases and Kitchins for the Priests.*

x. *The House or Temple which (together with the Treasure Chambers y, and Buildings zz on each side of the Separate Place) is more particularly describ'd on the second Plate.*

A Description of the Inner Court & Buildings for the Priests in Solomons Temple.

ABCD. *The Separate Place.*

ABEF. *The Inner Court, or Court of the Priests, parted from the Separate Place, and and Pavement on the other three sides, by a marble rail.*

G. *The Altar.*

HHH. *The East, South, & North Gates of the Priests Court.*

III. *&c. The Cloysters supporting the Buildings for the Priests.*

KK. *Two Courts in which were Stair Cases and Kitchins for the Priests.*

L. *Ten Steps to the Porch of the Temple.*

M. *The Porch of the Temple.*

N. *The Holy Place.*

O. *The most Holy Place.*

PPPP. *Thirty Treasure-Chambers, in two rows, opening into a gallery, door against door, and compassing three sides of the Holy & most Holy Places.*

Q. *The Stairs leading to the Middle Chamber.*

RRRR. *&c. The buildings for the four and twenty Courses of Priests, upon the Pavement on either side of the Separate Place, three Stories high without Cloysters, but the upper Stories narrower than the lower, to make room for Galleries before them. There were 24 Chambers in each Story and they opend into a walk or alley, SS. between the Buildings.*

TT. *Two Courts in which were Kitchins for the Priests of the twenty four Courses.*

A Particular Description of one of the Gates of the Peoples Court, with part of the Cloyster adjoyning.

uw. *The inner margin of the Pavement compassing three sides of the Peoples Court.*

xxx. *&c. The Pillars of the Cloyster supporting the Buildings for the People.*

yyyy. *Double Pillars where two Exhedræ joyned, and whose interstices in the front zz were filled up with a square Column of Marble.*

Note *The preceding letters of this Plate refer to the description in pag. 344 345.*

CHAP. VI

Of the Empire of the Persians.

CYRUS having translated the Monarchy to the *Persians,* and Reigned seven years, was succeeded by his son *Cambyses,* who Reigned seven years and five months, and in the three last years of his Reign subdued Egypt: he was succeeded by *Mardus,* or *Smerdis* the *Magus,* who feigned himself to be *Smerdis* the brother of *Cambyses.*

Smerdis Reigned seven months, and in the eighth month being discovered, was slain, with a great number of the Magi; so the *Persians* called their Priests, and in memory of this kept an anniversary day, which they called, *The slaughter of the* Magi. Then Reigned *Maraphus* and *Artaphernes* a few days, and after them *Darius* the son of *Hystaspes,* the son of *Arsamenes,* of the family of *Achæmenes,* a *Persian,* being chosen King by the neighing of his horse: before he Reigned his[479] name was *Ochus.* He seems on this occasion to have reformed the constitution of the *Magi,* making his father *Hystaspes* their Master, or *Archimagus;* for *Porphyrius* tells us,[480] that *the* Magi *were a sort of men so venerable amongst the* Persians, *that* Darius *the son of* Hystaspes *wrote on the monument of his father,* amongst other things, *that he had been the Master of the* Magi. In this reformation of the *Magi, Hystaspes* was assisted by *Zoroastres:* so Agathias; *The* Persians *at this day say simply that* Zoroastres *lived under* Hystaspes: and *Apuleius; Pythagoram, aiunt, inter captivos* Cambysæ Regis *[ex Ægypto Babylonem abductos] doctores habuisse Persarum Magos, & præcipue Zoroastrem, omnis divini arcani Antistitem.* By *Zoroastres's* conversing at *Babylon* he seems to have borrowed his skill from the *Chaldæans;* for he was skilled in Astronomy, and used their year: so *Q. Curtius;*[481] *Magi proximi patrium carmen canebant: Magos trecenti & sexaginta quinque juvenes sequebantur, puniceis amiculis velati, diebus totius anni pares numero:* and *Ammianus; Scientiæ multa ex Chaldæorum arcanis Bactrianus addidit Zoroastres.* From his conversing in several places he is reckoned a *Chaldæan,* an *Assyrian,* a *Mede,* a *Persian,* a *Bactrian. Suidas* calls him[482] a *Perso-Mede,* and saith that he was *the most skilful of Astronomers, and first author of the name of the* Magi *received among them.* This skill in Astronomy he had doubtless from the *Chaldæans,* but *Hystaspes* travelled into *India,* to be instructed by the *Gymnosophists:* and these two conjoyning their skill and authority, instituted a new set of Priests or *Magi,* and instructed them in such ceremonies and mysteries of Religion and Philosophy as they thought fit to establish for the Religion and Philosophy of that Empire; and these instructed others, 'till from a small number they grew to a great multitude: for *Suidas* tells us, that *Zoroastres gave a beginning to the name of the* Magi: and *Elmacinus;* that *he reformed the religion of the* Persians, *which before was divided into many sects:* and *Agathias;* that *he introduced the religion of the* Magi *among the* Persians, *changing their ancient sacred rites, and bringing in several opinions:* and *Ammianus*[483] tells us, *Magiam esse divinorum incorruptissimum cultum, cujus scientiæ seculis priscis multa ex Chaldæorum arcanis Bactrianus addidit Zoroastres: deinde Hystaspes Rex prudentissimus Darii pater; qui quum superioris Indiæ secreta fidentius penetraret, ad nemorosam quamdam venerat solitudinem, cujus tranquillis silentiis præcelsa Brachmanorum ingenia potiuntur; eorumque monitu rationes mundani motus & siderum, purosque sacrorum ritus quantum colligere potuit eruditus, ex his quæ didicit, aliqua sensibus Magorum infudit; quæ illi cum disciplinis præsentiendi futura, per suam quisque progeniem, posteris ætatibus tradunt. Ex eo per sæcula multa ad præsens, una eademque prosapia multitudo creata, Deorum cultibus dedicatur. Feruntque, si justum est credi, etiam ignem coelitus lapsum apud se sempiternis foculis custodiri, cujus portionem exiguam ut faustam præisse quondam Asiaticis Regibus dicunt: Hujus originis apud veteres numerus erat exilis, ejusque mysteriis Persicæ potestates in faciendis rebus divinis solemniter utebantur. Eratque piaculum aras adire, vel hostiam contrectare, antequam Magus conceptis precationibus libamenta diffunderet præcursoria. Verum aucti paullatim, in amplitudinem gentis solidæ concesserunt & nomen: villasque inhabitantes nulla murorum firmitudine communitas & legibus suis uti permissi, religionis respectu sunt honorati.* So this Empire was at first composed of many nations, each of which had hitherto its own religion: but now *Hystaspes* and *Zoroastres* collected what they conceived to be best, established it by law, and taught it to others, and those to others, 'till their disciples became numerous enough for the Priesthood of the whole Empire; and instead of those various old religions, they set up their own institutions in the whole Empire, much after the manner that *Numa* contrived and instituted the religion of the *Romans:* and this religion of the *Persian* Empire was composed partly of the institutions of the *Chaldæans,* in which *Zoroastres* was well skilled; and partly of the institutions of the ancient Brachmans, who are supposed to derive even their name from the *Abrahamans,* or sons of *Abraham,* born of his second wife *Keturah,* instructed by their father in the worship of ONE GOD without images, and sent into the east, where *Hystaspes* was instructed by their successors. About the same time with *Hystapes* and *Zoroastres,* lived also *Ostanes,* another eminent *Magus: Pliny* places him under *Darius Hystaspis,* and *Suidas* makes him the follower of *Zoroastres:* he came into *Greece* with Xerxes, and seems to be the *Otanes* of *Herodotus,* who discovered *Smerdis,* and formed the conspiracy against him, and for that service was honoured by the conspirators, and exempt from subjection to *Darius.*

In the sacred commentary of the *Persian* rites these words are ascribed to *Zoroastres,*[484] [Greek: Ho Theos esti kephalên echôn hierakos. houtos estin ho prôtos, aphthartos, aidios, agenêtos, amerês, anomoiotatos, hêniochos pantos kalou, adôrodokêtos, agathôn agathôtatos, phronimôn phronimôtatos; esti de kai patêr eunomias kai dikaiosynês, autodidaktos, physikos, kai teleios, kai sophos, kai hierou physikou monos heuretês.] Deus est accipitris capite: hic est primus, incorruptibilis, æternus, ingenitus, sine partibus, omnibus aliis dissimillimus, moderator omnis boni, donis non capiendus, bonorum optimus, prudentium prudentissimus, legum æquitatis ac justitiæ parens, ipse sui doctor, physicus & perfectus & sapiens & sacri physici unicus inventor: and the same was taught by *Ostanes,* in his book called *Octateuchus.* This was the Antient God of the *Persian Magi,* and they worshipped him by keeping a perpetual fire for Sacrifices upon an Altar in the center of a round area, compassed with a ditch, without any Temple in the place, and without paying any worship to the dead, or any images. But in a short time they declined from the worship of this Eternal,

Invisible God, to worship the Sun, and the Fire, and dead men, and images, as the *Egyptians, Phoenicians*, and *Chaldæans* had done before: and from these superstitions, and the pretending to prognostications, the words *Magi* and *Magia*, which signify the Priests and Religion of the *Persians*, came to be taken in an ill sense.

Darius, or *Darab*, began his Reign in spring, in the sixteenth year of the Empire of the *Persians, Anno Nabonass. 227*, and Reigned 36 years, by the unanimous consent of all Chronologers. In the second year of his Reign the Jews began to build the Temple, by the prophesying of *Haggai* and *Zechariah*, and finished it in the sixth. He fought the *Greeks* at *Marathon* in *October, Anno Nabonass.* 258, ten years before the battel at *Salamis*, and died in the fifth year following, in the end of winter, or beginning of spring, *Anno Nabonass.* 263. The years of Cambyses and *Darius* are determined by three Eclipses of the Moon recorded by *Ptolemy*, so that they cannot be disputed: and by those Eclipses, and the Prophesies of *Haggai* and *Zechariah* compared together, it is manifest that the years of *Darius* began after the 24th day of the eleventh *Jewish* month, and before the 24th day of *April*, and by consequence in *March* or *April*.

Xerxes, Achschirosch, Achsweros, or Oxyares, succeeded his father *Darius*, and spent the first five years of his Reign, and something more, in preparations for his Expedition against the Greeks: and this Expedition was in the time of the Olympic Games, in the beginning of the first year of the 75th Olympiad, *Callias* being *Archon* at *Athens*; as all Chronologers agree. The great number of people which he drew out of *Susa* to invade *Greece*, made *Æschylus* the Poet say[485]:

[Greek: To d' asty Sousôn exekeinôsen peson.]
It emptied the falling city of Susa.

The passage of his army over the Hellespont began in the end of the fourth year of the 74th Olympiad, that is in *June, Anno Nabonass.* 268, and took up a month; and in autumn, after three months more, on the 16th day of the month *Munychion*, at the full moon, was the battel at *Salamis;* and a little after that an Eclipse of the Moon, which by the calculation fell on *Octob.* 2. His first year therefore began in spring, *Anno Nabonass.* 263, as above: he Reigned almost twenty one years by the consent of all writers, and was murdered by *Artabanus*, captain of his guards; towards the end of winter, *Anno Nabonass.* 284.

Artabanus Reigned seven months, and upon suspicion of treason against *Xerxes*, was slain by *Artaxerxes Longimanus*, the son of *Xerxes.*

Artaxerxes began his Reign in the autumnal half year, between the 4th and 9th *Jewish* months, *Nehem.* i. 1. & ii. 1, & v. 14. and *Ezra* vii. 7, 8, 9. and his 20th year fell in with the 4th year of the 83d Olympiad, as *Africanus*[486] informs us, and therefore his first year began within a month or two or the autumnal Equinox, *Anno Nabonass.* 284. *Thucydides* relates that the news of his death came to *Athens* in winter, in the seventh year of the *Peloponnesian* war, that is *An.* 4. Olymp. 88. and by the Canon he Reigned forty one years, including the Reign of his predecessor *Artabanus*, and died about the middle of winter, *Anno Nabonass.* 325

ineunte: the *Persians* now call him *Ardschir* and *Bahaman,* the Oriental Christians *Artahascht.*

Then Reigned Xerxes, two months, and *Sogdian* seven months, and *Darius Nothus,* the bastard son of *Artaxerxes,* nineteen years wanting four or five months; and *Darius* died in summer, a little after the end of the *Peloponnesian* war, and in the same Olympic year, and by consequence in *May or June, Anno Nabonass.* 344. The 13th year of his Reign was coincident in winter with the 20th of the *Peloponnesian* war, and the years of that war are stated by indisputable characters, and agreed on by all Chronologers: the war began in spring, *Ann.* 1. Olymp. 87, lasted 27 years, and ended Apr. 14. An. 4. Olymp. 93.

The next King was *Artaxerxes Mnemon,* the son of *Darius:* he Reigned forty six years, and died *Anno Nabonass.* 390. Then Reigned Artaxerxes Ochus twenty one years; *Arses,* or *Arogus,* two years, and *Darius Codomannus* four years, unto the battel of Arbela, whereby the *Persian* Monarchy was translated to the Greeks, *Octob. 2. An. Nabonass.* 417; but *Darius* was not slain untill a year and some months after.

I have hitherto stated the times of this Monarchy out of the *Greek* and *Latin* writers: for the Jews knew nothing more of the *Babylonian* and *Medo-Persian* Empires than what they have out of the sacred books of the old Testament; and therefore own no more Kings, nor years of Kings, than they can find in those books: the Kings they reckon are only *Nebuchadnezzar, Evilmerodach, Belshazzar, Darius* the *Mede, Cyrus, Ahasuerus,* and *Darius* the *Persian;* this last *Darius* they reckon to be the *Artaxerxes,* in whose Reign *Ezra* and *Nehemiah* came to *Jerusalem,* accounting *Artaxerxes* a common name of the *Persian* Kings: Nebuchadnezzar, they say, Reigned forty five years, 2 King. xxv. 27. *Belshazzar* three years, *Dan.* viii. 1. and therefore *Evilmerodach* twenty three, to make up the seventy years captivity; excluding the first year of *Nebuchadnezzar,* in which they say the Prophesy of the seventy years was given. To *Darius* the *Mede* they assign one year, or at most but two, *Dan.* ix. 1. to *Cyrus* three years incomplete, *Dan.* x. 1. to *Ahasuerus* twelve years 'till the casting of *Pur, Esth.* iii. 7. one year more 'till the *Jews* smote their enemies, *Esth.* ix. 1. and one year more 'till *Esther* and *Mordecai* wrote the second letter for the keeping of *Purim, Esth.* ix. 29. in all fourteen years: and to *Darius* the *Persian* they allot thirty two or rather thirty six years, *Nehem.* xiii. 6. So that the *Persian* Empire from the building of the Temple in the Second year of *Darius Hystaspis,* flourished only thirty four years, until *Alexander* the great overthrew it: thus the *Jews* reckon in their greater Chronicle, *Seder Olam Rabbah. Josephus,* out of the sacred and other books, reckons only these Kings of *Persia; Cyrus, Cambyses, Darius Hystaspis, Xerxes, Artaxerxes,* and *Darius:* and taking this *Darius,* who was *Darius Nothus,* to be one and the same King with the last *Darius,* whom *Alexander* the great overcame; by means of this reckoning he makes *Sanballat* and *Jaddua* alive when *Alexander* the great overthrew the *Persian* Empire. Thus all the *Jews* conclude the *Persian* Empire with *Artaxerxes Longimanus,* and *Darius Nothus,* allowing no more Kings of *Persia,* than they found in the books of *Ezra* and *Nehemiah;* and referring to the Reigns of this *Artaxerxes,* and this *Darius,* whatever they met with in profane history concerning the following Kings of the same names: so as to take *Artaxerxes Longimanus, Artaxerxes Mnemon* and *Artaxerxes Ochus*, for one and the same *Artaxerxes;* and *Darius Nothus,* and *Darius Codomannus,* for one and the same *Darius;* and *Jaddua,* and *Simeon Justus,* for one and the same High-Priest. Those Jews who took *Herod* for the *Messiah,* and were thence called *Herodians,* seem to have grounded their opinion upon the seventy weeks of years, which they found between the Reign of *Cyrus* and that of *Herod:* but afterwards, in applying the Prophesy to *Theudas,* and *Judas* of *Galilee,* and at length to *Barchochab,* they seem to have shortned the Reign of the Kingdom of *Persia.* These accounts being very imperfect, it was necessary to have recourse to the records of the *Greeks* and *Latines,* and to the Canon recited by *Ptolemy,* for stating the times of this Empire. Which being done, we have a better ground for understanding the history of the Jews set down in the books of *Ezra* and *Nehemiah,* and adjusting it; for this history having suffered by time, wants some illustration: and first I shall state the history of the *Jews* under *Zerubbabel,* in the Reigns of *Cyrus, Cambysis,* and *Darius Hystaspis.*

This history is contained partly in the three first chapters of the book of *Ezra,* and first five verses of the fourth; and partly in the book of *Nehemiah,* from the 5th verse of the seventh chapter to the 9th verse of the twelfth: for *Nehemiah* copied all this out of the Chronicles of the *Jews,* written before his days; as may appear by reading the place, and considering that the Priests and Levites who sealed the Covenant on the 24th day of the seventh month, *Nehem.* x. were the very same with those who returned from captivity in the first year of *Cyrus, Nehem.* xii. and that all those who returned sealed it: this will be perceived by the following comparison of their names.

The Priests who returned	The Priests who sealed.
Nehemiah. Ezra ii. 2.	*Nehemiah.*
Serajah.	*Serajah.*
*	*Azariah.*
Jeremiah.	*Jeremiah.*
Ezra.	*Ezra. Nehem.* 8.
*	*Pashur.*
Amariah.	*Amariah.*
Malluch: or *Melicu, Neh. xii.* 2, 14.	*Malchijah.*
Hattush	*Hattush.*
Shechaniah or *Shebaniah Neh. xii.* 3, 14.	*Shebaniah.*
*	*Malluch.*
Rehum: or *Harim, ib.* 3, 15.	*Harim.*
Meremoth.	*Meremoth.*
Iddo	*Obadiah* or *Obdia.*
*	*Daniel.*
Ginnetho: or *Ginnethon, Neh. xii.* 4, 16.	*Ginnethon.*
*	*Baruch.*
*	*Meshullam.*
Abijah.	*Abijah.*

Miamin.	*Mijamin.*
Maadiah.	*Maaziah.*
Bilgah.	*Bilgai.*
Shemajah.	*Shemajah.*
Jeshua.	*Jeshua.*
Binnui.	*Binnui.*
Kadmiel.	*Kadmiel.*
Sherebiah. [Hebrew: shrbjh].	*Shebaniah. [Hebrew: shbnjh].*
Judah: or Hodaviah, Ezra ii. 40. & iii. 9.	
[Greek: Ôdouia]; Septuag.	*Hodijah.*

The *Levites, Jeshua, Kadmiel,* and *Hodaviah* or *Judah,* here mentioned, are reckoned chief fathers among the people who returned with *Zerubbabel, Ezra* ii. 40. and they assisted as well in laying the foundation of the Temple, *Ezra* iii. 9. as in reading the law, and making and sealing the covenant, *Nehem.* viii. 7. & ix. 5. & x. 9, 10.

Comparing therefore the books of *Ezra* and *Nehemiah* together; the history of the *Jews* under *Cyrus, Cambyses,* and *Darius Hystaspis,* is that they returned from captivity under *Zerubbabel,* in the first year of *Cyrus,* with the Holy Vessels and a commission to build the Temple; and came to *Jerusalem* and *Judah,* every one to his city, and dwelt in their cities untill the seventh month; and then coming to *Jerusalem,* they first built the Altar, and on the first day of the seventh month began to offer the daily burnt-offerings, and read in the book of the Law, and they kept a solemn fast, and sealed a Covenant; and thenceforward the Rulers of the people dwelt at *Jerusalem,* and the rest of the people cast lots, to dwell one in ten at *Jerusalem,* and the rest in the cities of *Judah:* and in the second year of their coming, in the second month, which was six years before the death of *Cyrus,* they laid the foundation of the Temple; but *the adversaries of* Judah *troubled them in building, and hired counsellors against them all the days of* Cyrus, and longer, *even until the Reign of* Darius King of Persia: but in the second year of his Reign, by the prophesying of *Haggai* and *Zechariah,* they returned to the work; and by the help of a new decree from *Darius,* finished it on the third day of the month *Adar,* in the sixth year of his Reign, and kept the Dedication with joy, and the Passover, and Feast of Unleavened Bread.

Now this *Darius* was not *Darius Nothus,* but *Darius Hystaspis,* as I gather by considering that the second year of this *Darius* was the seventieth of the indignation against *Jerusalem,* and the cities of *Judah,* which indignation commenced with the invasion of *Jerusalem,* and the cities of *Judah* by *Nebuchadnezzar,* in the ninth year of *Zedekiah, Zech.* i. 12. *Jer.* xxxiv. 1, 7, 22. & xxxix. 1. and that the fourth year of this *Darius,* was the seventieth from the burning of the Temple in the eleventh year of *Zedekiah, Zech.* vii. 5. & *Jer.* lii. 12. both which are exactly true of *Darius Hystaspis:* and that in the second year of this *Darius* there were men living who had seen the first Temple, *Hagg.* ii. 3. whereas the second year of *Darius Nothus* was 166 years after the desolation of the Temple and City. And further, if the finishing of the Temple be deferred to the sixth year of *Darius Nothus, Jeshua* and *Zerubbabel* must have been the one High-

Priest, the other Captain of the people an hundred and eighteen years together, besides their ages before; which is surely too long: for in the first year of *Cyrus* the chief Priests were *Serajah, Jeremiah, Ezra, Amariah, Malluch, Shechaniah, Rehum, Meremoth, Iddo, Ginnetho, Abijah, Miamin, Maadiah, Bilgah, Shemajah, Joiarib, Jedaiah, Sallu, Amok, Hilkiah, Jedaiah:* these were Priests in the days of *Jeshua,* and the eldest sons of them all, *Merajah* the son of *Serajah, Hananiah* the son of *Jeremiah, Meshullam* the son of *Ezra,* &c. were chief Priests in the days of *Joiakim* the son of *Jeshua: Nehem.* xii. and therefore the High Priest-hood of *Jeshua* was but of an ordinary length.

I have now stated the history of the *Jews* in the Reigns of *Cyrus, Cambyses,* and *Darius Hystaspis:* it remains that I state their history in the Reigns of *Xerxes,* and *Artaxerxes Longimanus:* for I place the history of *Ezra* and *Nehemiah* in the Reign of this *Artaxerxes,* and not in that of *Artaxerxes Mnemon:* for during all the *Persian* Monarchy, until the last Darius mentioned in Scripture, whom I take to be *Darius Nothus,* there were but six High-Priests in continual succession of father and son, namely, *Jeshua, Joiakim, Eliashib, Joiada, Jonathan, Jaddua,* and the seventh High-Priest was *Onias* the son of *Jaddua,* and the eighth was *Simeon Justus,* the Son of *Onias,* and the ninth was *Eleazar* the younger brother of *Simeon.* Now, at a mean reckoning, we should allow about 27 or 28 years only to a Generation by the eldest sons of a family, one Generation with another, as above; but if in this case we allow 30 years to a Generation, and may further suppose that *Jeshua,* at the return of the captivity in the first year of the Empire of the *Persians,* was about 30 or 40 years old; *Joiakim* will be of about that age in the 16th year of *Darius Hystaspis, Eliashib* in the tenth year of *Xerxes, Joiada* in the 19th year of *Artaxerxes Longimanus, Jonathan* in the 8th year of *Darius Nothus, Jaddua* in the 19th year of *Artaxerxes Mnemon, Onias* in the 3d year of *Artaxerxes Ochus,* and *Simeon Justus* two years before the death of *Alexander* the Great: and this reckoning, as it is according to the course of nature, so it agrees perfectly well with history; for thus *Eliashib* might be High-Priest, and have grandsons, before the seventh year of *Artaxerxes Longimanus, Ezra* x. 6. and without exceeding the age which many old men attain unto, continue High-Priest 'till after the 32d year of that King, *Nehem.* xiii. 6, 7. and his grandson *Johanan,* or *Jonathan,* might have a chamber in the Temple in the seventh year of that King, *Ezra* x. 6. and be High-Priest before Ezra wrote the sons of *Levi* in the book of *Chronicles; Nehem.* xii. 23. and in his High-Priesthood, he might slay his younger brother *Jesus* in the Temple, before the end of the Reign of *Artaxerxes Mnemon: Joseph. Antiq.* l. xi. c. 7. and *Jaddua* might be High-Priest before the death of *Sanballat, Joseph. ib.* and before the death of *Nehemiah, Nehem.* xii. 22. and also before the end of the Reign of *Darius Nothus;* and he might thereby give occasion to *Josephus* and the later *Jews,* who took this King for the last *Darius,* to fall into an opinion that *Sanballat, Jaddua,* and *Manasseh* the younger brother of *Jaddua,* lived till the end of the Reign of the last *Darius: Joseph. Antiq.* l. xi. c. 7, 8. and the said *Manasseh* might marry *Nicaso* the daughter of *Sanballat,* and for that offence be chased from *Nehemiah,* before the end of the Reign of *Artaxerxes Longimanus; Nehem.* xiii. 28. *Joseph. Antiq.* l. xi. c. 7, 8. and *Sanballat* might at that time be *Satrapa* of *Samaria,* and in the Reign of *Darius Nothus,* or soon after, build the Temple of the *Samaritans* in *Mount Gerizim,* for his son-in-law *Manasseh,* the first High-Priest of that Temple; *Joseph. ib.* and *Simeon Justus* might be High-Priest when the *Persian* Empire was invaded by *Alexander* the Great, as the *Jews* represent, *Joma* fol. 69. 1. *Liber Juchasis. R. Gedaliah,* &c. and for that reason he might be taken by some of the *Jews* for the same High-Priest with *Jaddua,* and be dead some time before the book of *Ecclesiasticus* was writ in *Hebrew* at *Jerusalem,* by the grandfather of him, who in the 38th year of the *Egyptian Æra* of *Dionysius,* that is in the 77th year after the death of *Alexander* the Great, met with a copy of it in *Egypt,* and there translated it into *Greek: Ecclesiast.* ch. 50. & *in Prolog.* and *Eleazar,* the younger brother and successor of *Simeon,* might cause the Law to be translated into *Greek,* in the beginning of the Reign of *Ptolemaus Philadelphus: Joseph. Antiq.* l. xii. c. 2. and *Onias* the son of *Simeon Justus,* who was a child at his father's death, and by consequence was born in his father's old age, might be so old in the Reign of *Ptolemæus Euergetes,* as to have his follies excused to that King, by representing that he was then grown childish with old age. *Joseph. Antiq.* l. xii. c. 4. In this manner the actions of all these High-Priests suit with the Reigns of the Kings, without any straining from the course of nature: and according to this reckoning the days of *Ezra* and *Nehemiah* fall in with the Reign of the first *Artaxerxes;* for *Ezra* and *Nehemiah* flourished in the High Priesthood of *Eliashib, Ezra* x. 6. *Nehem.* iii. 1. & xiii. 4, 28. But if *Eliashib, Ezra* and *Nehemiah* be placed in the Reign of the second *Artaxerxes,* since they lived beyond the 32d year of *Artaxerxes, Nehem.* xiii. 28, there must be at least 160 years allotted to the three first High-Priests, and but 42 to the four or five last, a division too unequal: for the High Priesthoods of *Jeshua, Joiakim,* and *Eliashib,* were but of an ordinary length, that of *Jeshua* fell in with one Generation of the chief Priests, and that of *Joiakim* with the next Generation, as we have shewed already; and that of *Eliashib* fell in with the third Generation: for at the dedication of the wall, *Zechariah* the son of *Jonathan,* the son of *Shemaiah,* was one of the Priests, *Nehem.* xii. 35, and *Jonathan* and his father *Shemaiah,* were contemporaries to *Joiakim* and his father Jeshua*: Nehem.* xii. 6, 18. I observe further that in the first year of *Cyrus, Jeshua,* and *Bani,* or *Binnui,* were chief fathers of the *Levites, Nehem.* vii. 7. 15. & *Ezra* ii. 2. 10. & iii. 9. and that *Jozabad* the son of *Jeshua,* and *Noadiah* the son of *Binnui,* were chief Levites in the seventh year of *Artaxerxes,* when *Ezra* came to *Jerusalem, Ezra* viii. 33. so that this *Artaxerxes* began his Reign before the end of the second Generation: and that he Reigned in the time of the third Generation is confirmed by two instances more; for *Meshullam* the son of *Berechiah,* the son of *Meshezabeel,* and *Azariah* the son of *Maaseiah,* the son of *Ananiah,* were fathers of their houses at the repairing of the wall; *Nehem.* iii. 4, 23. and their grandfathers, *Meshazabeel* and *Hananiah,* subscribed the covenant in the Reign of *Cyrus: Nehem.* x. 21, 23. Yea *Nehemiah,* this same *Nehemiah* the son of *Hachaliah,* was the *Tirshatha,* and subscribed it, *Nehem.* x. 1, & viii. 9, & *Ezra* ii. 2, 63. and therefore in the 32d year of *Artaxerxes Mnemon,* he will be above 180 years old, an age surely too great. The same may be said of *Ezra,* if he was that Priest and Scribe who read the Law, *Nehem.* viii. for he is the son of *Serajah,* the son of

Azariah, the son of *Hilkiah*, the son of *Shallum*, &c. *Ezra* vii. 1. and this *Serajah* went into captivity at the burning of the Temple, and was there slain, 1 *Chron.* vi. 14. 2 *King.* xxv. 18. and from his death, to the twentieth year of *Artaxerxes Mnemon*, is above 200 years; an age too great for *Ezra*.

I consider further that *Ezra*, chap. iv. names *Cyrus*, *, *Darius*, *Ahasuerus*, and *Artaxerxes*, in continual order, as successors to one another, and these names agree to *Cyrus*, *, *Darius Hystaspis*, *Xerxes*, and *Artaxerxes Longimanus*, and to no other Kings of *Persia*: some take this *Artaxerxes* to be not the Successor, but the Predecessor of *Darius Hystaspis*, not considering that in his Reign the *Jews* were busy in building the City and the Wall, *Ezra* iv. 12. and by consequence had finished the Temple before. *Ezra* describes first how the people of the land hindered the building of the Temple all the days of *Cyrus*, and further, untill the Reign of *Darius;* and after the Temple was built, how they hindered the building of the city in the Reign of *Ahasuerus* and *Artaxerxes*, and then returns back to the story of the Temple in the Reign of *Cyrus* and *Darius;* and this is confirmed by comparing the book of *Ezra* with the book of *Esdras:* for if in the book of *Ezra* you omit the story of *Ahasuerus* and *Artaxerxes*, and in that of *Esdras* you omit the same story of *Artaxerxes*, and that of the three wise men, the two books will agree: and therefore the book of *Esdras*, if you except the story of the three wise men, was originally copied from authentic writings of Sacred Authority. Now the story of *Artaxerxes*, which, with that of *Ahasuerus*, in the book of *Ezra* interrupts the story of *Darius*, doth not interrupt it in the book of *Esdras*, but is there inferred into the story of *Cyrus*, between the first and second chapter of *Ezra;* and all the rest of the story of *Cyrus*, and that of *Darius*, is told in the book of *Esdras* in continual order, without any interruption: so that the *Darius* which in the book of *Ezra* precedes *Ahasuerus* and *Artaxerxes*, and the *Darius* which in the same book follows them, is, by the book of *Esdras*, one and the same *Darius;* and I take the book of *Esdras* to be the best interpreter of the book of *Ezra:* so the *Darius* mentioned between *Cyrus* and *Ahasuerus*, is *Darius Hysaspis;* and therefore *Ahasuerus* and *Artaxerxes* who succeed him, are *Xerxes* and *Artaxerxes Longimanus;* and the *Jews* who came up from *Artaxerxes* to *Jerusalem*, and began to build the city and the wall, *Ezra* iv. 13. are *Ezra* with his companions: which being understood, the history of the Jews in the Reign of these Kings will be as follows.

After the Temple was built, and *Darius Hystaspis* was dead, the enemies of the *Jews* in the beginning of the Reign of his successor *Ahasuerus* or *Xerxes*, wrote unto him an accusation against them; *Ezra* iv. 6. but in the seventh year of his successor *Artaxerxes*, *Ezra* and his companions went up from *Babylon* with Offerings and Vessels for the Temple, and power to bestow on it out of the King's Treasure what should be requisite; *Ezra* vii. whence the Temple is said to be finished, *according to the commandment of* Cyrus, *and* Darius, *and Artaxerxes King of* Persia: *Ezra* vi. 14. Their commission was also to set Magistrates and Judges over the land, and thereby becoming a new Body Politic, they called a great Council or Sanhedrim to separate the people from strange wives; and they were also encouraged to attempt the building of *Jerusalem* with its wall: and thence

Ezra saith in his prayer, that *God had extended mercy unto them in the sight of the Kings* of Persia, *and given them a reviving to set up the house of their God, and to repair the desolations thereof, and to give them a WALL in* Judah, *even in* Jerusalem. *Ezra* ix. 9. But when they had begun to repair the wall, their enemies wrote against them to *Artaxerxes: Be it known,* say they, *unto the King, that the* Jews *which came up from thee to us, are come unto* Jerusalem, *building the rebellious and the bad city, and have set up the walls thereof, and joined the foundations,* &c. And the King wrote back that the *Jews* should cease and the city not be built, until another commandment should be given from him: whereupon their enemies *went up to* Jerusalem, *and made them cease by force and power; Ezra* iv. but in the twentieth year of the King, *Nehemiah* hearing that the Jews were in great affliction and distress, and that the wall of *Jerusalem,* that wall which had been newly repaired by *Ezra, was broken down, and the gates thereof burnt wth fire;* he obtained leave of the King to go and build the city, and the Governour's house, *Nehem.* i. 3. & ii. 6, 8, 17. and coming to *Jerusalem* the same year, he continued Governor twelve years, and built the wall; and being opposed by *Sanballat, Tobiah* and *Geshem,* he persisted in the work with great resolution and patience, until the breaches were made up: then *Sanballat* and *Geshem* sent messengers unto him five times to hinder him from setting up the doors upon the gates: but notwithstanding he persisted in the work, until the doors were also set up: so the wall was finished in the eight and twentieth year of the King, *Joseph. Antiq.* l. xi. c. 5. in the five and twentieth day of the month *Elul,* or sixth month, in fifty and two days after the breaches were made up, and they began to work upon the gates. While the timber for the gates was preparing and seasoning, they made up the breaches of the wall; both were works of time, and are not jointly to be reckoned within the 52 days: this is the time of the last work of the wall, the work of setting up the gates after the timber was seasoned and the breaches made up. When he had set up the gates, he dedicated the wall with great solemnity, and appointed Officers *over the chambers for the Treasure, for the Offerings, for the First-Fruits, and for the Tithes, to gather into them out of the fields of the cities, the portions appointed by the law for the Priests and Levites; and the Singers and the Porters kept the ward of their God;* Nehem. xii. *but the people in the city were but few, and the houses were unbuilt: Nehem.* vii. 1, 4. and in this condition he left *Jerusalem* in the 32d year of the King; and after sometime returning back from the King, he reformed such abuses as had been committed in his absence. *Nehem.* xiii. In the mean time, the Genealogies of the Priests and Levites were recorded in the book of the *Chronicles,* in the days of *Eliashib, Joiada, Jonathan,* and *Jaddua,* until the Reign of the next King *Darius Nothus,* whom *Nehemiah* calls *Darius* the *Persian: Nehem.* xii. 11, 22, 23. whence it follows that *Nehemiah* was Governor of the *Jews* until the Reign of *Darius Nothus.* And here ends the Sacred History of the Jews.

The histories of the *Persians* now extant in the East, represent that the oldest Dynasties of the Kings of Persia, were those whom they call *Pischdadians* and *Kaianides,* and that the Dynasty of the *Kaianides* immediately succeeded that of the *Pischdadians.* They derive the name *Kaianides* from the word *Kai,* which, they say, in the old *Persian* language signified a Giant or great King; and they call the first four Kings of this Dynasty, *Kai-Cobad, Kai-Caus, Kai-Cosroes,* and *Lohorasp,* and by *Lohorasp* mean *Kai-Axeres*, or *Cyaxeres*: for they say that *Lohorasp* was the first of their Kings who reduced their armies to good order and discipline, and *Herodotus* affirms the same thing of *Cyaxeres:* and they say further, that *Lohorasp* went eastward, and conquered many Provinces of *Persia*, and that one of his Generals, whom the *Hebrews* call *Nebuchadnezzar*, the *Arabians Bocktanassar*, and others *Raham* and *Gudars*, went westward, and conquered all *Syria* and *Judæa*, and took the city of *Jerusalem* and destroyed it: they seem to call *Nebuchadnezzar* the General of *Lohorasp*, because he assisted him in some of his wars. The fifth King of this Dynasty, they call *Kischtasp*, and by this name mean sometimes *Darius Medus*, and sometimes *Darius Hystaspis:* for they say that he was contemporary to *Ozair* or *Ezra*, and to *Zaradust* or *Zoroastres*, the Legislator of the *Ghebers* or fire-worshippers, and established his doctrines throughout all *Persia;* and here they take him for *Darius Hystaspis:* they say also that he was contemporary to *Jeremiah*, and to *Daniel*, and that he was the son and successor of *Lohorasp*, and here they take him for *Darius the Mede*. The sixth King of the *Kaianides*, they call *Bahaman*, and tell us that *Bahaman* was *Ardschir Diraz*, that is *Artaxerxes Longimanus*, so called from the great extent of his power: and yet they say that *Bahaman* went westward into *Mesopotamia* and *Syria*, and conquered *Belshazzar* the son of *Nebuchadnezzar*, and gave the Kingdom to *Cyrus* his Lieutenant-General over *Media:* and here they take *Bahaman* for *Darius Medus*. Next after *Ardschir Diraz*, they place *Homai* a Queen, the mother of *Darius Nothus*, tho' really she did not Reign: and the two next and last Kings of the *Kaianides*, they call *Darab* the bastard son of *Ardschir Diraz*, and *Darab* who was conquered by *Ascander Roumi*, that is *Darius Nothus*, and *Darius* who was conquered by *Alexander* the *Greek:* and the Kings between these two *Darius's* they omit, as they do also *Cyrus, Cambyses*, and Xerxes. The Dynasty of the *Kaianides*, was therefore that of the *Medes* and *Persians*, beginning with the defection of the *Medes* from the *Assyrians*, in the end of the Reign of *Sennacherib*, and ending with the conquest of *Persia* by *Alexander* the Great. But their account of this Dynasty is very imperfect, some Kings being omitted, and others being confounded with one another: and their Chronology of this Dynasty is still worse; for to the first King they assign a Reign of 120 years, to the second a Reign of 150 years, to the third a Reign of 60 years, to the fourth a Reign of 120 years, to the fifth as much, and to the sixth a Reign of 112 years.

This Dynasty being the Monarchy of the *Medes*, and *Persians;* the Dynasty of the *Pischdadians* which immediately preceded it, must be that of the *Assyrians:* and according to the oriental historians this was the oldest Kingdom in the world, some of its Kings living a thousand years a-piece, and one of them Reigning five hundred years, another seven hundred years, and another a thousand years.

We need not then wonder, that the *Egyptians* have made the Kings in the first Dynasty of their Monarchy, that which was seated at *Thebes* in the days of *David, Solomon*, and *Rehoboam*, so very ancient and so long lived; since the *Persians* have done the like to their Kings, who began to Reign in *Assyria* two hundred years after the death of *Solomon;* and the *Syrians* of *Damascus* have done the like to their Kings *Adar* and *Hazael,* who Reigned an hundred years after the death of *Solomon, worshipping them as Gods, and boasting their antiquity, and not knowing, saith Josephus, that they were but modern.*

And whilst all these nations have magnified their Antiquities so exceedingly, we need not wonder that the *Greeks* and *Latines* have made their first Kings a little older than the truth.

FINIS.

ENDNOTES

[1]   *In the life of* Lycurgus.
[2]   In the life of Solon.
[3]   Herod. l. 2.
[4]   Plutarch. de Pythiæ Oraculo.
[5]   Plutarch. in Solon
[6]   Apud Diog. Laert. in Solon p. 10.
[7]   Plin. nat. hist. l. 7. c. 56.
[8]   Ib. l. 5. c. 29.
[9]   Cont. Apion. sub initio.
[10]   In [Greek: Akousilaos].
[11]   Joseph. cont. Ap. l. 1.
[12]   Dionys. l. 1. initio.
[13]   Plutarch. in Numa.
[14]   Diodor. l. 16. p. 550. Edit. Steph.
[15]   Polyb. p. 379. B.
[16]   In vita Lycurgi, sub initio.
[17]   In Solone.
[18]   Plutarch. in Romulo & Numa.
[19]   In Æneid. 7. v. 678.
[20]   Diodor. l. 1.
[21]   Plutarch. in Romulo.
[22]   Lib. I. in Proæm.
[23]   Plutarch. in Lycurgo sub initio.
[24]   Pausan. l. 4. c. 13. p. 28. & c. 7. p. 296 & l. 3. c. 15. p. 245.
[25]   Pausan. l. 4. c. 7. p. 296.
[26]   Herod. l. 7.
[27]   Herod. l. 8.
[28]   Plato in Minoe.
[29]   Thucyd. l. 1. p. 13.
[30]   Athen. l. 14 p. 605
[31]   Pausan. l. 5. c. 8.
[32]   Pausan. l. 6. c. 19.
[33]   Plutarch. de Musica. Clemens Strom. l. 1. p. 308.
[34]   Herod. l. 6. c. 52.
[35]   Pausan. l. 5. c. 4.
[36]   Pausan. l. 5. c. 1, 3, 8. Strabo, l. 8, p. 357.
[37]   Pausan. l. 5. c.4.
[38]   Pausan. l. 5. c.18.
[39]   Solin. c. 30.
[40]   Dionys. l. 1. p. 15.
[41]   Apollon. Argonaut. l. 1. v. 101.
[42]   Plutarch. in Theseo.
[43]   Diodor. l. 1. p. 35.

[44]   Joseph. Antiq. l. 4. c. 8
[45]   Contra Apion. l. 1.
[46]   Hygin. Fab. 144.
[47]   Gen. i. 14. & viii. 22. Censorinus c. 19 & 20. Cicero in Verrem. Geminus
c. 6.
[48]   Cicero in Verrem.
[49]   Diodor. l. 1.
[50]   Cicero in Verrem.
[51]   Gem. c. 6.
[52]   Apud Laertium, in Cleobulo.
[53]   Apud Laertium, in Thalete. Plutarch. in Solone.
[54]   Censorinus c. 18. Herod. l. 2. prope initium.
[55]   Apollodor l. 3. p. 169. Strabo l. 16. p. 476. Homer. Odyss. [Tau]. v. 179.
[56]   Herod. l. 1.
[57]   Plutarch. in Numa.
[58]   Diodor. l. 3. p. 133.
[59]   Diodor. l. 1. p. 13.
[60]   Apud Theodorum Gazam de mentibus.
[61]   Apud Athenæum, l. 14.
[62]   Suidas in [Greek: Saroi].
[63]   Herod. l. 1.
[64]   Julian. Or: 4.
[65]   Strabo l. 17. p. 816.
[66]   Diodor. l. 1. p. 32.
[67]   Plutarch de Osiride & Iside. Diodor. l. 1. p. 9.
[68]   Hecatæus apud Diodor. l. 1. p. 32.
[69]   Isagoge Sect. 23, a Petavio edit.
[70]   Hipparch. ad Phænom. l.2. Sect. 3. a Petavio edit.
[71]   Hipparch. ad Phænom. l.1. Sect. 2.
[72]   Strom. 1. p. 306, 352.
[73]   Laertius Proem. l. 1.
[74]   Apollodor. l. 1. c. 9. Sect. 16.
[75]   Suidas in [Greek: Anagallis].
[76]   Apollodor. l. 1. c. 9. Sect. 25.
[77]   Laert. in Thalete. Plin. l. 2. c. 12.
[78]   Plin. l. 18. c. 23.
[79]   Petav. Var. Disl. l. 1. c. 5.
[80]   Petav. Doct. Temp. l. 4. c. 26.
[81]   Columel. l. 9. c. 14. Plin. l. 18. c. 25.
[82]   Arrian. l. 7.
[83]   In Moph.
[84]   Euanthes apud Athenæum, l. 67. p. 296.
[85]   Hyginus Fab. 14.
[86]   Homer. Odyss. l. 8. v. 292.
[87]   Hesiod. Theogon. v. 945.

[88] Pausan. l. 2. c. 23.
[89] Strabo l. 16.
[90] Isa. xxiii. 2. 12.
[91] 1 Kings v. 6
[92] Steph. in Azoth.
[93] Conon. Narrat. 37.
[94] Nonnus Dionysiac l. 13 v. 333 [alpha]   sequ.
[95] Athen. l. 4. c. 23.
[96] Strabo. l. 10. p. 661. Herod. l. 1.
[97] Strabo. l. 16.
[98] 2 Chron. xxi. 8, 10. & 2 Kings. viii. 20, 22.
[99] Herod. l. 1. initio, & l. 7. circa medium.
[100] Solin. c. 23, Edit. Salm.
[101] Plin. l. 4. c. 22.
[102] Strabo. l. 9. p. 401. & l. 10. p. 447.
[103] Herod. l. 5.
[104] Strabo. l. 1. p. 42.
[105] Strabo. l. 1. p. 48.
[106] Bochart. Canaan. l. 1. c. 34.
[107] Strabo. l. 3. p. 140.
[108] Vid. Phil. Transact. N°. 359.
[109] Canaan, l. 1. c. 34. p. 682.
[110] Aristot. de Mirab.
[111] Plin. l. 7. c. 56.
[112] Canaan. l. 1. c. 39.
[113] Philostratus in vita Apollonii l. 5. c. 1. apud Photium.
[114] Arnob. l. 1.
[115] Bochart. in Canaan. l. 1. c. 24.
[116] Oros. l. 5. c. 15. Florus l. 3. c. 1. Sallust. in Jugurtha.
[117] Antiq. l. 8. c. 2, 5. & l. 9. c. 14.
[118] Thucyd. l. 6. initio. Euseb. Chr.
[119] Thucyd. ib.
[120] Apud Dionys. l. 1. p. 15.
[121] Herod. l. 8. c. 137.
[122] Herod. l. 8.
[123] Herod. l. 8. c. 139.
[124] Thucyd. l. 2. prope finem.
[125] Herod l. 6. c. 127.
[126] Strabo. l. 8. p. 355.
[127] Pausan. l. 6. c. 22.
[128] Pausan. l. 5. c. 9.
[129] Strabo. l. 8. p. 358.
[130] Phanias Eph. ap. Plut. in vita Solonis.
[131] Vid. Dionys. Halicarnass. l. 1. p. 44, 45.
[132] Pausan. l. 2. c. 6.

[133]   Hygin. Fab. 7 & 8.
[134]   Homer. Iliad. [Omicron].
[135]   Homer. Odys. [Eta]. Diodor. l. 5. p.237.
[136]   Diodor. l. 1. p.17.
[137]   Pausan. l. 2. c. 25.
[138]   Apollodor. l. 2. Sect. 5.
[139]   Herod l. 7.
[140]   Bochart. Canaan part. 2. cap. 13.
[141]   Apollon. Argonaut. l. 1. v. 77.
[142]   Conon. Narrat. 13.
[143]   Pausan. l. 5. c. 1. Apollodor. l. 1. c. 7.
[144]   Pausan. l. 7. c. 1.
[145]   Pausan. l. 1. c. 37. & l. 10. c. 29.
[146]   Pausan. l. 7. c. 1.
[147]   Hesych. in [Greek: Kranaos].
[148]   Themist. Orat. 19.
[149]   Plato in Alcib. 1.
[150]   Pausan. l. 8. c. 1, 2, 3, 4, 5.
[151]   Pausan. l. 8. c. 4. Apollon. Argonaut. l. 1. v. 161.
[152]   Pausan. l. 8. c. 4.
[153]   Herod. l. 5. c. 58.
[154]   Strabo l. 10. p. 464, 465, 466.
[155]   Solin. Polyhist. c. 11.
[156]   Isidor. originum. lib. xi. c. 6.
[157]   Clem. Strom. l. 1.
[158]   Pausan. l. 9. c. 11.
[159]   Strabo l. 10. p. 472, 473. Diodor. l. 5. c. 4.
[160]   Strabo l. 10. p. 468. 472. Diodor. l. 5. c. 4.
[161]   Lucian de sacrificiis. Apollod. l. 1. c. 1. sect. 3. & c. 2. sect. 1.
[162]   Boch. in Canaan. l. 1. c. 15.
[163]   Athen. l. 13. p. 601.
[164]   Plutarch in Theseo.
[165]   Homer Il. [Nu]. & [Xi]. & Odys. [Lambda]. & [Tau].
[166]   Herod. l. 1.
[167]   Apollod. l. 3. c. 1. Hygin. Fab. 40, 41, 42. 178.
[168]   Lucian. de Dea Syria.
[169]   Diodor. l. 5. c. 4,
[170]   Argonaut. l. 2. v. 1236.
[171]   Lucian. de sacrificiis.
[172]   Porphyr. in vita Pythag.
[173]   Cicero de Nat. Deor. l. 3.
[174]   Callimac. Hymn 1. v. 8.
[175]   Cypr. de Idolorum vanitate.
[176]   Tert. Apologet. c. 10.
[177]   Macrob. Saturnal. lib. 1. c. 7.

[178] Pausan. l. 5. c. 7, vid. et. c. 13. 14. & l. 8. c. 2.
[179] Pausan. l. 8. c. 29.
[180] Diodor. l. 5. p. 183.
[181] Pausan. l. 5. c. 8. 14.
[182] Herod. l. 2. c. 44.
[183] Cic. de natura Deorum. lib. 3.
[184] Diodor. p. 223.
[185] Dionys. l. 1. p. 38, 42.
[186] Lucian. de saltatione.
[187] Arnob. adv. gent. l. 6. p. 131.
[188] Herod. l. 2. initio.
[189] Diodor. l. 1. p. 8.
[190] Hesiod. opera. v. 108.
[191] Apollon. Argonaut. l. 4. v. 1643.
[192] Vita Homeri Herodoto adfer.
[193] Herod. l. 2.
[194] 1 Sam. ix. 16. & xiii. 5. 19, 20.
[195] Clem. Al. Strom. 1. p. 321.
[196] Plin. l. 7.
[197] Plato in Timæo.
[198] Apollodor. l. 3. c. 1.
[199] Herod. l. 2.
[200] Hygin. Fab. 7.
[201] Apollodor. l. 3. c. 6.
[202] Homer. Il. [Gamma]. vers 572.
[203] Thucyd. l. 2. p. 110. & Plutarch. in Theseo.
[204] Strabo. l. 9. p. 396.
[205] Apud Strabonem, l. 9. p. 397.
[206] Pausan. l. 2. c. 15.
[207] Strabo. l. 8. p. 337.
[208] Pausan. l. 8. c. 1. 2.
[209] Plin. l. 7. c. 56.
[210] Dionys. l. 1. p. 10.
[211] Dionys. l. 2. p. 126.
[212] Diodor l. 5. p. 224. 225. 240.
[213] Ammian. l. 17. c. 7.
[214] Plin. l. 2. c. 87.
[215] Diodor. l. 5. p. 202. 204.
[216] Apud Diodor. l. 5. p. 201.
[217] Dionys. l. 1. p. 17.
[218] Dionys. l. 1. p. 33. 34.
[219] Dionys. ib.
[220] Ptol. Hephæst. l. 2.
[221] Dionys. l. 2. p. 34.
[222] Diodor. l. 5. p. 230.

[223]   Ister apud Porphyr. abst. l. 2. s. 56.
[224]   Bochart. Canaan. l. 1. c. 15.
[225]   Apud Strabonem. lib. 14. p. 684.
[226]   Strabo. l. 17. p. 828.
[227]   Diodor. l. 3. p. 132.
[228]   Herod. l. 1.
[229]   1 King. xx. 16.
[230]   Genes. xiv. Deut ii. 9. 12. 19.-22.
[231]   Exod. i. 9. 22.
[232]   Job xxxi. 11.
[233]   Job xxxi. 26.
[234]   1 Chron. xi. 4. 5. Judg. i. 21. 2 Sam v. 6.
[235]   Vide Hermippum apud Athenæum, I.
[236]   Argonaut. l. 4. v. 272.
[237]   Diodor. l. 1. p. 7.
[238]   Apud Diodorum l. 3. p. 140.
[239]   Diodor. l. 3. p. 131. 132.
[240]   Pausan. l. 2. c. 20. p. 155.
[241]   Diodor. l. 3. p. 130 & Schol. Apollonii. l. 2.
[242]   Ammian. l. 22. c. 8.
[243]   Justin. l. 2. c. 4.
[244]   Diodor. l. 1. p. 9.
[245]   Apud Diodor. l. 3. p. 141.
[246]   Step. in [Greek: Ammônia].
[247]   Plin. l. 6. c. 28.
[248]   Ptol. l. 6. c. 7.
[249]   D. Augustin. in exposit. epist. ad Rom. sub initio.
[250]   Procop. de bello Vandal. l. 2. c. 10.
[251]   Chron. l. 1. p. 11.
[252]   Gemar. ad tit. Shebijth. cap. 6.
[253]   Manetho apud Josephum cont. Appion. l. 1. p. 1039.
[254]   Herod. l. 2.
[255]   Jerem. xliv. 1. Ezek. xxix. 14.
[256]   Menetho apud Porphyrium [Greek: peri aponês**] l. 1. Sect. 55. Et.
Euseb. Præp. l. 4. c. 16. p. 155.
[257]   Diodor. l. 3. p. 101.
[258]   Diodor. apud Photium in Biblioth.
[259]   Herod. l. 2.
[260]   Plutarch. de Iside. p. 355. Diodor. l. 1. p. 9.
[261]   Augustin. de Civ. Dei. l. 18. c. 47.
[262]   Apud Photium, c. 279.
[263]   Fab. 274.
[264]   Apud Euseb. Chron.
[265]   Plin. l. 6. c. 23, 28. & l. 7. c. 56.
[266]   Diodor. l. 1. p. 17.

[267]   Pausan. l. 4. c. 23.
[268]   Apollodor. l. 2. c. 1.
[269]   Dionys. in Perie. v. 623.
[270]   Fab. 275.
[271]   Saturnal. l. 5. c. 21.
[272]   Lucan. l. 10.
[273]   Lucan. l. 9.
[274]   Herod. l. 1.
[275]   Diodor. l. 1. p. 35. Herod. l. 2 c. 102, 103, 106.
[276]   Pausan. l. 10. Suidas in [Greek: Parnasioi].
[277]   Lucan l. 5.
[278]   Argonaut. l. 4. v. 272.
[279]   Herod. l. 2. c. 109.
[280]   In vita Pythag. c. 29.
[281]   Diodor. l. 1. p. 36
[282]   Dionys. de situ Orbis.
[283]   Diodor. l. 1. p. 39.
[284]   Plutarch. de Iside & Osiride.
[285]   Diodor. l. 1. p. 8.
[286]   Lucian. de Dea Syria
[287]   Exod. xxxiv. 13. Num. xxxiii. 52. Deut. vii. 5. & xii. 3.
[288]   2 Sam. viii. 10. & 1 King. xi. 23.
[289]   Antiq l. 9. c. 2.
[290]   Justin. l. 36.
[291]   Diodor. l. 5. p. 238.
[292]   Suidas in [Greek: Sardanapalos].
[293]   Apollod. l. 3.
[294]   Argonaut. l. 4. v. 424. & l. 1. v. 621.
[295]   Homer Odyss. [Theta]. v. 268. 292. & Hymn. 1. & 2. in Venerem. &
Hesiod. Theogon. v. 192.
[296]   Pausan. l. 1. c. 20.
[297]   Clem. Al. Admon. ad Gent. p. 10. Apollodor. l. 3. c. 13. Pindar. Pyth.
Ode 2. Hesych. in [Greek: Kinyradai]. Steph. in [Greek: Amathous]. Strabo. l.
16, p. 755.
[298]   Clem. Al. Admon. ad Gent. p. 21. Plin. l. 7. c. 56.
[299]   Herod. l. 2.
[300]   Herod. l. 3. c. 37.
[301]   Bochart. Canaan. l. 1. c. 4.
[302]   Apud Athenæum l. 9. p. 392.
[303]   Ptol. l. 2.
[304]   Diod. l. 3. p. 145.
[305]   Vas. Chron. Hisp. c. 10.
[306]   Strabo l. 16. p. 776.
[307]   Homer.
[308]   Diodor. l. 3. p.132, 133

[309]   Plato in Timæo. & Critia.
[310]   Apud Diodor. l. 5. p. 233.
[311]   Pamphus apud Pausan. l. 7. c. 21.
[312]   Herod. l. 2. c. 50.
[313]   Plutarch in Iside.
[314]   Lucian de Saltatione.
[315]   Agatharc. apud Photium.
[316]   Hygin. Fab. 150.
[317]   Plutarch. in Iside.
[318]   Diodor. l. 1. p. 10.
[319]   Pindar. Pyth. Ode 9.
[320]   Diodor. l. 1. p. 12.
[321]   Plin. l. 6. c. 29.
[322]   Herod. l. 2. c. 110.
[323]   Manetho apud Josephum cont. Apion. p. 1052, 1053.
[324]   Diodor. l. 1. p. 31.
[325]   Herod. l. 2.
[326]   Strabo. l. 1. p. 48.
[327]   Pindar. Pyth. Ode 4.
[328]   Strabo. l. 1. p. 21, 45, 46.
[329]   Diodor. l. 1. p. 29.
[330]   Manetho
[331]   Herod. l. 2
[332]   Herod. l. 2.
[333]   Ammian. l. 17. c. 4.
[334]   Strabo. l. 17. p. 817.
[335]   Annal. l. 2. c. 60.
[336]   Diodor. l. 1. p. 32.
[337]   Diodor. l. 1. p. 51.
[338]   Joseph. Ant. l. 1. c. 4.
[339]   Heordot. l. 2. c. 141.
[340]   Isa. xix. 2, 4, 11, 13, 23.
[341]   Herod. l. 2. c. 148, &c.
[342]   Plin. l. 36. c. 8. 9.
[343]   Diodor. l. 1 p. 29, &c.
[344]   Diodor. l. 2, p. 83.
[345]   Amos vi. 13, 14.
[346]   Amos vi. 2.
[347]   2 Chron. xxvi. 6.
[348]   2 King. xiv. 25.
[349]   2 King. xix. 11.
[350]   Isa. x. 8.
[351]   1 Chron. v. 26. 2 King. xvi. 9 & xvii. 6, 24. & Ezra iv. 9.
[352]   Isa. xxii. 6.
[353]   2 King. xvii. 24, 30, 31. & xviii. 33, 34, 35. 2 Chron. xxxii. 15.

[354]   2 Chron. xxxii. 13, 15.
[355]   Hosea v. 13. & x. 6, 14.
[356]   Herod. l. iii. c. 155.
[357]   Herod. l. i. c. 184.
[358]   Beros. apud Josep. contr. Appion. l. 1.
[359]   Curt. l. 5. c. 1.
[360]   Apud Euseb. Præp. l. 9. c. 41.
[361]   Doroth. apud Julium Firmicum.
[362]   Heren. apud Steph. in Βαβ.
[363]   Abyden apud Euseb. Præp. l. 9. c. 41.
[364]   Isa. xxiii. 13.
[365]   Tobit. i. 13. Annal. Tyr. apud Joseph. Ant. l. 9. c. 14.
[366]   Hosea x. 14.
[367]   Tobit. i. 15.
[368]   Tobit. i. 21. 2 King. xix. 37. Ptol. Canon.
[369]   Isa. xx. 1, 3, 4.
[370]   Herod. l. 1. c. 72. & l. 7. c. 63.
[371]   Apud Athenæum l. xii. p. 528.
[372]   Herod. l. 1. c. 96. &c.
[373]   Athenæus l. 12. p. 529, 530.
[374]   Herod. l. 1. c. 102.
[375]   Herod. l. 1. c. 103. Steph. in Παρθυαιοι.
[376]   Alexander Polyhist. apud Euseb. in Chron. p. 46 & apud Syncellum. p. 210.
[377]   2 Kings xxiv. 7. Jer. xlvi. 2. Eupolemus apud Euseb. Præp. l. 9. c. 35.
[378]   2 King. xxiii. 29, &c.
[379]   Eupolemus apud Euseb. Præp. l. 9. c. 39. 2 King. xxv. 2, 7.
[380]   Dan. i. 1.
[381]   Dan. i. 2. 2 Chron. xxxvi. 6.
[382]   Jer. xlvi. 2.
[383]   Apud Joseph. Antiq. l. 10. c. 11.
[384]   Beros. apud Joseph. Ant. l. 10. c. 11.
[385]   2 King. xxiv. 12, 14. 2 Chron. xxxvi. 10.
[386]   2 Kings xxiv. 17. Ezek. xvii. 13, 16, 18.
[387]   Ezek. xvii. 15.
[388]   2 King. xxv. 1, 2, 8. Jer. xxxii. 1, & xxxix 1, 2.
[389]   Canon. & Beros.
[390]   2 King. xxv. 27.
[391]   Hieron. in Isa. xiv. 19.
[392]   2 King. xxv. 27. 29, &c.
[393]   Dan. v. 2.
[394]   Jos. Ant. l. 10. c. 11.
[395]   Herod. l. 1. c. 184, 185.
[396]   Philost. in vita Apollonii. l. 1. c. 15.
[397]   Jos. cont. Apion. l. 1. c. 21.

[398] Herod. l. 1. c. 189, 190, 191. Xenoph. l. 7. p. 190, 191, 192. Ed. Paris.

[399] Dan. v. 30, 31. Joseph. Ant. l. 10. c. 11.

[400] Æsch. Persæ v. 761.

[401] Herod. l. 1. c. 107, 108. Xenophon Cyropæd. l. 1. p. 3.

[402] Cyropæd. l. 1. p. 22.

[403] Cyropæd. l. viii. p. 228, 229.

[404] Herod. l. 1. c. 73.

[405] Herod. l. 1. c. 106, 130.

[406] Herod. l. 1. c. 103.

[407] Herod. ib.

[408] Jer. xxv.

[409] Herod. l. 1. c. 73, 74.

[410] Herod. Ibid. Plin. l. 2. c. 12.

[411] The Scythians.

[412] Jer. xxvii. 3, 6. Ezek. xxi. 19, 20 & xxv. 2, 8, 12.

[413] Ezek. xxvi. 2. & xxix. 17, 19.

[414] Ezek. xxix. 19. & xxx. 4, 5.

[415] Suid. in Δαρεικος & Δαρεικους. Harpocr. in Δαρεικος. Scoliast in Aristophanis. Εκκλησιαζουστον. v. 598.

[416] Herod. l. 1. c. 71.

[417] Isa. xiii. 17.

[418] Plin. l. 33. c. 3.

[419] Herod. l. 1. c. 94.

[420] Theogn. Γνωμαι, v. 761.

[421] Ibid. v. 773.

[422] Cyrop. l. 8.

[423] Comment. in Dan. v.

[424] Strabo. l. 16. initio.

[425] Strab. l. 16. p. 745.

[426] Herod. l. 1. c. 192.

[427] Herod. l. 1. c. 178, &c.

[428] Isa. xxiii. 13.

[429] Diod. l. 1. p. 51.

[430] Herod. l. 1. c. 181.

[431] Suidas in Αρισταρχος. Herod. l. 1. c. 123, &c.

[432] Strabo. l. 15. p. 730.

[433] Herod. l. 1. c. 127, &c.

[434] Cyrop. l. 8. p. 233.

[435] See Plate I. & II.

[436] Ezek. xli. 13, 14.

[437] Ezek. xl. 47

[438] Ezek. xl. 29, 33, 36.

[439] Ezek. xl. 19, 23, 27. 2 King xxi. 5. 2 Chron. iv. 9.

[440] Ezek. xl. 15, 17, 21. 1 Chron. xxviii. 12.

[441] Ezek. xl 5, xlii. 20, & xlv. 2.

[442] 2 King. xxi.5.
[443] Ezek. xl.
[444] Plate III.
[445] Plate I.
[446] 1 Chron. xxvi. 17.
[447] Ezek. xlvi. 8, 9.
[448] Ezek. xliv. 2, 3.
[449] 1 Chron. xxvi. 15, 16, 17, 18.
[450] Ezek. xl. 22, 26, 31, 34, 37.
[451] Plate II & III.
[452] 1 King. vi. 36. & vii. 13. Ezek. xl. 17, 18.
[453] Ezek. xl. 10, 31, 34, 37.
[454] Plate I.
[455] 1 King. vi. 36, & vii. 12.
[456] Ezek. xl. 17.
[457] Plate III.
[458] Plate I & II.
[459] Ezek. xlvi. 21, 22.
[460] Ezek. xl. 45.
[461] Ezek. xl. 39, 41, 42, 46.
[462] Plate II.
[463] Ezek. xlii. 1, 2, 3, 4, 6, 8, 13, 14.
[464] Ezek. xlvi. 19, 20.
[465] Ezek. xlii. 5, 6.
[466] 1 King. vi. 2. Ezek. xli. 2, 4, 12, 13, 14.
[467] 1 King. vi. 3. Ezek. xli. 13.
[468] Ezek. xli. 6, 11.
[469] 1 King. vi. 6.
[470] Ezek. xli. 6.
[471] 2 Chron. iii. 4.
[472] 1 King. vi. 8.
[473] 2 Chron. xx. 5.
[474] 2 King. xvi. 18.
[475] Ezra vi. 3, 4.
[476] Plate I
[477] Plate III.
[478] Plate I.
[479] Valer. Max. l. 9. c. 2.
[480] Porph. de Abstinentia, lib. 4.
[481] Q. Curt. Lib. iii. c. 3.
[482] Suidas in Ζωροαστρης.
[483] Ammian. l. 23. c. 6.
[484] Euseb. Præp. Evang. l. 1. c. ult.
[485] Æsch. Persæ v. 763.
[486] Apud. Hieron in Dan. viii.

Echo Library
www.echo-library.com

Echo Library uses advanced digital print-on-demand technology to build and preserve an exciting world class collection of rare and out-of-print books, making them readily available for everyone to enjoy.

Situated just yards from Teddington Lock on the River Thames, Echo Library was founded in 2005 by Tom Cherrington, a specialist dealer in rare and antiquarian books with a passion for literature.

Please visit our website for a complete catalogue of our books, which includes foreign language titles.

The Right to Read

Echo Library actively supports the Royal National Institute for the Blind's Right to Read initiative by publishing a comprehensive range of Large Print (16 point Tiresias font as recommended by the RNIB) and Clear Print (13 point Tiresias font) titles for those who find standard print difficult to read.

Customer Service

If there is a serious error in the text or layout please send details to feedback@echo-library.com and we will supply a corrected copy. If there is a printing fault or the book is damaged please refer to your supplier.

Printed in the United States
107506LV00003B/238/A